Performance Assessment in Education and Training: Alternative Techniques

Performance Assessment in Education and Training: Alternative Techniques

Michael Priestley

National Evaluation Systems, Inc.

Educational Technology Publications
Englewood Cliffs, New Jersey 07632

Library of Congress Cataloging in Publication Data

Priestley, Michael.
    Performance assessment in education and training.

    Includes bibliographical references and index.
    1. Criterion-referenced tests. 2. Educational tests
and measurements. I. Title.
LB3060.32.C74P74   371.2'64   81-19598
ISBN 0-87778-181-8   AACR2

Printed in the United States of America.

Library of Congress Catalog Card Number:
81-19598.

International Standard Book Number:
0-87778-181-8.

First Printing: April, 1982.

Acknowledgments

Many of my colleagues at National Evaluation Systems, Inc. (NES), deserve to be acknowledged for their efforts and support in developing innovative assessment techniques, but a few stand out above the rest. My special thanks go to Paula Nassif, for her personal and professional guidance and encouragement in this and in all of my other work at NES, and for her helpful review of this manuscript in its first draft.

My gratitude to Bill Gorth, whose generosity made possible the writing of this book. And, for their assistance in work that led to the birth of this book, I would like to thank David L. Gere, Stacey Sparks Williams, and Lise Gordon of the Test Development Department; and Susan Torrey and Kathleen Adams for their help in preparing this manuscript.

Finally, I would like to express my appreciation to the exemplary men and women of all the organizations and associations, particularly those cited herein, whose pioneering efforts in performance assessment represent a commitment to creativity and progress in a most constructive sense.

Preface

Interest in performance testing has flourished in recent years for a number of reasons: a growing faith in the idea that people should learn how to apply what they know; a disenchantment with traditional standardized tests, particularly of the multiple-choice variety; an increase in adult education, community education, and vocational training; and a thriving interest in occupational and professional licensing and certification. As the world and its technology become more complex and more specialized, the need for specialized training—and subsequent assessment—increases.

The purpose of this book is simply stated: to provide practical information on alternative methods of assessing performance. The range of skills that can be measured by multiple-choice tests, or by any single means of assessment, is necessarily limited. What we need are alternatives to choose from that will enable us to measure whatever skills need to be assessed. That is what I hope to provide here: alternatives.

In concept, performance assessment is not new: the original Olympic games held in ancient Greece were tests of athletic ability; many American Indian tribes required young men and women to pass rigid tests before entering adulthood; and, at least since Napoleon, soldiers have used war games to test and strengthen their skills. But the term itself can be misleading, depending on how it is defined.

Although "performance tests" and "applied performance testing" often refer to on-the-job activity, this view is unnecessarily restrictive. Drawing from resources and experience in several areas that require assessment, I hope to illustrate the practical applications of performance assessment techniques in education, vocational and professional training, and in the professions themselves. Assessment methods can be used as training devices, as techniques for evaluation, and as instruments designed to fulfill many other purposes, in all aspects of "performance."

The ten chapters of this book consider alternative assessment methods from all of these perspectives. Illustrative examples sprinkled throughout the book have been drawn from a large domain in an effort to meet the needs of educators, trainers, and other professional personnel who are involved with, or simply interested in, alternative performance assessments.

Chapter One provides an illustration of how to design an assessment program; without a program design, there will be no basis for evaluating the relative merits of various assessment methods. Chapters Two and Three, respectively, provide an overview of types of assessment methods and procedures for designing an actual test, or assessment instrument. Later chapters explore a number of assessment techniques, most of which emphasize actual or simulated performance. Finally, the last chapter deals with assessment centers and how to integrate the preliminary developmental work to construct an assessment program, based on the original design.

Before proceeding, however, I would like to include some notes here on the technical context of this book.

First, two technical qualifications: although the title of this work refers to "alternative" assessments, I do include discussions of standard paper-and-pencil approaches to measurement, such as multiple-choice questions. My approach here is to apply the widely disseminated and highly advanced technology for producing standardized paper-and-pencil tests to the development of alternatives. This seems to be a sound approach because the same basic principles apply to assessments of all kinds. Discussion of paper-and-pencil tests is also included to provide a basis for comparison with the alternatives: those who are familiar with traditional approaches to testing can see clearly how the alternatives differ from standardized test methods.

The second technical qualification is the type of test referred to here. One of the superior characteristics of the growing technology in performance assessment is its ability to measure a clearly defined domain. All discussion of actual assessment techniques in this book refers to *criterion-referenced* test development procedures; applications of these procedures to normative-referenced testing would require modifications in various stages of the process. The key here is to consider tests that enable the examiner or trainer to assess a candidate's knowledge and performance in relation to a specified domain of knowledge and skills, not in relation to the performance of other candidates. An additional note: I use the term *criterion-referenced test* as a general term that subsumes objective-referenced, competency-based, and domain-referenced tests. Distinctions among these types of tests are negligible in the present context.

Criterion-referenced assessment instruments provide a means for determining whether or not a candidate has the knowledge and skills required for job performance or successful completion of a training or educational program. This domain of knowledge and skills must be clearly defined, through a job analysis, task analysis, or other procedure; and some sort of cut-off score (or standard) must be determined. A performance rated at or above the cut-off yields a passing score on the test; below it yields a failing score. This is the essence of the widely touted *minimum competency* approach to assessment, as applied to criterion-referenced testing. Minimum competency requirements, which are especially useful in training, licensing, and certification, serve to identify those candidates who cannot make the grade—those who require further training or education to become "minimally competent."

The past decade has borne a proliferation of standardized tests to measure everything from aardvark husbandry to zygote production. It has also spawned a "back-to-basics" movement, demanded assurances that our high school graduates are functionally literate, called for demonstrations of minimum competency, and suggested that all of us might need to improve our life skills.

With increasing demands for more comprehensive education and training programs comes a demand for more comprehensive and sophisticated methods of assessment, to emphasize the accountability of training and education agencies.

It is our responsibility in assessment to provide the best

assessment techniques available and the latest technology extant. I sincerely hope that this book will aid you in your efforts.

Michael Priestley
November, 1981

Table of Contents

Performance Assessment in Education and Training: Alternative Techniques

Chapter One

Designing an Assessment Program

Anyone who builds an assessment program without a preliminary design faces the same risk as an architect who begins
construction of a house before drawing the blueprint: the
structure may collapse. Regardless of the types of materials used
to build the house, or the assessment techniques used to build the
program, they must be supported by a solid foundation.

An *assessment program* is a unified approach to assessment for
a specific purpose; it is not synonymous with a test. An assessment
program may include a number of requirements, all designed to
assess various aspects of a candidate's qualifications; one or more
of these requirements may be a test, but this is only one aspect of
the program. For example, a company may require a prospective
employee to furnish proof of having earned a college degree, go
through an interview, and then take two tests, one written and one
practical examination. This entire set of requirements, which the
company has deemed necessary to provide sufficient information
for assessing the candidate, is an assessment program. Each
requirement is measured by an assessment technique.

The steps in designing a program appear to be straightforward,
as shown below, but the importance of the issues that must be
considered before taking each step should not be underestimated.

Steps in Designing an Assessment Program

1. Define the purpose.
2. Identify resources.
3. Decide who is to be assessed and when.

4. Define what to assess.
5. Decide how to assess.
6. Draft a preliminary plan.
7. Evaluate the plan.

Each step is considered individually here, and in the specified sequence; but, in any particular situation, the steps may run together and occur all at once, or at least in a different sequence.

Define the Purpose

Defining the purpose sounds simple enough and is obviously required; but the number of assessment programs built for unstated purposes is large enough to defy the imagination.

Whether an assessment is part of an occupational training program, professional licensing or certification, or educational program, its purpose must be specified precisely. Different needs require different approaches to assessment; the stated purpose of an assessment program will govern its construction, from start to finish.

For example, the purposes of most assessment programs fall into one of two major categories: *screening* or *selection*. A screening test must be capable of identifying those who have not attained the minimum level of required qualifications. A selection test must identify those who are most qualified, or those who would be "selected" as prime candidates for a job, training, or educational program.

Within either of these two categories, the specific purpose of an assessment program requires a more precise definition. "Why an assessment program?" is the basic question to answer. The response to this question is the program's purpose. A screening test may be used as a certification or licensing requirement to ensure that all candidates are minimally competent; as an achievement test; as a diagnostic or placement test to identify strengths and weaknesses; as an entrance or qualifying test; and so on. Selection tests may include instruments used to measure aptitude, potential for promotion or advancement, college admissions, etc. One or both of these types, selection or screening, may also be used in program evaluation to assess the effectiveness of a training or educational program. A program may be designed to fulfill more than one of these needs, but this must be specified in the stated purpose of the program.

Each purpose mentioned above has its own particular requirements which the design of the program must satisfy. The assessment techniques discussed later in this book, for example, may be useful in some contexts but not in others. Without a clear statement of its purpose to serve as a foundation, the program may not support its own weight.

Identify Resources

Loosely defined, *resources* may include money, time and personnel, technical expertise, materials, and equipment. After defining the purpose of an assessment program, look at the resources available—the purpose may be unrealistic. (Again, these steps may not occur in the sequence presented: a more practical approach might be to look at available resources first, then begin designing the program to fit within whatever constraints may exist.) The initial version of the program's purpose may have to be modified in these early stages of preparation.

Although it is difficult at this stage to know exactly how much of these types of resources the program will require, the questions and notes below might be helpful in making a fair estimation.

- *Is there enough money to fund the program?* Most likely, initial costs of developing the program will exceed annual maintenance costs, especially if candidates will be required to pay fees for applications or testing. These two types of funds should be estimated separately.
- *How much time is there? When should (or must) the program be implemented?* A complex assessment program with considerable test development may take several years to get off the ground. If the implementation date has already been mandated, plans may have to proceed from that date backwards in outlining the program.
- *Are there enough personnel to do the job?* Personnel may include in-house staff, consultants, volunteers, test administrators, and so on.

- *Is the technical expertise available? In-house experts or expert consultants?*
- *What materials and equipment will be needed? Are they available?* For example, a large-scale assessment of thousands of people will probably require computer scoring and analysis of some type. Are these facilities accessible?

Some idea of what is available and what is needed will facilitate the completion of all the remaining steps. As with many steps in this kind of project, the most practical approach may be to begin with an ideal plan, then work toward achieving whatever portions of that ideal are realistic.

Decide Who Is to Be Assessed and When

This decision can be made in response to the stated purpose of the program. For example, if the purpose is to assess physicians' assistants for certification, then the candidates may be assessed before, during, and after their training program. Before, to assess their aptitude; during, to assess their progress; and after, to assess their achievement. A somewhat more complicated example might involve a state mandate that requires all students to pass a test before receiving a high school diploma. The mandate determines *who* is to be tested—every student in the state; but the question of *when* must still be decided. At the end of twelfth grade? At the end of tenth grade, so that those who fail will have time to take it again? In the fall? In the spring?

Who is to be tested and when depend on the program's purpose, but these questions must be answered before the next step can occur.

Define What to Assess

An assessment program may involve a number of requirements that candidates must satisfy. If the purpose is to assess electronic technicians in a training program, there may be three types of requirements: mathematical ability, aptitude for learning on the job, and manual dexterity. Each would require a different type of assessment.

Essentially, the task here is to define the qualifications and the competencies that a candidate must possess in order to pass the assessment requirements. Depending on the situation, these competencies may be dictated by the legislature, established by a school board or company personnel office, or identified by a licensing or certification board. In all of these cases, the use of *job analysis* or *task analysis* might be helpful.

A licensing test, for example, is usually designed to measure the skills that the licensee needs on the job. These skills can be defined through a comprehensive analysis of what people on the job actually do. Educational or training requirements can be defined through an analysis of the expectations brought to bear on a person who completes the education or training (e.g., ability to read and write, ability to repair a television set). The results of the analysis will produce a set of skills or competencies that represent the *domain* of the assessment—those skills or competencies on which the assessment will be based. (References for information on job analysis and task analysis are listed at the end of this chapter.)

Defining specific knowledge and skills in the total domain to be assessed is one aspect of this step; the second aspect is to define subtests (or subdomains) in relation to a scoring model. An example may be helpful here. In Massachusetts, persons seeking drivers' licenses must be at least 17 years of age (without driver education) and must pass a three-part exam. The first part is a written test, the second is an eye test, and the third is a road test (performance). In this program, the scoring model is *disjunctive*: the candidate must pass all three tests in order to receive a license. With a *compensatory* scoring model, a candidate who earns a very high score on one section of the exam could fail another section and still receive a license (the high score *compensates* for the low score).

The same general principle applies to an entire assessment program and to a single test. In defining what to assess, identify those requirements that are most essential and be sure that the program's scoring model accommodates this identification.

Decide How to Assess

A cartoon that once appeared in *The New Yorker* magazine

portrays a cigar-smoking corporate executive looking at his undistinguished subordinate. The caption reads: "That's the gist of what I want to say. Now get me some statistics to base it on." If this man were directing an assessment program and determining the results before conducting the assessment, his unwitting victims might find serious cause for alarm in his approach.

Procedures for deciding how to assess certain knowledge and skills should take the opposite direction from the one in the cartoon. First, specify the domain; second, decide how to assess the domain; then gather information by conducting the assessment.

Ideally, the determination of assessment methods follows directly from the specific knowledge and skills that must be measured. For example, a test designed to measure writing skills should be a writing test. But at this stage in designing the program, there are larger decisions to make first, before getting down to measuring each skill.

Reviewing the purpose of the program will help to clarify the significant issues to be considered here. If the purpose of the program is to certify tax collectors, then ask this question: what does a person need to know or be able to do in order to function as a certified tax collector? The answer might be in three parts: he or she must have an irreproachable personal tax record, mathematical skills and knowledge of tax laws, and a command of the interpersonal skills needed to extract taxes from unwilling citizens. Based on this answer, the assessment program begins to take shape. It will have three parts: an examination of the candidate's past history, for which he or she could be required to verify tax payments made over the last ten years; a paper-and-pencil test on math and tax laws; and an assessment instrument designed to measure the candidate's ability to deal with people, especially recalcitrant types.

This unorthodox example illustrates the point of this task, deciding how to assess. The overall decisions needed to plan the basic structure of a comprehensive assessment program should be based on the program's purpose and whatever domain is specified to satisfy that purpose. Particular skills and assessment techniques can be defined later, but initial planning requires an outline of what the ultimate program will look like.

As with all other aspects of this kind of program, its basic structure may be dictated by practical constraints, such as time and money. In general, paper-and-pencil tests are less expensive to develop and use than most other forms of assessment; but alternative methods can provide more validity or relevance to the program. Consider the practical aspects of the program before deciding how to assess the specified knowledge and skills, then make the decisions. Specify all the components of the assessment program (e.g., qualifications for application, training or education, testing, interviewing, placement); then proceed to the next step.

Draft a Preliminary Plan

With an outline of the assessment program completed, the next step is to sketch the preliminary assessment plan. Components of the assessment should correspond to the components of the outline of the program. Preliminary plans are just that—preliminary; but a sketch of the program now will help to define all subsequent steps in implementing the plan. At any point in the program's maturation, it may be necessary to go back and revise the plan to accommodate unforeseen developments.

Consider the hypothetical example below, which provides a tentative answer to each question raised thus far.

Preliminary Plans for an Assessment Program

Agency: National Association of Automobile Salespersons (NAAS).

Program Purpose: To certify automobile salespersons by verifying that they have attained the minimum level of knowledge and skills required to sell automobiles.

Identify Resources: Unlimited.

Define What to Assess: An automobile salesperson must have some knowledge of automobile manufacturing, engines, pricing, and distribution. He or she must have interpersonal skills needed to deal with potential buyers, and must have mathematical skills needed to calculate costs, interest rates, commissions, and discounts.

Define How to Assess: The assessment program will include: (1) a test of practical knowledge related to automobiles and their manufacture; (2) an assessment of relevant interpersonal skills; and (3) a test of practical mathematical skills.

This case study demonstrates the extent and usefulness of a preliminary plan for an assessment program. The "NAAS" now has a design from which to develop the instruments needed to assess and certify candidates for automobile sales. However, this plan is only preliminary, and it is only a beginning, however helpful. There are a number of legal and technical issues to consider very carefully before implementing this plan. All of these issues, explored in the following pages, constitute the criteria for the final step: evaluating the plan.

Evaluate the Plan

The purpose of this last step in designing the program is to evaluate the degree to which the plan satisfies the purpose of the program—legally, technically, and practically. Anything that affects a large number of people will have significant implications, and thus must be planned carefully. All of the ramifications inherent in the program must be considered in depth, particularly in a program that may affect a person's career and ability to earn wages in a desired occupation, or a program that affects a person's educational standing. Licensing, certification, training assessment, and educational assessment—particularly exit examinations—all fall into this category of programs that may affect a large number of people, some of them adversely.

Most significant of the reasons for planning an assessment program carefully are these three: (1) to provide a fair assessment of all candidates who might be affected; (2) to protect the health, safety, and welfare of the public; and (3) to protect yourself. Any candidate who applies for a job, a training program, or a license not only deserves fair, unbiased treatment, but demands it by law. On the other hand, programs such as those which grant licenses are established for good reason—to maintain the standards of the profession which, in turn, protects the public by denying licensure to candidates who are incompetent. This, to most people, is a necessity; but it must be done fairly. Finally, protecting yourself and the program is strong motivation for sound planning. A legal challenge to a test, for example, could drag people into court, ruin their reputations, and destroy an assessment program that took years to develop.

Avoiding all of these dire consequences requires planning and careful consideration of all the issues involved. The following section presents many of the most significant issues to be aware of; although perhaps not all of them will affect a given program directly, it is worth the time at least to consider each one and cross it off as inapplicable to the situation.

Federal guidelines. In addition to the federal laws, constitutional amendments, and civil rights legislation that affect everyone, there is a set of federal guidelines developed by the Equal Employment Opportunity Commission (1978) intended to govern the development and use of employee selection procedures. These guidelines apply to tests and other procedures used as a basis for any employment decision, including licensing and certification. General principles stated by the guidelines which apply to testing and alternative assessment techniques are summarized below.

Essentially, any instrument or procedure used in employee selection that results in *adverse impact* must be proven valid for the purpose for which it is used. ("A selection rate for any race, sex, or ethnic group which is less than 4/5 or 80 percent of the rate for the group with the highest rate will be regarded as evidence of adverse impact.") The burden of proof lies with the employer who uses the test or procedure.

Procedures resulting in adverse impact are not permissible unless justified by "business necessity," which is established through a validity study showing the relationship between the selection procedure and performance on the job. In conducting a validity study, the employer must consider available *alternative* procedures that will achieve the assessment program's legitimate business purpose with less adverse impact. Also, if a procedure of several components results in adverse impact, each component of the procedure or program must be validated.

EEOC guidelines also state the standards for acceptability of validity studies, in accordance with standards set forth by the American Psychological Association, the American Educational Research Association, and the National Council on Measurement in Education (1974). Criterion-related validity is acceptable if, among other things, the criteria are justified by job analysis, are measures of job training progress, or are otherwise shown to be relevant. ("Criterion measures consisting of paper-and-pencil tests will be closely reviewed for job relevance.") Content validity is a way to establish that the test or procedure measures a representative sample of knowledge, skills, or abilities; and that the knowledge, skills, or abilities are prerequisite to the performance of critically important work behavior(s). Procedures may deal with work behaviors or work products, but the closer the relationship of the test to the work situation, work-sample, or work behavior, the stronger the basis for content validity.

The guidelines go on to spell out standards for reliability, job analysis, documentation, retesting, fairness studies, etc.; but the gist of the guidelines is this: any test that results in discrimination must be able to be proven valid. Thus, an assessment program which may, at any time, be used in employee selection, licensing, job training, or certification should be developed in such a way that it is legally and technically defensible.

Job analysis. One step toward developing a valid test is to define the domain of the test through a job or task analysis. Basically, this analysis is done by surveying or interviewing job incumbents to determine what tasks they perform on the job, and what skills and knowledge are required to perform those tasks. A technically sound analysis will provide an empirical basis for determining what should be measured by a test or by alternative assessment methods.

Implementation. Deciding when to implement an assessment program is also important. In Florida, a test of functional literacy used as a requirement for high school diplomas was challenged in court because it resulted in adverse impact (*Debra P. v. Turlington*, 1978). The court declared that the test was valid, but it had been implemented too soon; students who were juniors at the time it was implemented did not have adequate time to prepare for a test that would determine whether or not they received diplomas at graduation. The court's decision delayed enforcement of the test requirement for two years.

Retesting/remediation. EEOC guidelines state that "users" should provide reasonable opportunity for retesting and reconsideration. Educators who use tests as requirements, such as Connecticut's Ninth-Grade Proficiency Test, often develop remediation programs to help students improve their skills if they fail the test the first time. Both of these aspects emphasize the same goal: assessment programs are designed to make sure that students, trainees, and job applicants possess the skills required. Thus, an assessment program should provide for retesting and, in some cases, additional training or educational remediation.

Setting standards. A phrase commonly heard in relation to assessment, "setting standards" often refers to one of two activities: (1) determining the standards of minimum competency which candidates must achieve, i.e., the competencies they must master; or (2) setting the cut-off score or standard on a test. The first activity is closely related to defining the domain of knowledge or skills to be tested; the second is a highly technical, statistical procedure which the EEOC examines very closely in court cases. Both instances of setting standards require careful thought: How high should the standards be? How high does an examinee have to score in order to pass? And both sets of standards must be defined carefully, in a technically sound manner—not in an arbitrary or capricious way.

Consequences to examinees. Perhaps most important of all the issues considered here is this one: the consequences of the assessment program. The seriousness of the consequences—to examinees, to the public, and to the program administrators—will often determine the procedures to be used throughout the program. For example, an informal training program in a vocational field, for which trainees take an end-of-course test for a grade, is not nearly as consequential as a national licensing examination. Assessment instruments in the training program need not be developed as rigidly as in the licensing exam.

All of these issues should be considered during this final step of planning the program: evaluating the plan. Awareness of these issues will help in defining a program that serves its purpose technically, legally, and fairly. When a preliminary plan has been sketched out, go back to each one of these issues and compare it to the plan. If, after this evaluation, the plan appears to be sound, then proceed to the next stage of development: considering various types of alternative assessment methods.

Selected References

Job Analysis
Baehr, M.E. Job analysis: Objectives, approaches, and applications. In Miller, E.A., Burack, E.H., and Albrecht, M. (Eds.), *Human Resource Management Readings.* Englewood Cliffs, N.J.: Prentice-Hall, Inc., 1979.
Fine, S., and Wiley, W.W. *An Introduction to Functional Job Analysis.* Kalamazoo, Mich.: Upjohn Institute for Employment Research, 1971.
Flanagan, J.C. The critical incidents technique. *Psychological Bulletin,* 1954, *51,* 327-358.
Levine, E.L. Exploratory comparative study of four job analysis methods. *Journal of Applied Psychology,* October 1980, *65*(5), 524-535.
Primoff, E.S. *How to Prepare and Conduct Job-Element Examinations.* Washington, D.C.: Personnel Research and Development Center, Bureau of Policies and Standards, 1976.

Testing Guidelines
American Psychological Association, American Educational Research Association, and National Council on Measurement in Education. *Standards for Educational and Psychological Tests.* Washington, D.C.: American Psychological Association, Inc., 1974.
Division of Industrial-Organizational Psychology, American Psychological Association. *Principles for the Validation and Use of Personnel Selection Procedures.* Dayton, OH: Industrial-Organizational Psychologist, 1975.
Erickson, J.R., and McGovern, K.S. (Eds.) *Equal Employment Practice Guide, Volume 1.* Washington, D.C.: Committee on Equal Employment

Opportunity of the Council on Labor Law and Labor Relations, Federal Bar Association, March 1979.

U.S. Equal Employment Opportunity Commission. Uniform guidelines on employee selection procedures. *Federal Register,* 1978, *43*(166), 38290-38309.

U.S. Equal Employment Opportunity Commission. Adoption of questions and answers to clarify and provide a common interpretation of the uniform guidelines on employee selection procedures. *Federal Register,* 1979, *44*(43), 11996-12009.

Setting Standards

Angoff, W.H. Scales, norms, and equivalent scores. In R.L. Thorndike (Ed.), *Educational Measurement, Second Edition.* Washington, D.C.: American Council on Education, 1971.

Berk, R.A. Determination of optimal cutting scores in criterion-referenced measurement. *Journal of Experimental Education,* 1976, *45,* 4-9.

Nassif, P.M. Setting standards. In Gorth, W.P., and Perkins, M.R. (Eds.), *A Study of Minimum Competency Testing Programs: Final Program Development Resource Document.* Washington, D.C.: National Institute of Education, December 1979.

Assessment Program Planning

Airasian, P.W., Madaus, G.F., and Pedulla, J.J. (Eds.) *Minimal Competency Testing.* Englewood Cliffs, N.J.: Educational Technology Publications, 1979.

Brickell, H.M. Seven key notes on minimal competency testing. In B.S. Miller (Ed.), *Minimal Competency Testing: A Report of Four Regional Conferences.* St. Louis, Mo.: CEMREL, 1978.

Jaeger, R.M., and Tittle, C.K. *Minimum Competency Achievement Testing.* Berkeley, Calif.: McCutchan Publishing Corporation, 1980.

Chapter Two

Types of Assessment Techniques

Conventional tests of paper-and-pencil varieties, if well-constructed, are adequate to measure cognitive skills. A student's ability to supply a word to complete a sentence, or a dental hygienist's ability to identify a picture of a bicuspid, can be measured by fill-in-the-blank or multiple-choice items. If the student were required to write a sentence, however, or the hygienist to clean someone's teeth—these skills would require performance, which could not be measured directly by paper-and-pencil tests. Measuring skills beyond the cognitive domain requires other types of assessment.

Alternatives have always been available and have been used in a multitude of ways, but in recent years, the related technology—methods of construction, administration, and scoring—has become more refined and more accessible to practitioners. The purpose of this chapter is to introduce various approaches to assessment; later chapters explore the technology related to the assessment techniques. All of the techniques considered here can be classified in six categories, as follows:

Actual Performance Assessments
Simulations
Observational Assessments
Oral Assessments
Paper-and-Pencil Assessments
Program Requirements

Although these categories are not totally independent—different approaches often depend on one another for their practical use—they help provide an organized framework for discussion.

Types of assessment vary significantly, but every type has three basic elements: a task to perform, conditions which govern the performance, and a method of scoring the result. An understanding of the variations on these elements, which are what make one assessment technique differ from another, requires a handful of terms and working definitions. First, how the task is presented to the examinee is the *mode of assessment*, which may be in written, visual, verbal, or kinetic form (denoting physical movement or manipulation); or in some combination of these. The mode of assessment may include instructions to the examinee, stimulus material, and additional relevant information needed to formulate a response. Second, how the examinee performs the task is the *mode of response*, which may also be in written, visual, verbal, or kinetic form. Third, each type of assessment has a *method of scoring* the response, which may incorporate a number of specific criteria. Fourth, each one has a *mode of administration*, which denotes the number of people who can be assessed at one time with the technique: individual, small group (two to ten persons), or large group (more than ten).

Every assessment technique can be defined in terms of these basic characteristics. The simplest example of these elements is a standard multiple-choice test. Each examinee receives a printed booklet of questions (mode of assessment) and answers them by filling in circles on an answer sheet (mode of response), while sitting in an auditorium filled with people taking the same test (mode of administration). All the tests are then graded by machine, either right or wrong for each question (method of scoring).

For a more complex example, consider an assessment of five students in a film class. The instructor shows a two-minute film on the Clio awards, which are given for excellence in advertising, then asks factual questions of the students orally. Each student responds orally, and the instructor checks off "yes" or "no" for each student's answer to each question given. Both the film (stimulus) and the instructor's questions constitute the mode of

assessment, which is a combination of visual and oral presentations. The students' mode of response is oral; and the instructor
uses a yes/no checklist (method of scoring) to record the responses
by each member of a small group (mode of administration).

The techniques introduced in this chapter have been classified
by their mode of response (actual performance, paper-and-pencil,
etc.). Unfortunately, since abstract concepts can seldom be
pigeonholed without a struggle, this neat scheme of classification
has two exceptions: observational assessment and program requirements. By nature, these two categories resist pigeonholing.

For an overview of the six categories and how they differ from
one another, consider the informal example of professional
baseball players. Every spring the teams attend spring training
camps where they hold practice and play in exhibition games. The
team's coach must assess each player before the official season's
opening game. During exhibition games, the coach observes each
player as he performs. The coach uses *observational assessment* to
evaluate each player's *actual performance.* Between games, the
players might take batting practice by hitting balls pitched from a
pitching machine (*simulation*). Later, in a team meeting, the coach
tests the players' knowledge of a new rule passed by the baseball
commissioner by asking questions (*oral assessment*). And finally,
just to make sure that everyone knows all the rules of the game, he
administers a *paper-and-pencil* test to every member of the squad.

In this particular training camp, the coach uses five types of
assessment; in four of them, the players are given tasks to perform.
As the example demonstrates, however, observational assessment
is done by the "evaluator" while observing the "examinee," an
approach that varies in principle from other types. *Program
requirements* would consist of those conditions which the players
must meet before they show up for practice. For example, they
must be of a certain age, they must have demonstrated a certain
level of competence in previous situations, and so on. A formal
assessment program often stipulates qualifications or prerequisites
that the candidate must satisfy before he or she can be considered
for final assessment.

Continuing with the professional baseball players: from the

information gathered in these assessments, the coach can select his final roster of players who make the team. He can also use his assessment results to identify the strengths and weaknesses of each player, which can then be used to plan later practices and "instruction." Obviously, when he must decide which player will start at each position, information from some types of assessment (actual and simulated performances) will be more reliable and more relevant than others (paper-and-pencil tests).

Each assessment technique has its ideal purpose, but the ideal is seldom attainable in a real situation. Program constraints such as cost, time, and defensibility may all influence the choice of which assessment techniques to use. Beyond the practical constraints, however, are a number of other factors to consider. Before evaluating the merits (or demerits) of each type of assessment, it is necessary to clarify what is to be measured (product or process), how realistic the assessment should be, how precisely to measure it (directness of measure), and the ultimate use of the information obtained from the assessment. All of these factors, as defined below, must be weighed before choosing one assessment technique over another.

Product vs. Process Evaluation

The first distinction to make is in what to measure: product or process, or some combination of both. *Product* refers, in most cases, to a tangible object resulting from a person's performance. It can be evaluated on the basis of its quality, appearance, conformance to predetermined specifications, and many other criteria. *Process* refers to the procedures or methods used to arrive at a particular point, which may or may not result in a product. Processes are often more difficult to assess because of their subjective and/or complex nature; but they are usually evaluated on the basis of quality and efficiency, through observational assessment techniques.

Again, the most important criterion in comparing assessment techniques for a particular purpose is the skill defined for assessment. If the essential aspect of the skill is the process, then a measure of process would assess the skill most realistically and most directly. Similarly, if the product is more important than how it is produced, then the product must be assessed.

Evaluators often disagree on what is most important, depending on which school of thought they belong to: "If you're going to do the job, do it right," or "I don't care how you do it, just give me the finished product." In certain situations, as when the process is not practically measurable, the question is moot. This holds true for most creative and artistic endeavors: an essay or a pastel portrait is a product that can be judged, but the creative process involved usually defies exact definition and inspection.

Regarding other skills, the question of whether to assess the process or the product is more straightforward. A sales trainee must have an appropriate sales pitch and approach to customers (process), but the product of the performance (whether or not the person sells something) may be non-existent or unimportant during the training stages. Similarly, for a factory worker who assembles electronic components, the quality of the product is essential; but there may be only *one* method for assembly. If the product is satisfactory, the process *must* have been adequate.

Many skills, by definition, require both process and product assessment. In a typing test, a typed letter is a product; the "hunt and peck" method is a process. Few typing tests are designed to measure only one or the other: the letter, the time it takes, and the method used by the typist are *all* important, especially for beginning typists who have yet to learn the proper techniques. A house painter whose finished product is magnificent may not have demonstrated an adequate process (e.g., the job may have taken six months and 30 gallons of paint).

Some situations require step-by-step procedures that must be followed to prevent serious consequences (such as learning to handle nitroglycerine). Others have procedures designed to teach beginners how to approach and solve a given problem, with the intent of inculcating the student with a method for approaching larger, more complex problems beyond the protective world of instruction. Both of these situations require assessment of the process used by the examinee, and perhaps of the product as well.

To summarize, the essential task is to distinguish between

measures of process and of product. Which type of measure would be most appropriate for a given purpose depends on the skill to be assessed and the practical constraints that might influence the decision. One constraint, of a more technical nature, is the degree of realism which the assessment must achieve.

Degree of Realism

The degree of realism in particular techniques is important to understanding types of assessment and, later, to selecting the ones that best fit program needs.

As Fitzpatrick and Morrison (1971) indicate, a "performance test is one that is *relatively* realistic." The inference here is that all techniques vary in their degree of realism. A test designed to evaluate auto mechanics is most realistic if it requires the examinees to work on actual automobiles, e.g., to adjust the carburetor; less realistic if it requires a written description of how to make the adjustment. Likewise, with architects: a test for licensing architects is more realistic if it requires them to create a design than it is if it requires an essay on design history.

In the past, realism in testing was simply more desirable than lack of realism; now it is required by law in many cases. Federal guidelines not only state that any instrument used for licensing or selection must be a representative measure of the actual domain of skills used on the job (see Chapter One), but also that the instrument must measure these skills under conditions which approximate the actual job setting as closely as possible.

Tests in education that are used for similar purposes must comply with the same guidelines. Two examples of such tests are the competency-based teacher certification tests required by the state of Georgia and Florida's test of functional literacy, which high-schoolers must pass before they can receive diplomas (Priestley and Nassif, 1979).

The degree to which an assessment technique approximates actual job conditions has been called its degree of *realism, fidelity,* or *authenticity.* This varies from one assessment technique to another. Actual performance techniques are generally most realistic, i.e., they most faithfully approximate real working conditions.

Other techniques provide less realism, but they may be more desirable for other reasons such as cost, time, or reliability of the measure. (The "as closely as possible" clause in the guidelines applies to these "other reasons.") If a test administrator unobtrusively observes an apprenticed electrician at work on a job, for example, this would demonstrate a high degree of realism. On the other end of the spectrum, this same apprentice could sit in a classroom and write an essay describing what he or she does on the job and how well he or she does it. The latter approach has low realism because the assessment result would be a written description of performance, not the performance itself.

As a criterion for judging assessment techniques, the degree of realism is most useful in comparison to practical constraints. For instance, actual performance tests are often expensive to administer and difficult to score reliably, while paper-and-pencil tests are less expensive and easier to administer and score. The most important criterion, however, is the domain of skills and knowledge to be measured.

Directness of Measure

Closely related to an assessment's degree of realism is the *directness* of measure, which is a function of both the skill measured and the technique used to measure it. The skills measured by an assessment instrument fall into four domains: cognitive, affective, psychomotor, and perceptual. (Some experts cite a fifth domain called psychomotor-perceptual, because the two are interrelated and seldom occur independently.) Cognitive skills refer to intellectual or mental skills, such as analyzing, identifying, calculating, and comparing, which can be measured objectively. The affective domain refers to attitudes and behaviors, which cannot be measured objectively because they are neither "right" nor "wrong"; rather, they are "there" or "not there," to some degree. Psychomotor skills are those which require physical movement or manipulation, and perceptual skills include those which specifically require the use of the body's sense organs.

The most direct measure of a cognitive, psychomotor, or perceptual skill is the application of that skill in a real situation.

Assessment techniques other than actual performance measure these skills less directly. A student's ability to draw a picture would be assessed most directly by having the student actually draw a picture to satisfy certain requirements; less directly, it might be assessed by having the student choose the picture that best fits the requirements; or by having the student describe what the picture would look like.

The ideal assessment technique is the one that measures a given skill most directly, but practical restrictions may make the ideal option impossible. To most people concerned with writing skills, for example, there is no substitute for testing students by having them write. But educators who must assess thousands of students statewide may find the most direct method too expensive and time-consuming; they may decide to measure writing skills indirectly by administering multiple-choice tests that require students to choose the most clearly written selections.

Instruction vs. Evaluation

Another important factor that influences the use of assessment techniques is the kind of information desired from the assessment, and how it will be used. This factor requires careful scrutiny of the relationship between instruction and evaluation, teaching and testing. Summative evaluation refers to terminal assessment—end-of-term, end-of-course, end-of-year. A final examination used for summative purposes must determine whether or not an examinee has learned sufficiently what he or she has been taught. Formative evaluation, on the other hand, attempts to provide "formative" information to the instructor. Daily quizzes in the classroom and practice tests in a job training course may both be used to indicate what the student has and has not learned thus far.

This distinction is important when considering different types of assessment. Some techniques provide feedback to the examinee, which may be more helpful to the teacher for formative purposes than other techniques which provide little or no feedback. Those which provide only a total score, or scores by subtest, may be sufficient if the program's purpose is summative (e.g., Did the student pass the course or not?).

The remainder of this chapter comprises the introductory descriptions of assessment types. For each type, the description indicates the mode of assessment, mode of response, mode of administration, and method of scoring. Examples of each assessment technique are provided, as well as brief discussions of its technical characteristics, advantages, and disadvantages. Evaluative comments on the various types derive from comparisons made across all types of assessment, in terms of the criteria discussed thus far: product vs. process evaluation, degree of realism, directness of measure, and instruction vs. evaluation.

Actual Performance Assessments

Actual performance assessments include those techniques which are administered in actual work or classroom settings, and which generally require actual performance of some kind. Actual performance tests provide the most realistic assessment of job-related competencies, but they are often time-consuming and expensive to design, administer, and score. They may be used to evaluate a product, a process, or both; and they may be used to test skills in the affective, cognitive, psychomotor, and perceptual domains.

This category includes the following specific techniques: work-sample tests, identification tests, supervisor ratings, peer ratings, and self-assessment. In most of these techniques, the examinee is assessed individually while performing a given task, usually through observation. Thus, actual performance and observational assessment are interdependent. Although the subjective nature of observational judgment can cause difficulties in achieving reliable results, instruments designed to measure actual performance can be fairly objective and reliable if constructed carefully.

Work-Sample Tests

Work-sample tests cover a broad range of assessment techniques which may focus on product, process, or both. They may be closely controlled for assessment purposes, or they may not be controlled at all. Essentially, a task is assigned to the examinee and the result is evaluated, usually by judges using checklists or rating scales (see Chapter Six). If the assessment is intended to measure process, then observational judgment occurs as the examinee performs the task; judgment of a product may occur afterwards. A test of process is usually administered and scored individually, while a product test may be administered to a large group and scored for each individual.

Work-sample tests have been widely used to assess products in many areas, such as food preparation (a loaf of bread), office skills (a typed letter or transcription), industry, plastic arts (sculpture, film-making), construction, and manufacturing. Tests of process have been used in vehicle operation (road test required for a driver's license), the performing arts (auditions for performers), physical fitness, laboratory research, sales, personnel, and office skills. Many of these uses have, in the past, been relatively informal; for example, a director who wishes to choose a chorus line of dancers is unlikely to use a carefully constructed checklist to rate each applicant. But in a formal assessment program, the mode of assessment, mode of response, and method of scoring must all be defined and implemented with care.

Identification Tests

As its name implies, an identification test measures an individual's ability to identify something—a tool, object, material, problem, function, or quality—in a job or performance context. For example, a dentist might be asked to identify the specific tools required to cap a tooth. The term *identification test*, however, has been used to refer to actual performance, simulated performance, and objective (paper-and-pencil) tests. And, it often refers to something that requires more than identification.

In relation to actual performance, the examinee taking an identification test must often perceive and respond to some form of perceptual input. Troubleshooting skills, for example, are frequently measured by identification tests. An electronics technician might be handed a radio with a malfunction; the technician's task would be to listen, to *identify* the malfunction, and perhaps to fix it. Other perceptual stimuli might be auditory (listening to a car engine), gustatory (tasting wines or bread), tactile (feeling the texture of fabrics or wood), olfactory (smelling laboratory chemicals or medical antiseptics), or visual (judging colors by sight). In response to the stimuli, the examinee must identify each stimulus and/or what is wrong with it. The examinee's response may be expressed in oral or written form, indicated by motion, or implied by what the examinee does next. Theoretically, an identification test requires only identification, but many are constructed with further steps dependent on the identification. An auto mechanic, for instance, may have to listen to an engine, locate the problem, then fix it. When additional steps are added, the test often becomes a combination of identification and work-sample test. When it is simply an identification test, it is most useful as a vocational training device, or for screening out those candidates who cannot identify the basic tools or functions of a given trade (Gronlund, 1977).

Supervisor and Peer Ratings

Whether by the supervisor or a peer, *ratings* are evaluative judgments about an employee or trainee (or possibly, of a student) based on observation of and interaction with that person in an actual job situation. Most often these judgments are based on the individual's performance, attitude, and competencies; and they are more often made over a period of time than in a controlled testing situation. The supervisor or peer records his or her ratings on a checklist or rating scale. For example, a teacher training supervisor may rate a student teacher on the basis of a semester's work in the classroom; or the owner of a plumbing firm may rate an employee engaged as an apprentice. In some cases, peers make similar judgments from their perspectives (which are theoretically similar to the examinee's).

Ratings by supervisors and peers are most often used in training programs, as with apprentices or student teachers, and in employee evaluations (e.g., for promotions to better jobs within a company). They are not widely credited for their reliability because of their inherent subjectivity, particularly with peers. (If they are peers, i.e., trainees or fellow employees, they are seldom qualified to judge others at the same level; also, they may be vying for the same promotion as those whom they rate.) In fact, supervisor ratings have been declared unacceptable in court cases (*Brito et al. v. Zia Company,* 1973; *Moody v. Albemarle Paper Company,* 1975), because they were based on vague and subjective criteria, and because their use in personnel selection procedures resulted in adverse impact.

Self-Assessment

Various forms of self-assessment require the examinee or trainee to evaluate his or her own performance. This may involve an introspective observation, a product assessment, or an actual test, self-administered in an uncontrolled situation. The primary use of self-assessment is actually for instruction and not testing; it can provide the examinee with a view of his or her own strengths and weaknesses, illustrate the value of quality control guidelines, and impress upon the examinee the importance of assessment criteria.

Simulations

In a certain World War II movie, a number of British military personnel entered a classroom on the first day of their training course for espionage work. Just as everyone sat down and the instructor began to introduce himself, a woman charged through the door at the back of the room, raced up the aisle, shot the instructor in the chest, grabbed a document from his desk, and ran out again—all in about five seconds. The ensuing pandemonium lasted only about a minute, until the instructor hopped up, wiped the ketchup off his shirt front, and began asking questions: "Was that a man or a woman? How many shots were fired? What did the person take from the desk?" Etc.

This is a wonderful example of a simulated performance test or simulation, a type most often used in situations in which actual performance tests are impractical, for any of a number of reasons: cost, danger, the serious consequences of mistakes, or the impossibility of arranging actual performance situations. For these same reasons, simulations are more often used as training tools than as instruments for evaluation. In the spy school example, the trainer could hardly afford to plan a real event like the one used; but the simulation worked ideally, particularly as a sort of "pretest" to show the new trainees what they did not know and would have to learn.

Simulations have been used to train and to evaluate pilots, surgeons, blasters, management trainees, psychiatrists, physicians, and many others. These types of tests provide less direct measures of job skills and behaviors than actual performance tests, but are more direct than paper-and-pencil objective tests. Also, simulations generally enable the assessor to control most of the variables in the testing situation (unlike in a real job), to standardize the test across candidates and situations, to present the test in a fairly realistic context, and to measure on-the-job behaviors and skills.

This category includes five different types of assessments: simulated performance tests, simulated identification tests, written simulations, management exercises, and simulator machines. All five types are designed to simulate actual job or work situations; but even within one particular type, the degree of fidelity to the real situation may vary significantly. For example, the mode of response in a simulated identification test may be kinetic, written, oral, or visual. Each would provide a more or less direct measure of whatever skill is tested.

Simulated Performance Tests

A simulated performance test is one that requires physical performance in a simulated setting. The performance itself must resemble the actual on-the-job performance as closely as possible, but the testing conditions usually vary from the real conditions. Most simulated performance tests are used to measure the examinee's competence in technical procedures, management skills, and behavior (usually under pressure). Most often, simulated performance tests are used instead of actual performance in situations in which errors could have serious consequences. For example, the National Registry of Emergency Medical Technicians conducts simulated performance tests in which candidates for certification as EMTs have to administer first aid (to actors pretending injury) or apply cardiopulmonary resuscitation (to a mannequin). The use of simulated performance tests also tends to improve test reliability, over that attainable in actual performance, because the test situation can be standardized. However, in return for improved reliability, the realism of the context decreases.

Simulated Identification Tests

As mentioned earlier, identification tests may be used in actual or simulated performance, or in paper-and-pencil assessment. Primarily, simulated identification tests differ from actual performance in that the examinee does not actually perform a particular function in a real situation. The context of the test is a controlled situation, as opposed to a real job or work situation, in which the examinee either identifies parts or problems and does nothing more, or responds by manipulating a model. For example, the dentist who handles each tool in actual performance might only handle plastic tools here; or a medical student might identify the parts of the body on a mannequin and describe how an operation would be performed, but would not actually perform the operation. Simulated identification tests usually measure an examinee's cognitive understanding of how to perform a task, but not his or her actual ability to do it.

Written Simulations

A written simulation is a paper-and-pencil exercise designed to simulate a decision-making process in which the examinee must make inquiries, make decisions based on the results of those inquiries, and take action. The simulation begins with the presentation of a realistic situation, information related to it, and a written problem. By working through the written problem step-by-step, the examinee either solves the problem or faces unacceptable consequences resulting from his or her own decisions.

This type of simulation has a number of significant characteristics that distinguish it from actual performance and from paper-and-pencil tests: (1) the exercise requires a series of sequential, interdependent decisions analogous to the various stages of solving a problem—presentation, interpretation, analysis, resolution; (2) the examinee receives feedback after each action taken, but the examinee's decision cannot be retracted (on the basis of that feedback); and (3) a written simulation can be constructed to allow for a number of different, but acceptable, solutions, thereby permitting the examinee to pursue any of several reasonable approaches.

This type of exercise was first developed by the military to train and to test technicians in how to go about solving a technical problem, e.g., repairing an electronic transmitter, which requires a methodical procedure. It is now used in many fields—from training young people how to survive alone in the wilderness with only limited equipment, to testing sales approaches, to testing police investigators, to training and evaluating management personnel. In particular, written simulations—also called "clinical simulations" or "patient management problems"—are used widely in the medical field to train and test physicians and other medical personnel. Given a summary of the condition of a patient entering the out-patient clinic, the examinee must choose questions to ask the patient, diagnose the patient's problem, and prescribe treatment; the examinee receives feedback after each choice.

As with most types of simulations, written ones are useful both for teaching and testing. The American Academy of Family Physicians (AAFP), for example, has developed a self-assessment program for its members as part of a continuing medical education program. Each unit of the six-year program includes a monograph, a series of tests, and a patient management problem in which to apply newly acquired knowledge to a realistic situation.

Finally, as Fitzpatrick and Morrison (1971) note, some types of simulations have another distinct advantage: they test the examinee's ability to decide which information is most critical to solving the problem *and* which information is too costly or impractical to use (and should be discarded). Glaser, Damrin, and Gardner (1952) used "Tab Items" (simulations in which the choices and the feedback responses were printed on opposite sides of index cards) to achieve this in an exam for repairpersons who had to determine which tests to make. The AAFP's patient management problems include such a component: physicians are penalized for choosing lab tests or treatments for the hypothetical patient that are unnecessary, too costly, or too dangerous.

Management Exercises

In a formal assessment, management exercises are situational tests which require the examinee to assume a role and act according to the needs of the situation. They are designed primarily to measure, through an elaborate simulation, how a person would act in certain circumstances, in order to predict how the person will act when placed in the real situation. The term *management*, in this case, is not confined to the realm of the business executive; it refers to the skills needed for "management" of people and situations. These skills include the ability to analyze the situation, consider alternatives, evaluate information, solve problems, and make decisions.

Situational tests and management exercises have been used for centuries in diverse contexts, most likely beginning with the earliest versions of tactical war games. Today in occupational and educational assessment, the most useful forms of this type of exercise are role-playing situations in general and in-basket tests in particular.

In a role-playing situation, the examinee receives instructions and information about the role he or she is to play. The situation generally involves a problem and requires the examinee to use interpersonal skills to interact with other "players" (who may be examinees, examiners, instructors, or professional actors) and solve the problem. Observational judgment is used in scoring the person's actions. For example, a trainee at a police academy might be asked to role-play the officer in charge of an interrogation; his or her job is to question possible witnesses, played by other trainees. The instructor watches, rates the trainee's performance, then provides feedback as to which skills are adequate and which need improvement. As with other forms of simulated performance assessment, role-playing provides a direct measure of certain skills, such as those required to communicate with others, in a relatively realistic setting; but it is more useful as a training technique than as an assessment instrument.

The in-basket test, developed primarily by Fredericksen (1960) of Educational Testing Service, is essentially a specialized role-playing situation customized for business executives. It has been refined, however, to a point where observational judgments and rating procedures can be executed objectively and reliably—unlike many other types of role-playing assessments, which continue to be informal and subjectively scored. As its name implies, this test requires a person to assume the role of a management executive and deal with a day's worth of typical "in-basket" information, problems, and so on. Two particular virtues of this approach are: (1) it measures an examinee's abilities to manage time and personnel, and (2) it does so in a fairly realistic setting.

Simulator Machines

A simulator machine is an apparatus that closely approximates an actual piece of equipment or component of a larger machine. As an assessment or training device, it is used to measure technical or repair skills, particularly when the actual apparatus would be impossible to use because of danger, expense, or other impracticalities. Aircraft pilots are trained and tested with simulators (for obvious safety considerations), as are astronauts (for practical reasons); some people learn with simulators to drive automobiles; and many technicians are trained and tested on devices that simulate such equipment as washing machines, radar, and transistor radios.

Tests involving simulator machines may require the examinee to locate and repair a malfunction, or may assess the examinee's abilities to operate the device properly under specified conditions. For example, pilots must maneuver the simulated airplane through rough weather, emergency situations, or programmed malfunctions. Within the constraints of most assessment programs, particularly in education, simulator machines are too expensive to utilize. On the other hand, they are less expensive than the real devices (e.g., an automobile or a space capsule), and they provide a fairly direct measure of skills in a setting that is only slightly less realistic than the actual.

Observational Assessments

Observational assessments are used primarily as methods of scoring an examinee's performance in a controlled testing situation, or in a naturally occurring situation. The former is *obtrusive* observation: watching the performance of someone who knows you are watching and judging him or her. *Unobtrusive* observation refers to observation of someone in a natural situation, in which the examinee is usually unaware of being observed for the purpose of evaluation. Elementary school teachers use unobtrusive observation continually to assess children's skills, attitudes, and behaviors. A supervisor who evaluates his or her employees might observe them "unobtrusively" every day—although employees generally know they are always being assessed—or obtrusively during certain predetermined situations.

Observational assessments permit an evaluator to assess performance or behaviors that require subjective judgments, and that cannot be measured adequately by other, more objective kinds of tests. The observer watches the examinee's performance, then records his or her observations on one of four types of instruments: checklists, rating scales, ranking scales, or anecdotal records. Thus, what people often refer to as an "observational test" is actually a scoring instrument which is seldom used independently; it is almost always used in combination with another type of assessment such as actual or simulated performance, oral presentation, or interview. This scoring instrument, however, provides the framework and the criteria for the observation: it specifies what to look for, and how closely.

Instruments for recording observations vary in purpose, format, specificity, and formality. Checklists, which generally require a yes/no judgment, may be quantitative or qualitative. On a quantitative checklist, the observer marks "yes" if an event takes place (e.g., the student drew a picture) and "no" if it does not (this type of checklist may also include how many times an event occurs, e.g., the student tied her shoes by herself three times this week). Qualitative checklists also require yes/no judgments, but the criteria generally involve some evaluation of quality (e.g., yes, the student drew a colorful picture; but no, the object pictured was not clear).

Rating scales may require numerical ratings, graphic ratings, descriptive-graphic ratings, or rankings. Basically, all of these scales require judgment as to where a product, performance, or attitude falls on a spectrum from good to bad, high to low, etc. In a numerical rating scale, each number represents a value; the observer circles the most appropriate number. For example:

The individual is:	Never				Always
punctual	1	2	3	4	5
reliable	1	2	3	4	5
self-motivating	1	2	3	4	5

A graphic rating scale uses language rather than numbers, as in this example:

Dimension / Neatness

Distressing   Sloppy   Fairly Neat   Meticulous   Impeccable

The observer marks the place on the line that indicates the individual's propensity for neatness. The most common ratings in this type of scale extend from "poor" to "excellent."

Descriptive-graphic scales also use words to denote ratings, but the gradations are more clearly defined. For example, a rating of "excellent" in organizational skills may be defined as "labels each part clearly, maintains consistent level of specificity," etc.

All of these various scales may be used in the assessment of products or processes, attitudes or behaviors. The standard for assessing each one by a rating scale or checklist is embodied within the instrument; that is, a behavior might be compared to a written description of various behaviors. With a ranking scale, the standard of comparison changes. For example, a set of products might be ranked from best to worst within a group. If the products are compared to one another, then the ranking scale may serve a normative-referenced purpose: examinees are compared within a group, and their ranks may vary if compared to any other group.

A different type of ranking scale is the product scale, which is essentially criterion-referenced. With the product scale, a representative sample of products (e.g., model buildings by construction designers) is collected and arranged in order of quality (to serve as the criterion); all other products are judged against the criterion.

Finally, the fourth type of observational assessment is the anecdotal record, which is a factual written description of significant events in a person's life or work. Anecdotal records are most often used by elementary school teachers, but they may also be used by employers to record commendable (or uncommendable) accomplishments or behaviors by their staff members. The purpose of these records is to set down, as objectively as possible, events that might otherwise be forgotten or remembered incorrectly. By referring to accumulated records in a personnel file, for example, a supervisor may become aware of patterns of behavior, or may refresh his or her memory for an annual evaluation of an employee.

The major advantages to observational assessment are these: (1) they provide for the most direct measure of certain skills, and (2) they provide detailed criteria for observing and evaluating complex products and procedures. However, observational tests are expensive and time-consuming to develop and to administer because they are so detailed and are administered individually. Also, the subjectivity of observation—which cannot be totally eliminated—must be minimized through careful construction, training of observers, and, if possible, observation by more than one judge. These procedures will improve the reliability of the instruments, but will also increase costs and time required for administration.

Oral Assessments

Oral assessments require some form of oral response from the examinee, they must be administered on an individual or small-group basis, and must usually be scored during the administration (unless the response is such that a tape recording can be used). The three assessment techniques in this category are: interviews, oral examinations, and prepared presentations. Time and cost may be relatively high for these techniques, and scoring is difficult to accomplish in a valid and reliable manner; but oral-response tests can be used to measure skills and behaviors, such as speaking skills, which cannot be measured adequately by other techniques. Oral-response tests are perhaps best suited to fields that require oral communication skills, such as foreign language teaching or public speaking; but they have been widely used in other fields for screening or selecting applicants for any number of positions.

Interviews may be used for screening or selection and may require the interviewee to answer questions designed to elicit attitudes, values, content knowledge, communication skills, or experience. Job interviews are used for selection purposes: the intent is to select the best candidate from a pool of applicants, based on personal qualifications and the results of personal interviews. Screening interviews are used in many licensing and certification programs to "screen out" those applicants who may have all the necessary qualifications, but should not be granted licenses or certificates, for one reason or another. For example, the Wisconsin Examining Board of Architects, Designers, Land Surveyors, and Engineers interviews every candidate who has satisfied all other program requirements for licensure. In California, however, the Board of Architectural Examiners requires each candidate to pass an oral examination, after passing all other requirements. The oral exam consists of content-based, technical questions.

Oral examinations may be "quizzes," or they may be "oral defenses"; both are designed to assess either factual or comprehensive in-depth knowledge of a particular subject. Oral quizzes usually require the examinee to answer a series of questions designed to assess a store of information necessary for professional competence; or they may be used in education to assess skills in language, public speaking, and so on. An oral defense consists of questions based on a particular product (e.g., a design, a thesis or dissertation, a research experiment) which the examinee has developed and must defend before the examining board. Both these approaches are widely used in academic settings to assess knowledge of subject matter, interpretive and problem-solving skills, and oral communication skills.

As an assessment technique, the prepared presentation is used in many professional areas: candidates applying for jobs (e.g., in the dramatic arts), student teachers, product demonstrations, design projects—all of these may involve prepared presentations. The presentation itself may utilize visual or audio aids, such as filmstrips or overhead transparencies, in addition to the oral component. Primarily, the purpose is to assess the candidate's professional presence and ability to communicate information in a specified context; for example, prepared presentations of research papers are common at professional association conventions. With the possible exceptions of student teaching and sales/marketing businesses, however, prepared presentations are more likely to be for selection purposes than for screening to determine those who have attained a specified level of competence. They are also valuable training aids in certain professions, used to help persons improve their skills of presentation.

Paper-and-Pencil Assessments

Although these techniques are often called *objective* tests, the term *paper-and-pencil* seems clearer and less confusi. g. Calling one type of test "objective" implies that other tests are subjective, which may be a relative truth but certainly not an absolute. Also, confusion with *objective-referenced* tests and *objectives* themselves may cause unnecessary problems. An objective test is one that can be measured objectively—it includes only questions that can be answered right or wrong; an objective test is *not* necessarily one that is based on objectives (although it may be).

Paper-and-pencil assessments include standard objective tests such as multiple-choice and supply-type questions, and non-standard computer-adaptive tests; they also include essay tests, written reports, and design problems (which are not usually considered "objective," but may well be so).

Since we are concerned primarily with *alternative* assessments in this book, standard paper-and-pencil tests receive little attention, except as standards of comparison to the alternatives. As mentioned earlier in this chapter, selection- and supply-type questions (e.g., multiple-choice items and fill-ins) may be quite adequate for measuring cognitive skills and factual knowledge; they are usually the least expensive techniques to use in large-scale assessments because they can be administered to large groups and scored manually or by machine.

Computer-adaptive tests also utilize paper-and-pencil items, which are sequenced by the computer and presented to the examinee. The primary virtue of this type is the computer's ability to select items of specific levels of difficulty and present them in an order determined by the examinee's performance on previous items. Essentially, the computer tailors the test to each examinee by administering items that increase in difficulty until the examinee answers incorrectly, then an easier item is administered. Item selection occurs spontaneously as the examinee takes the test. Although this approach has been used in programmed learning contexts by the military, it has little practical value in most assessment programs at this time. Proliferation of inexpensive computers in the future may change this, however, and make computer-adaptive testing more feasible for individualized instruction and assessment.

Essay Tests

The "back-to-basics" movement that gathered steam in the 70s has led to widespread use of essay tests in writing assessment programs. Proponents of writing assessment remind us that the only direct way to teach or test writing skills is by having the students or examinees write. Essay tests need not be the types we have all taken in the past, which would require the examinee, for example, to "write a five-page essay on the history of human-kind." Essay tests may include extended writing samples or brief responses on any subject. Recent trends have manifested a penchant for writing as a "life skill," e.g., write a letter to your representative, or to the editor of your local newspaper.

In certain professional contexts, such as bar examinations for lawyers, essay tests may be considered actual or simulated performance. That is, lawyers must be able to write briefs and other legal documents; thus, essay tests may be realistic and directly related to job performance. Educators have also begun to use large-scale writing assessments in high school minimum competency programs to ensure that high school graduates have acquired some level of writing skills. The Connecticut Ninth-Grade Proficiency Test (1979), which all ninth-graders must pass, is an example; it includes sections on mathematics, reading, and language arts—and a writing sample for which students must produce essays on very specific subjects of relevance to all ninth-graders.

Written Reports

As assessment instruments, written reports are used either like the essay, to evaluate an examinee's in-depth knowledge of a given subject; or, like the prepared presentation, to assess written communication skills, and the ability to select, effectively organize, and present materials and ideas. Essentially, the examinee chooses or is assigned a subject and prepares a report, then submits it as a basis for evaluation.

Beyond the academic context where written reports are common, this technique may be used by any profession which requires writing skills, e.g., proposal writing for marketing, advertising copywriting, script writing, and technical writing. Writing samples, which may be considered work-sample tests in these contexts, or as program requirements, are often required as part of job applications for positions that require writing skills.

Design Problems

Design problems, as such, are almost unique to professional fields that require design skills, such as architecture and engineering. The National Council of Engineering Examiners (NCEE) now includes design problems on its test of engineering fundamentals, as does the National Council of Architectural Registration Boards (NCARB) on its Professional Examination for architect licensure candidates. Like essay tests in certain contexts, design problems may be considered work-sample tests for some professions.

In most design problems, the examinee receives a packet of information, from which he or she must produce a design. The

NCARB test, for example, provides examinees with topographical maps of a proposed building site and a set of building requirements; the examinee must draw a site plan to satisfy the requirements and fit in with the features of the site. Examinees' designs are then scored by three judges who are professional architects.

Standard design problems are limited to the professional fields mentioned, but we might also consider other types of design problems. For example, elementary school students who must draw geometric figures, or art students who must sketch a model, are required to solve "design problems" of a sort.

Program Requirements

The last category of assessment techniques is called *program requirements,* which is a specific label for a miscellany of various types of assessment. An assessment program, whether occupational or educational, may have a number of requirements; one or more of these requirements may be examinations constructed with any of the techniques discussed previously. But the program may also have other requirements that each candidate must satisfy. This category is concerned with the "other" requirements which are not examinations, but are still techniques of assessing an individual's qualifications.

Program requirements may include personal records (educational background, transcripts, recommendations), required submissions (such as portfolios), internships, and a number of others. The purpose of the program normally dictates its requirements. If the program requirements are stipulated by law, as in licensing procedures, then they must conform to federal guidelines; i.e., they must be closely related to skills required for the job itself.

Architect licensing provides a good example. The California Board of Architectural Examiners currently requires candidates for architect licensing to complete an architectural degree program at an accredited institution, or pass a qualifying test (NCARB). The candidate must also complete up to eight years of job experience (internship) and must pass NCARB's Professional Examination. Following the completion of all these requirements, the candidate submits to an interview and an oral examination. In this procedure for licensing architects, the program requirements are the degree and the internship; other requirements are forms of examinations.

Summary
This chapter has covered a number of assessment techniques classified in six categories: actual performance assessments, simulations, observational assessments, oral and paper-and-pencil assessments, and program requirements. Each technique has a mode of assessment, mode of response, method of scoring, and mode of administration. In addition, the techniques vary in relation to other factors: product vs. process evaluation, degree of realism, directness of measure, and instruction vs. evaluation.

With this information about assessment techniques, the process of designing a test can begin. This process involves decisions as to which techniques to use and how to put them together in an assessment instrument. Once completed, the test design will guide the development of specific techniques for the instrument.

Each assessment technique introduced and briefly described here is explored in depth in the chapters following test design. Emphases in these later chapters include how to construct each type of assessment, how to administer it, and how to score the results.

Selected References

Boyd, J.C., Jr., and Shimberg, B. *Handbook of Performance Testing: A Practical Guide for Test Makers.* Princeton, N.J.: Educational Testing Service, 1970.

Brito et al. v. Zia Company, 478 F 2d 1200 (1973).

Connecticut Ninth-Grade Proficiency Test. Hartford, Conn.: State Board of Education, 1979.

Erickson, R.C., and Wentling, T.L. *Measuring Student Growth.* Boston: Allyn and Bacon, Inc., 1976.

Fitzpatrick, R., and Morrison, E.J. Performance and product evaluation. In R.L. Thorndike (Ed.), *Educational Measurement, Second Edition.* Washington, D.C.: American Council on Education, 1971.

Fredericksen, N. In-basket tests and factors in administration performance. *Procedures of the International Conference on Testing Problems—1960.* Princeton, N.J.: Educational Testing Service, 1960.

Glaser, R., Damrin, D.E., and Gardner, F.M. *The Tab Item: A Technique for the Measurement of Proficiency in Diagnostic Problem-Solving Tasks.* Urbana: University of Illinois, College of Education, Bureau of Research and Service, 1952.

Gronlund, N.E. *Constructing Achievement Tests, Third Edition.* Englewood Cliffs, N.J.: Prentice-Hall, Inc., 1977.

Moody v. Albemarle Paper Company, 9 EPC 10, 230 (1975), 94 S. Ct. 2513.

Nunnally, J.C. *Educational Measurement and Evaluation, Second Edition.* New York: McGraw-Hill Book Company, 1972.

Priestley, M., and Nassif, P.M. From here to validity: Developing a conceptual framework for test item generation in criterion-referenced measurement. *Educational Technology,* February 1979, *19*(2).

Sanders, J.R., and Sachse, T.P. Applied performance testing in the classroom. *Journal of Research and Development in Education,* 1977, *10*(3).

U.S. Equal Employment Opportunity Commission. Guidelines on employee selection procedures. *Federal Register,* 1978, *43*(166), 38290-38309.

Chapter Three

Test Design

Designing an assessment instrument, or test, requires an overall program design and some familiarity with various types of assessment methods. Chapters One and Two cover these prerequisites; the purpose of this chapter is to begin integrating this information. The ideal test design takes into consideration each important facet of the program context and attempts to meet the program's ultimate goal(s); it also utilizes available assessment methods to the best advantage, i.e., to collect useful measurement data.

The basic aim of this chapter is to provide a model for creating a test design by matching test content with testing methods: what is to be tested with how to test it most effectively. Fundamental concepts covered in this chapter include the following:

Considerations for Test Design
Test Blueprinting
Sample Test Specifications
Item Specifications

All of these concepts and procedures may occur in the development of an assessment program, although the sequence in which they occur may vary from one program to another. Some programs may require only some of these steps.

Considerations for Test Design

The purpose of test design is twofold: to ensure that the final product will meet the goals of the assessment program and to plan in advance for test development. All of the issues discussed here should be considered in the initial stages of test design. Decisions made in relation to these issues should govern every stage of the developmental process.

Purpose of program. The assessment instrument designed at this stage must be constructed to meet the program goals or purpose, which may be defined as a sort of "mission statement." If the program's purpose is to license barbers, for example, then one component of the program will be an assessment instrument designed for licensing. Essentially, this assessment will certify that each candidate for licensure possesses the knowledge, skills, training, and personal attributes necessary to practice a barber's profession. A different program might be designed to *screen* applicants for admission to an apprenticeship program, or to gauge a student's *achievement* in a training program, or to *place* applicants in a suitable career position. Each assessment instrument must serve its stated purpose: screening, achievement, placement.

Practical issues. Factors such as time and money may dictate test design from the very beginning, particularly in a program mandated by law or developed by an agency with limited resources. If a state legislature decides that the Department of Education must implement a basic skills testing program within one year, then the Department cannot design a testing program that will take two years to develop.

The important point here is to consider practical issues before designing the test, just as these issues were considered earlier in designing the overall assessment program. How much money is available? How much time is available? Are the required personnel available to develop, administer, and score the test? Is the required technical expertise available to do the job; and, if not, can it be obtained?

Technical issues. Technical considerations are likely to be the most complex and extensive issues in developing the program. Professional expertise may be required to answer many of the questions raised here—questions that are essential to any assessment program.

A test design must provide for the validity and reliability of the assessment instrument. Simply stated, *validity* refers to whether or not a test measures what it purports to measure; *reliability* refers to whether or not test scores actually reflect an examinee's performance, knowledge, or skills. In practical terms, these issues require careful planning to ensure that the test is constructed properly, that it is long enough to be reliable, that the assessment devices or items measure the competencies identified, and so on. (Each of these requirements is discussed in more depth in later sections.)

A vital requirement here is to plan for the future, assuming that the assessment program will be continuous or cyclical; that is, tests will be administered periodically in the years ahead. If this is the case, then the test design must incorporate provisions for developing parallel or equivalent test forms; for revising the test enough to prevent a breach of test security (but not enough to decrease its reliability); and for developing future tests cost-effectively.

In relation to the program goals, a test must produce the results expected and required. This means, for example, that a test must be designed to produce useful scores. Scoring issues must be considered at the outset to ensure an accommodating test design. A certification program, for example, may require a written test of three content areas: must an applicant pass all three areas independently, or will a *compensatory* score (a high score on one area may compensate for a low score in another) be sufficient? The answers to this kind of question help to determine the number of subareas in a test, if any, and how many items must be included in each.

The type of test, its length, and types of items should also be considered during the planning stages. The purpose of the test, what it measures, its level of difficulty, and the need for reliability all contribute to these determinations, which must be decided before completing the test blueprint.

Legal issues. As discussed in Chapter One, legal issues related to assessment will influence the planning and development of a test. Federal guidelines may require test developers to prove that a test is job-related, valid, reliable, and free of bias. Procedures used in test development must be planned with legal requirements in mind, and every step of the process should be clearly, comprehensively documented. This is particularly true of licensing and employee selection programs, those which are most likely to come under scrutiny; but every type of assessment should be planned and documented carefully.

Test Blueprinting

When all of the preceding issues—practical, technical, and legal—have been considered in depth and the determinations incorporated in the program planning, then development of a test blueprint can begin. The primary purposes of a test blueprint, or test specifications, are to: (1) ensure that the test meets the program's goals, and (2) provide a plan for test development. A blueprint should be specific and lucid enough to enable any test developer to use it in developing or understanding the structure of a test, today or five years from today.

Some test developers use the terms *test blueprint* and *test specifications* interchangeably, but there is a distinction between them. As the name implies, *test specifications* are more detailed and more specific than a blueprint. The two terms derive from architecture and engineering; an architect may draw a blueprint to illustrate the overall structure of a building and its components; then he or she draws up specifications that list the quantity and quality of materials to be used in constructing the building.

In this book, the term *test blueprint* refers to the general design of a test, and *test specifications* refers to the detailed versions of the general design. The test blueprint is normally developed first, then specifications are developed from the information in the blueprint.

Common features of a test blueprint (for a criterion-referenced test) include the following:

- test length,
- domain specifications,
- proportionality design,
- type and number of measures, and
- scoring methods.

Each feature is described below, and a number of examples follow these descriptions.

Test length. At this point, overall test length is most practically stated as an expression of the time required for test administration. Specifications for a one-hour test and a 32-hour test will vary significantly, so the first decision to make is a determination of how long the test should be. As with all the features of a test blueprint, the length of the test may change later; but the preliminary blueprint should outline the characteristics of each feature as accurately as possible.

Ideally, test length depends on the domain to be measured and the techniques used for measurement, although cost and time factors may dictate the maximum test length. Also, certain types, e.g., minimum competency tests, should not have time limits during the administration (a test designed to assess whether or not a candidate possesses certain factual knowledge should not be dependent upon the candidate's ability to answer questions within a given time period). But practicality requires setting some sort of limits on the test, both in planning and administration.

A test should only be as long as is required to measure the specified domain reliably. To measure a person's writing skills, for example, might call for a 30-minute test composed of one essay question. Less than 30 minutes would probably be insufficient time for the examinee to develop an essay, but a test of two hours would probably not provide any more information on the examinee's writing skills than would the 30-minute test.

To approximate the length of the test, determine the most reliable method for measuring the specified domain, the number of items or assessment devices required, and the time needed to administer these items or devices. In reality, many test developers make this determination in reverse order: first they determine how long the test will be, then how many competencies can be measured within that length of time; but the *ideal* method is to begin with the domain or competencies to be measured, then determine how long the measurement will take.

Domain specifications. The most important feature of a test blueprint is the set of domain specifications which provide a definition of what the test measures. Domain specifications often comprise a list of subareas and a list of competencies within each subarea that identify the knowledge, skills, or attributes that the test must measure. Also, it is assumed that the domain has been defined through a technically sound job or task analysis. (There are other ways to define a field, job, or area of knowledge, but each one generally accomplishes the same goal: to analyze the domain and determine which parts of it are essential; essential parts should then be tested.)

Figure 3.1 is an example of domain specifications for a test of students in an industrial arts training program; it lists the content subareas included in the test and the number of competencies in each subarea.

The number of competencies per subarea has been defined on the basis of a hypothetical job analysis. A more detailed set of domain specifications would list each competency, as in the following brief example:

    I.   Industrial Technology
        Competency 1. Demonstrate the use of drafting instruments.
        Competency 2. Construct a working drawing from specifications.

(Note: This particular example will be expanded as each feature is added, but will not include lists of competencies due to space limitations.)

A test constructed to measure this domain in industrial arts would consist of six subareas and would measure 50 competencies. The next step is to determine the proportionality or "weighting" of each subarea.

Proportionality design. A job analysis provides two important pieces of information: those competencies which the test should measure and the relative importance of each area. For example, if 200 industrial arts teachers analyzed and rated 100 competency statements, the results might be a set of 50 competencies considered "important" or job-related, i.e., essential to the practice of industrial arts. A test based on these results would

Figure 3.1

Example: Domain Specifications

Field: Industrial Arts	
Subareas	# of Competencies
I. Industrial Technology	12
II. Graphic Arts	8
III. Electricity and Electronics	10
IV. Manufacturing and Construction	11
V. Power and Transportation	4
VI. Industry in America	5
Total:	50

measure the 50 competencies, and each subarea would reflect the importance of its competencies in the field. In the example specifications, subarea III, "Electricity and Electronics," includes ten of the 50 job-related competencies, or 20 percent. To determine the proportionality of the domain, calculate the percentage of the whole that each subarea represents. See Figure 3.2.

Following this design, a test would be constructed to measure the competencies in each subarea; each subarea of the test would be proportional to the relative importance of the subarea in the domain. Thus, measures of "Graphic Arts" competencies would represent 16 percent of the test; "Industry in America" would represent ten percent; and so on. (Some test developers, in addition to the empirical basis for determining proportionality, use expert judgment to determine the appropriate "weighting" of each subarea or skill. Thus, a certain portion of the test could

Figure 3.2

Example: Proportionality Design

Field: Industrial Arts		
Subareas	# of Competencies	%
I. Industrial Technology	12	24
II. Graphic Arts	8	16
III. Electricity and Electronics	10	20
IV. Manufacturing and Construction	11	22
V. Power and Transportation	4	8
VI. Industry in America	5	10
Totals:	50	100%

represent only 20 percent of the domain, but account for 80 percent of an examinee's score. This complex issue is considered in greater depth in later chapters.)

Type and number of measures. The domain specifications and proportionality design describe what the test will measure and the relative importance of each subarea. The next step is to determine how to measure the competencies: what type of assessment technique and how many.

To an extent, each competency determines the type of assessment required to measure it; but this ideal situation is seldom practical. Any competency may be assessed in a number of ways, with varying degrees of accuracy and directness (as explained in Chapter Two). The example competency "Construct a working drawing" may be assessed by performance, simulation, design problem, or by other forms of paper-and-pencil assessment. Most desirable would be a design problem: this would provide a direct measure of skills that could be scored analytically. In a design problem, the student would receive a set of specifications and instructions that say "Construct a working drawing from these specifications of a machine part." Least desirable would be to assess a student's drawing skills by asking him or her to inspect a drawing and determine what is wrong with it (Instructions: "Analyze this drawing of a machine part and list the errors made by the drafter."). This would test the candidate's knowledge of working drawings and how they should be drawn, but would not test the actual ability to draw. The most direct measure of this competency would actually require the examinee to "construct" a working drawing.

Ideally, each competency should be measured by the most direct, most reliable method; but the selection of assessment methods also depends on practical considerations, such as resources available, scoring, and administration procedures. An agency that wants to use a design problem may not have the time and money to develop, administer, and score it; thus, the agency might have to choose a second method, sacrificing directness and some degree of validity for savings and efficiency.

Determining how many items or assessment devices the measurement requires involves a number of considerations. Each measurement must be reliable, each subarea must reflect its relative importance in the test, and the total test must be feasible within given time and cost limits. A two-hour design problem could be used to assess a number of specific competencies (e.g., using instruments properly, drawing to scale, interpreting specifications). However, a broader competency such as "Identify tools used in electronics repair" might be measured by five to ten brief identification (fill-in-the-blank) items. The assessment techniques should permit a candidate to demonstrate competency in different ways and in different situations, if this is feasible; such an approach would minimize problems that might arise from a candidate's ability or inability to perform adequately in any one particular type of assessment.

Figure 3.3 is the test blueprint for Industrial Arts expanded to show the domain specifications (subareas, # of competencies), the

Figure 3.3

Example: Test Blueprint

Field: Industrial Arts				
Subareas	# of Competencies	%	Assessment Technique	# of Items
I	12	24	Design problem	1
II	8	16	Identification test	30
III	10	20	Work-sample	5
IV	11	22	Short-answer	60
V	4	8	Essay test	1
VI	5	10	Essay test	1
Totals:	50	100%		98

proportionality (%), the type of assessment technique used to measure competencies in each subarea, and the number of items or assessment devices to be constructed.

Each assessment technique has been selected to measure competencies in each subarea as directly as possible; the number of items has been determined by the need for reliability and the need to keep the test within a reasonable period of administration time. The number of items also reflects proportionality: 60 short-answer items measure knowledge of 11 competencies in "Manufacturing and Construction," while one design problem measures 12 competencies in "Industrial Technology." Each section would take 30-90 minutes to complete. An essay test of about 20 minutes, however, would be sufficient to measure four competencies in "Power and Transportation" (the goal here is to measure knowledge of power and transportation, not writing skills which could be minimally job-related in industrial arts).

Scoring methods. The next-to-last step in completing this test blueprint is to identify the method of scoring each section of the test and how to compile the scores for each candidate. Beginning with the method of scoring: the blueprint would be expanded to indicate the method used to score each assessment technique. For example:

> Design problem   — Analytical scoring
> Identification test — Observation/checklist

Procedures for compiling and reporting a candidate's score from different subareas and with different scoring methods would depend on the program's purpose. If this were a minimum competency test to assess the achievement of a student in a vocational training program, the program planners might decide that each student must attain a "pass" on the total test, or a "pass" on each subarea. In the first model, a student could pass sections I-IV, fail sections V-VI, and still receive a passing grade. In the second model, a student would have to pass each of the six sections in order to pass the total test.

The scoring methods for "pass" or "fail" would help to determine the requirements for each section, e.g., number of items. If the student were to receive scores by competency, for example, then each competency would have to be measured by enough items to provide a reliable score. Scoring by subarea requires fewer items per competency, but still enough to provide a reliable subarea score. If the only score generated is a total test score (e.g., 80 of 100 possible points), then reliability depends to some extent on the number of items or assessment devices in the entire test.

Summary. The last step in completing this blueprint is to go back to the first feature, test length. This blueprint now indicates the domain to be measured, the proportionality of subareas, assessment techniques, and number of items to be developed for reliable assessment on the basis of subarea. All of this information contributes to a determination of overall test length (in time). Familiarity with the assessment techniques will provide an estimate of the time required to complete some of the subareas; for example, at about one minute per item an identification test of 30 items will take approximately 30 minutes. Arbitrary decisions will determine the time required for other sections; for example, the test developer can decide that an essay test designed to measure five competencies should only take 20 minutes. He or she then develops a 20-minute essay question. But the developer could decide to use a two-hour essay test, then develop a test that would take two hours.

Assigning a time estimate to each subarea and adding up all six estimates will provide the approximate test length. If the development process includes a "field test" or "pilot test," designed to refine the test by administering it to a sample of candidates, then empirical data can be gathered and used to derive a more accurate determination of time required to complete the test. If a pilot test is not feasible, estimate conservatively; i.e., give the examinees more time than you expect the test to require. Examinees should not be penalized for low time estimates or for working slowly, unless time and speed are essential to successful performance (as in "track and field" trials, typing tests, or many types of normative-referenced tests).

Sample Test Specifications

This section of test design demonstrates the results of applying test blueprinting procedures to given domains. Included are specifications for three different tests in diverse areas: mathematics (Figure 3.4), dental hygiene (Figure 3.5), and sales management (Figure 3.6). Each test specification exemplifies specific features associated with certain types of tests in particular fields.

The first specification illustrates the plan for a test of high school mathematics composed entirely of paper-and-pencil items. (Note that the number of items in this test reflects the exact proportionality indicated by the percentage for each subarea.)

Time estimates for this test are based on approximately one minute per item; slightly more for problem-solving, slightly less for basic computation.

Specifications for a test for basic mathematics are fairly

Figure 3.4

Sample One: Mathematics Test for High School Students

Subareas	#of Competen-cies	%	Assessment Technique	#of Items	Time Required (Minutes)
I. Number Concepts	6	20	Multiple-choice	20	22
II. Computation	10	33.3	Short-answer	33	30
III. Geometry	3	10	Short-answer	10	10
IV. Algebra	3	10	Multiple-choice	10	10
V. Problem-Solving	5	16.6	Short-answer	17	20
VI. Measurement	3	10	Multiple-choice	10	8
Totals:	30	99.9%		100	100

Figure 3.5

Sample Two: Test for Vocational Training Program in Dental Hygiene

Subareas	#of Competen-cies	%	Assessment Technique	#of Items	Time Required
I. Health Sciences	20	25	Paper-and-pencil	80	90 min.
II. Dentistry	30	37.5	Paper-and-pencil	120	2 hours
III. Dental Techniques	25	31.3	Simulated per-formance tests	5	8 hours
IV. Office Procedures	5	6.2	Observation/rating scale	40	8 hours
Totals:	80	100%		245	19 hr., 30 min.

Figure 3.6

Sample Three: Sales Management Test

Subareas	#of Compe-tencies	%	Assessment Technique	#of Items	Time Required
I. Sales Techniques	5	20	Simulations	3	3 hours
II. Management Planning	5	20	Identifications; written simulations	15	3 hours
III. Administration Procedures	5	20	In-basket test	1	4 hours
IV. Interpersonal Skills	5	20	Simulations; role-playing	8	5 hours
V. Personnel Management	5	20	Interview	1	2 hours
Totals:	25	100%		28	17 hours

straightforward. The next specification becomes slightly more complicated: factual knowledge can be measured adequately by paper-and-pencil, but other skills required of dental hygienists cannot. These other skills require different types of assessment.

A number of unique characteristics emerge from this test specification. Sections I and II represent 62.5 percent of the test, include 200 paper-and-pencil items, and require 3½ hours to administer. Sections II and IV represent only 37.5 percent of the test, include 45 "items," and require 16 hours to administer. On paper this information can be deceptive, but in practice this plan is quite feasible.

Section III, "Dental Techniques," requires the student to participate in simulated performance exercises designed to assess his or her skills during a dental operation (e.g., cleaning instruments, checking teeth, cleaning teeth). The eight hours of simulated performance tests may occur over a 12-week semester; and the instructor scores the student's performance by observation. Similarly, Section IV tests the student's practice of office procedures, again scored by observation. In this case, the "40 items" refers to 40 procedures or steps the student must follow to satisfy five competencies (e.g., the competency "Implements billing procedures" may require filing, invoicing, follow-up, and so on). The "five simulated performance tests," however, measure 25 competencies; one simulation could measure eight competencies required for the performance of a dental check-up.

Sample three is more complicated than samples one or two because it includes no "objective" forms of paper-and-pencil assessment; all aspects of sales management are, in this example, assessed by alternative performance techniques.

All of the techniques here are simulation, performance, or oral assessments used to measure skills in various areas associated with sales management. The time required for the entire test is considerable (17 hours), because exercises such as interviews and role-playing are relatively long and complex. With the exception of written simulations and the four-hour in-basket test, all these exercises would be scored by observational ratings.

With the test blueprint completed, then expanded to serve as test specifications, the next step is to plan for the development of actual assessment instruments. The test specifications indicate how many instruments to develop, and of what type. This information serves as a guide for scheduling the development, selecting personnel, and completing all of the activities required to develop a test.

Depending on the kind of assessment instrument to be developed and the expertise of personnel involved, the planning for development might also include a step for generating item specifications.

Item Specifications

Like test specifications, item specifications are designed to improve the validity and reliability of test items or assessment devices; and, by extension, of the test as a whole. Essentially, an item specification is a set of criteria describing what an item developed to measure a given skill or competency will look like; it includes a number of detailed characteristics that govern item development.

Many researchers and test developers have designed various formats and procedures for producing items and assessment devices for criterion-referenced tests (CRTs). The key to a CRT is its ability to measure a clearly defined domain; thus, the clearer and more detailed the definition, the more likely is the development of a valid test. The ultimate purpose of an item specification is to guide the development of clearly defined, valid items.

Item forms (Hively, 1966; Hively, Patterson, and Page, 1968), general item types (Osburn, 1968), transformational item generation models (Bormuth, 1970), and Amplified Objectives (Popham, 1974) all strive to reduce subjectivity and human error in test development, in an effort to improve the validity of the item generation process. Each of these approaches is applicable to specific situations, usually involving multiple-choice items; but a broader approach could be applicable to all situations.

Developing item specifications for alternative performance assessment techniques can be a difficult, time-consuming task; but there are some general rules and procedures that can facilitate this effort. An item specification should include all of the following information:

- interpretation of the competency,
- description of the assessment method,
- prototype item,
- scoring guidelines,
- content or skill specifications, and
- list of equipment or resources.

Each of these is described briefly in the following pages.

Interpretation of the competency. A competency, skill statement, or objective may not always be clear to a writer trying to develop a test item designed to measure it. Different writers may interpret the statement differently and produce different types of items. Thus, the first task in developing an item specification is to define clearly the competency to be measured. This definition usually takes the form of a competency statement expanded to include conditions and standards, sometimes called simply a "restatement."

For example, consider this competency: "Apply the principles of soil conservation." This could mean "answer questions related to soil conservation," "practice soil conservation on your farm," or a number of other possibilities. Defining it more clearly in the item specification first requires looking at the context of the assessment. If it is decided that this competency will be measured by written simulation, not by actual performance, then the statement can be interpreted like this: "Given a description of the climate, soil, and farm products in a specific region, decide how to plow and irrigate the soil in a way that applies the principles of soil conservation."

Description of the assessment method. Part two of the item specification is a description of what method will be used to assess the clearly defined competency. All of the features of an item specification are interdependent. The competency may be defined first, which will govern all of the other features; or the assessment method may be selected first, which will govern the definition of the competency and all other features.

Essentially, the description of the assessment method or "item type" may be a word or two (e.g., "written simulation"), or it may be more detailed (e.g., "a written simulation of four parts, ten options to each part, accompanied by a graphic and textual information packet"). The key here is to define the *basic method* or type, its *stimulus materials,* its *mode of presentation,* and its *mode of response.* (The example specification following this section presents all of this information.)

Prototype item. The prototype is an example item written to illustrate the specifications more clearly. Some of the specifications may be difficult to understand or envision without the aid of a prototype. The example itself should be impeccable in terms of meeting the standards of the specification it is intended to illustrate.

Again, this step is closely related to all other features. Some test developers write a prototype item first, then fill out the specification accordingly. Others write the specification first, then the item; but when writing the item they find problems or omissions in the specification, so they go back and revise the specification. The point here is to work on both concurrently so that each component complements the other.

Scoring guidelines. This feature of the item specification describes the standards of "correctness," i.e., the performance required to get the item correct, the aspects of the item which must be corrected as scoring units, and the method by which to score the item itself. (Specific scoring criteria, as such, are developed as part of the items themselves; each set of actual criteria is related only to one item, while the specification defines guidelines for scoring all the items matched to the competency.)

Content or skill specifications. Part five defines the domain of content knowledge or skills which the items may assess. For example, if the competency says "Identify the tools used in household plumbing repairs," then the content specification would list all the tools that could be tested. Each identification item might use one of these tools (e.g., What is the tool pictured here?—a monkey wrench). No item matching this competency should test identification of any tool not included in the content specifications, although it may be necessary to review the list of tools periodically to include omissions or newly developed tools. Skill specifications function the same way, by defining the entire domain of specific skills that can be tested in relation to one competency.

List of equipment or resources. This final part simply lists any special equipment (e.g., an automobile engine, protractor, drafting table, sound booth) that must be provided for the examinee during the actual test. Anything listed here should be supplementary to what has already been listed above in part two as a description of "stimulus material."

Another feature that may be part of the item specifications, but is usually part of the test administration guidelines, is the "conditions" section. The conditions would describe in detail the circumstances or situation in which testing should occur. The conditions should be considered during the development of items or assessment methods, but need not be described in the item specifications.

Sample Specifications

Below are two samples of item specifications: the first is content-oriented (dealing primarily with knowledge of tools used in sheetmetal working), and the second is skill-oriented (dealing primarily with skills required in automotive mechanics).

Sample One: Item Specifications

Competency: Identify the basic tools used in sheetmetal working.

Interpretation: Given an actual tool to examine, identify the tool by name.

Description of the Assessment Method (Item Type): Actual identification test in which each item requires the examinee to identify one tool by naming it aloud.

> Stimulus: Test administrator (TA) shows the examinee a table of tools and devices used in sheetmetal work, points to each tool, one at a time, and asks this question: "What is the name of this tool?" or "What kind of . . . is this?"
>
> Response: Examinee looks at the tool and responds aloud. TA records the response on a checklist.

Prototype Item: Question: What is the name of this tool? (TA points to a standard type of micrometer lying on the table.)
> Response: Micrometer.
> (Any name other than "micrometer" is incorrect.)

Scoring Guidelines: For each item, the examinee must state the name of the tool, or one of the tool's names, as provided in the scoring criteria. The value of each item is one point. The test administrator will record each response, then label it as correct or incorrect by checking a checklist.

Content/Skill Specifications: Tools which may be included in the identification test items matched to this competency are as follows:

micrometer	"grips" or clamps	countersink
vernier scale	vise	lathe bits
metal files, rasps	rivet gun	spot welder

drills, bits	buffer	arc welder
mallet/hammer	shears or "snips"	solder gun
		punch press

Note: All these are hand-held tools, not machines.

Equipment/Resources: None, except the tools listed above.

This first example of an item specification is fairly straight-forward because it emphasizes factual knowledge of basic tools, the item type is simple, and the response is of the yes/no variety. In the second example (below), the item type is too complex to permit a prototype as such; instead it provides a brief description of an item.

Sample Two: Item Specifications

Competency: Perform basic repairs on an automotive engine.

Interpretation: Given an actual automobile with its engine intact, and the tools and parts required, complete a specified operation by making the repair or adjustment indicated.

Description of the Assessment Method (Item Type): Actual performance exercise, in which the TA instructs the examinee to perform a certain operation. The examinee then completes the work.

Prototype Item: TA instructs the examinee to replace the car's battery. Examinee removes old battery and installs new one. TA observes the work and scores the examinee's performance by observation.

Scoring Guidelines: For each exercise, the TA will have a rating scale that lists each step or procedure required. The TA must observe each step, task, or procedure and rate the examinee's performance on each one. The examinee must perform adequately on 90 percent of the criterion tasks (e.g., nine out of ten) in order to pass; and the engine part must function properly upon completion.

Content/Skill Specifications: The examinee may be required to demonstrate any or all of the following skills:
    Replace the battery.
    Replace a headlamp.
    Replace the alternator.
    Replace a fan or V-belt.

Replace the starter motor.
Replace the voltage regulator.
Replace the water pump.
Adjust the valves.
Change the oil.
Replace filters and PCV.
Complete an engine tune-up (points, plugs, rotor).
Adjust the timing.
Drain the brake fluid.
Replace the solenoid.

Equipment/Resources: An automobile and its engine, American-made, six- or eight-cylinder engine, no air conditioning, with manual brakes; tools and equipment necessary for the task; a garage bay and lift.

This specification is more complex than the first because it requires actual performance and application of specific skills, scored by observation and rating scales.

The most important aspect of item specifications is their ability to permit a test developer to interpret the actual intent of a given competency, then develop an instrument to assess the actual intent. Whether it is today or next year, anyone developing test items from properly constructed item specifications will produce comparable items, thereby improving the validity of the assessment instrument.

Summary

This chapter has presented the issues involved in test design, test blueprints, and test specifications. Based on the test specifications and plans for test development, item specifications were explored briefly.

The next six chapters are devoted to the various assessment techniques and how to develop each type. Chapter Ten integrates the principles of test design and the actual assessment methods developed. Most important at every stage of the development process, however, is to use the test design as a blueprint governing all construction; this foundation will support the validity and stability of the overall structure.

Selected References

Airasian, P.W., Madaus, G.F., and Pedulla, J.J. *Minimal Competency Testing.* Englewood Cliffs, N.J.: Educational Technology Publications, 1979.

Berk, R.A. (Ed.) *Criterion-Referenced Measurement: The State of the Art.* Baltimore: Johns Hopkins University Press, 1980.

Bormuth, J.R. *On the Theory of Achievement Test Items.* Chicago: University of Chicago Press, 1970.

Gronlund, N.E. *Constructing Achievement Tests, Third Edition.* Englewood Cliffs, N.J.: Prentice-Hall, Inc., 1977.

Hively, W. Preparation of a programmed course in algebra for secondary school teachers: A report to the National Science Foundation. Minnesota State Department of Education, Minnesota National Laboratory, 1966.

Hively, W., Patterson, H.L., and Page, S. A "universe-defined" system of arithmetic achievement tests. *Journal of Educational Measurement,* 1968, *5,* 275-290.

Osburn, H.G. Item sampling for achievement testing. *Educational and Psychological Measurement,* 1968, *28,* 95-104.

Popham, W.J. Selecting objectives and generating test items for objective-based tests: Problems in criterion-referenced measurement. *CSE Monograph Series in Evaluation.* Los Angeles: Center for the Study of Evaluation, UCLA, 1974.

Popham, W.J. *Criterion-Referenced Measurement.* Englewood Cliffs, N.J.: Prentice-Hall, Inc., 1978.

Thorndike, R.L. (Ed.) *Educational Measurement, Second Edition.* Washington, D.C.: American Council on Education, 1971.

Chapter Four

Actual Performance Assessment

Definitions of terms such as actual performance and performance testing vary widely, particularly when comparing the usage of these terms in work settings to their usage in educational settings. For the purposes of this book, we need to look at a few of these varied definitions in order to derive one that functions logically in training and education alike.

Fitzpatrick and Morrison (1971) define a performance test (which is an evaluation of a performance or a product) as a test in which a criterion situation, such as a job, is simulated to a relatively high degree. Both product and performance figure in Brown's (1971) definition: a performance item requires the students to make something, perform, or demonstrate a skill. Some of these performances may be assessed quantitatively (e.g., the number of words per minute in a typing test), but most would be assessed by qualitative observational ratings.

Sanders and Sachse (1977) define *applied* performance tests as instruments designed to measure performance in an actual or simulated setting. In the classroom, this type of test requires students to apply classroom learning to the performance of tasks. According to the authors, the distinctions between this and other types of test are the setting (degree of realism) in which the task must be performed and the value of the task performance. Literature from the Clearinghouse for Applied Performance Testing (NWREL, 1980) also posits this definition and includes the notion that in education such tests focus on the measurement of performance on tasks significant to adult life or to a student's life outside of school.

Thus far, the definitions have certain basic elements: performance or product, the realism of the setting, and the notion of applying skills to real tasks. Ebel (1979) limits his definition further by stating that a performance test requires the examinee to demonstrate his or her skill by manipulating objects or instruments, which implies physical movement.

Performance testing has often implied an evaluation of actual performance on the job, in an actual work setting. Instead of testing a candidate in a contrived setting and using the results to predict the candidate's degree of success on the job, performance tests assess the candidate's abilities while he or she performs the job itself in real life. *Applied* performance testing seems to denote similar performances in the classroom, based on the premise that a skill demonstrated in the classroom in a fairly realistic setting can be transferred to the job setting. Such testing in the classroom has often been defined in two categories: *performance*, which requires the demonstration of a task in a structured setting; and *verification*, which requires observation of a student's behavior or performance over a period of time in an unstructured context. But even these terms vary from one program to another, and from one age-group setting to another.

Taken literally, the term *performance* could denote anything from using an arc welder to writing a grammatical sentence. Some consider paper-and-pencil tests as measures of "performance in a classroom" (Coffman, 1971), because students are expected to demonstrate their skills by using pencils and paper. Turnbull (1980), for example, states that the Scholastic Aptitude Tests are "small work-samples of the kinds of thinking that college or graduate work demands." But this statement clouds the issue, because it stresses *thinking* and not actual performance (e.g., having high school students sit down and work through tasks in a college classroom).

Clearly, from all of these variations on a theme, we need one definition of actual performance assessment that will apply to both occupational and educational settings. The gist of performance tests used in occupational settings is that they require actual performance (physical movement or manipulation). Thus, when applied also to educational contexts, we can derive this definition:

> Actual performance assessment is the measurement of actual tasks performed in an actual on-the-job or in-the-classroom setting. The assessment of actual tasks may be accomplished by assessment of the performance process, its product, or both.

In accord with this definition, actual performance assessment in education and training can only be considered as such when the setting is "actual," i.e., essentially the same as it would be outside the school (metal shop, vehicle operation, home economics lab, etc.).

Within the context of this book, any performance carried out in a simulated setting is considered "simulated performance" (covered in Chapter Five). In addition, performance of an oral or paper-and-pencil nature (whether or not it could be considered "actual performance" for certain occupations, such as foreign language interpretation or journalism) is considered in depth in later chapters (Seven and Eight, respectively).

Actual performance assessment methods explored in this chapter include the following:

Work-Sample Test
Identification Test
Supervisor Ratings
Peer Ratings
Self-Assessment

Work-sample tests and identification tests are the primary focus of actual performance assessments, measured by observation and/or objective, quantitative methods. Supervisor ratings, peer ratings, and self-assessment are specialized approaches to assessing work-samples of process or product.

Each type is explored in depth in this chapter, with regard to its uses, advantages and disadvantages, and procedures for development, administration, and scoring.

Work-Sample Test

A work-sample test may assess a process, a product, or both. For example, a test of tractor trailer drivers might require each driver to shift gears properly, back into a parking space, and execute a hill-stop (process); a test for bakers might be based on the appearance and taste of a loaf of bread or a pastry (product); and a typing test might assess an examinee's typing technique and the finished letter itself (process and product).

Assessment of process is usually achieved by some form of observation (see Chapter Six) during or following the performance; assessment of a product may be achieved through observation of the product, with the use of quantitative and/or qualitative checklists or rating scales, or through quantitative analyses (e.g., an assembled computer component might be assessed by electronic testing).

Deciding whether to assess process, product, or both depends on the purpose of the program and the importance of each to the job or task performance. A training program might emphasize the teaching of a process or a procedure, as in the training of laboratory technicians, on the assumption that a trainee who has mastered the procedure will apply it successfully in working toward any given product. Industrial testing might emphasize the product (e.g., a widget) without concern for how it is produced.

As is true of all performance assessments, a work-sample test should be based on an analysis of the job or task performance. A clear definition of what is required for successful job performance will indicate those elements of the job which are most important and those which are performed most frequently; a comparison of these two scales, importance and frequency, will yield the most critical elements. A work-sample test should consist of a representative sample of all the job elements, or at least the set of those which are most critical.

Uses

Work-sample tests are used most often for job selection and training, where high fidelity between the work-sample and the job is possible (Knapp and Sharon, 1975). For example, a test for concrete or cement masons requires each candidate to pour and finish a section of a concrete sidewalk; criteria for performance include the use of wrist techniques, proper use of tools, and quality of the finished product indicated by such characteristics as a smooth surface and rounded corners.

Muchinsky (1975) cites the use of a work-sample test for selection of equipment mechanics, in which each mechanic must diagnose a malfunction (bad spark plug wire, inoperative taillight) based on the "customer's" complaints. Once diagnosed, the malfunction must be corrected. Criteria for performance include accuracy of diagnosis, efficiency, and not trying to fix something else that the "customer" did not complain about.

The Florida Department of Professional Regulation uses work-sample tests in a number of its screening tests for licensing programs. For example, candidates for licensure as dentists must often complete wax work and make dentures for their "clients" (persons who need dentures and agree to have them made as part of a test). Prospective licensed masseurs take a work-sample test that requires them to perform massage (on each other).

In business, selection tests for typists, stenographers, and keypunchers most often require work-samples. Industries and trades use work-sample tests extensively to assess welders, cosmetologists, electronic technicians, repair workers, plumbers, and many others. The key to the usefulness of work-sample tests in all of these areas is the facility with which actual job skills required can be identified and assessed in an efficient manner.

Work-sample tests can be useful in education as well, particularly in vocational areas and other fields which require performance of some kind. Performing arts, crafts, physical education, and driver education all fit into this latter category.

Advantages/Disadvantages

The advantages of work-sample tests are fairly obvious. Work-sample tests measure actual performance in realistic settings, thus exhibiting high face validity. They can measure skills not readily measurable by any other method, and they provide for direct observation of performance. Certainly the examinee would have a more difficult time bluffing through a work-sample test than through less direct forms of assessment. In situations where training is important, the observer of work-sample performance can provide specific, constructive feedback to the examinee, either at certain points during the test or after it has been completed.

Disadvantages of the work-sample test, unfortunately, are plentiful. Work-sample tests generally require one-to-one administration, a great deal of equipment, and much time; thus, they may be most feasible in industrial or trade settings which already have equipment available and rigid apprenticeship programs in place. Depending on how the work-sample test is developed and administered, it may suffer from lack of standardized testing conditions and, possibly, the use of equipment unfamiliar to some examinees. Observation of examinee performance may be subjective and less than reliable, particularly if observers are inexperienced or untrained. Work-sample tests are limited in their usefulness to jobs or tasks which are easily reduced to their simplest components (areas such as management, supervision, psychiatric counseling, and sales do not lend themselves to work-sample assessment). And, finally, due to cost and time limitations, work-sample tests are only that—samples; they cannot measure anywhere near the complete domain of required skills.

Developing a Work-Sample Test

Procedures for developing a work-sample test depend to some extent on the type of work to be assessed. Some work-sample tests may be developed for *unobtrusive observation* (in which the examinee does not know the assessment is in progress), others for *obtrusive observation* (in which the examinee knows from the start that a test is in progress). Unobtrusive observation requires no structuring of an assessment situation, but it requires careful planning to ensure that periodic observations yield a fair and representative sample of performance. Obtrusive observation calls for rigid structuring of the assessment situation itself, as well as careful planning for observances. Both approaches involve the following steps.

Step 1: Specify performances. Given a domain of performance skills, identify the most critical, or those constituting a representative sample, and state each one as a performance objective or task statement.

> *Example*:   A spot welder might have to demonstrate the ability to accomplish different types of welds. Task one might be stated as: Demonstrate a butt weld.

Step 2: Analyze the task. Given a specific performance task, analyze the activity required and break it down into measurable, identifiable components. Each task normally requires a number of steps or procedures for its completion. An important consideration here is to identify multiple steps which do not depend on one another, unless this dependence is essential to the job. Using multiple steps as criteria will help to avoid the chance that an error in an early step will cause failure in a later step, the performance of which might otherwise be considered adequate.

> *Example:*   Demonstrating a butt weld might require the following steps:
> 1. Prepare the spot welder.
> 2. Prepare the metal pieces.
> 3. Place the pieces on the machine.
> 4. Engage the welder.
> 5. Check the weld.

In a *product* work-sample test, this step would involve listing the characteristics of a satisfactory weld, such as accurate positioning, neatness, flatness of weld, smoothness of surface, lack of "blow-out," etc.

Step 3: Construct an assessment form. The steps or product characteristics identified in Step 2 can now be developed in an assessment format such as a checklist or rating scale, listing each step or characteristic and a numerical scale for scoring it. (Constructing observational assessment instruments is covered in detail in Chapter Six.) How you plan to use the results should be considered at this stage; it will govern, to some extent, the structure and format of the assessment form.

Step 4: Develop instructions. With the task defined, instructions to both the examinee and the observer(s) can be developed. These instructions should clearly state what is required of each person and what criteria will be applied to the performance process or product. It is important when developing instructions that they not include any references to proper procedures or to results of previous steps (e.g., do not say "Now that you've cleaned the welder points properly, proceed to . . .").

Step 5: Specify conditions, equipment, and materials. To complement the instructions, develop a clear definition of the conditions, equipment, and materials with which to complete the task. This step is essential to standardizing the procedures and criteria for product or process work-sample tests. Tests given under varying conditions, using different machines, or using different materials will not produce comparable results.

Example:	Conditions for the butt weld task might be defined as follows:
Equipment	—the Thompson 2200.
Materials	—two pieces of 1/8-inch cold-rolled stainless steel, measuring four inches by 12 inches.
	—one pint of toluol solvent, two clean rags.
	—steel wool.
Conditions	—a clean well-lit work area of at least 20 square feet.
	—examinee must wear regulation safety goggles, apron, and gloves.
	—examinee has a total of 12 minutes to complete the task.

When Steps 1 to 5 have been completed, the work-sample test is ready to be administered. A field test, pilot test, or prior run is highly advisable at this point to ensure that the work-sample test has been constructed properly, the task is feasible, the time limit is reasonable, and so on.

Administering and Scoring a Work-Sample Test

Administering and scoring a work-sample test requires as much standardization as possible. Conditions, materials, and equipment should be identical for each examinee. Each examinee should receive the same instructions, be allowed the same amount of time, and be observed in the same way.

Use the checklist or rating scale judiciously as a guideline to observation: what behaviors or steps to observe, the level of performance acceptable for each one, and the sequence of steps. Explain the procedures and criteria for performance to the examinee in advance, so he or she has fair expectations of what will occur. Complete the scoring sheet in conformity with pre-set criteria, following the established guidelines with each and every examinee.

Use the results of the assessment—product, process, or both—as determined by the purpose of the program. Notify the examinee of his or her score on the total test and/or on each of its components. If applicable, provide specific constructive feedback to the examinee after completing the administration. Feedback is essential in a training program designed to improve examinee performance.

Identification Test

Unlike the work-sample test, a true identification test does not *usually* require actual performance or physical completion of a task. What it does involve is the first step in an actual performance—identifying the material, the part, the malfunction, etc.—in preparation for using the part or repairing the malfunction. Because it involves identification of actual objects in a realistic setting, it is included in the actual performance category. (Modified versions of the identification test are included in Chapters Five and Seven.) Also, identification tests are often used in combination with other performance methods, such as work-sample tests.

An identification test provides the examinee with some form of perceptional stimulus requiring the use of sense organs. This stimulus may be visual, tactile, auditory, gustatory, or olfactory. The examinee then identifies each object (machine part, tool, fabric) or substance (metal, chemical); in some tests, the examinee must also explain the uses or characteristics of each object; and/or how to repair, improve, or replace it.

Uses

Because of its relatively simple requirement, i.e., identifying an object or problem, the identification test is most useful as a screening test for entry-level examinees. For example, someone applying for a training program in carpentry or nursing might be required to identify carpentry tools or medical instruments, in order to demonstrate a basic level of familiarity with the trade or profession (Gronlund, 1977). A carpenter or nurse prepared to take a final licensing test would presumably not have to be assessed for such basic knowledge.

In many occupations, the ability to identify something is an essential skill. For example: an anesthetist or a chemist might have to be able to identify gases by smell; a chef might have to identify spices (or lack of them) by tasting a stew or a sauce; and an air traffic controller might have to identify types of planes by the shape and size of blips on a radar screen. A relatively simple test format might, in these cases, be used to measure essential skills required for completion of a training program.

One of the most beneficial uses of the identification test is in the assessment of diagnostic or "troubleshooting" skills: by looking, listening, smelling, and so on, the examinee must identify a problem or a malfunction. This type of skill is part of a candidate's ability to perform in an actual work setting if it is part of the job itself. Auto mechanics may diagnose trouble by listening to an engine; television repair workers may diagnose a problem by looking at the picture on the screen; home economists may determine what ingredient was left out by looking at, tasting, and feeling the texture of a baked muffin.

The Wisconsin Board of Veterinary Examiners uses an identification test, or "Practical Exam," as a licensing requirement. Candidates go from booth to booth during the exam and must identify E. Coli bacteria, the dorsal flexor bone of a horse, etc. In addition, some of the booths require the examinee to diagnose an animal's condition, disease, or disorder based on symptoms, the animal's behavior, and so on.

Advantages/Disadvantages

Identification tests have some specific advantages related to their simplicity and the nature of the tasks included: they can measure perceptual competencies; they involve real objects or substances which the examinee identifies, but will later use in actual work settings; and they provide efficient measures of entry-level familiarity with basic requirements of a trade. Also, depending on the modes of assessment and response, an identification test may be administered to small groups instead of individuals. As stated earlier, its primary advantage is the ability to assess diagnostic or troubleshooting skills.

Its disadvantages are generally the converse applications of its advantages: an identification test may require expensive or difficult-to-locate objects, tools, and materials; it usually measures only simple skills or basic knowledge; and it does not directly measure an actual performance. The examinee that diagnoses an engine malfunction but does not fix it has not demonstrated an actual performance skill. These disadvantages are why identification tests are generally used as entry-level screening devices or are used in combination with other methods such as work-sample tests or simulations.

Developing an Identification Test

Generally, an identification test does not require extensive preparation of formal testing materials, but may require extensive efforts to secure the objects or substances to be identified.

Step 1: Define what is to be identified. As with the work-sample test, this first step derives from a job analysis or definition that indicates what tools, substances, materials, etc., are required for the job. A representative sample selected from the job-related domain will provide the basis for the test. These selections might be problems or malfunctions (to measure diagnostic or troubleshooting skills), objects, substances, materials, etc.

Step 2: Assess the feasibility of testing the selected domain. Within the context of the assessment program, determine whether the facilities and equipment for the test are available. Most important, determine whether or not you can secure the materials required. Determine whether to administer the test to small groups or to individuals.

Examples: In the veterinarian's practical exam mentioned earlier, the selection of identification tasks for the test depends on the availability of suitable "specimens" at the time of the test. Thus, the domain must be defined as, for instance, "any 20 of the 50 listed."

In an equipment repair test, the equipment (e.g., helicopter engine) must be available, programmed with a malfunction, and placed in a work area suitable for the job.

Some identification tests, such as identifying gases by smell, might be hazardous if the gases to be identified are not chosen and handled carefully.

Step 3: Structure the identification test. This step involves defining the logistics of the test: how to present the things to be identified, how the examinee should identify them, and how to score the responses. The logistics depend on what is to be measured and the time and facilities available.

Example: One common mechanic's test begins with a table covered with engine parts, most of which are worn or faulty. The examiner points to one part after another; for each one, the examinee names the part, explains its use, and diagnoses why the part is worn or faulty (e.g., brake shoe is worn on one side because the tires of the car were out of alignment). The examiner records each response.

Beyond the practical aspect of structuring the test are two considerations: (1) the test must be designed to permit replication; and (2) the test usually has to be designed to prevent breaches of test security. Proper replication of a test will ensure that each examinee is presented with the same situation. If a television repair examinee has to identify and replace a faulty tube as an assessment task, the examiner must put the faulty tube back in before giving the test to another candidate. Against the chance that the first person might describe the test to later examinees, it might be necessary to alternate different tubes for different examinees (as long as one problem is not significantly easier or more difficult than another).

Step 4: Secure the facilities, equipment, and materials. Decide where the test will occur (e.g., in a laboratory, in a service bay, in a classroom). Make sure that you have all the equipment and materials required. For example, in preparing for the mechanic's test described above, the sample of worn and faulty engine parts will have to be collected prior to the administration.

Step 5: Develop the assessment form. In general, preparing an observational checklist, a rating scale, or an answer sheet for an identification test is a fairly straightforward task: each identification will be a yes/no, correct/incorrect proposition. For group administrations, candidates would write their responses, which would require a standard answer sheet instead of a checklist.

Step 6: Develop instructions and scoring criteria. Instructions and scoring criteria for both the examinee and the examiner(s) must be developed in advance and, preferably, communicated to the examinee before the test administration.

> *Example:* The American Board of Clinical Pathologists uses an identification test to assess blood-typing skills for a blood bank. Given a live blood sample, the examinee identifies its type by marking any of the 44 choices. Each choice is worth up to four points, depending on its proximity to the correct answer. The only answers completely incorrect are those which would be dangerous if the two blood types were mixed together.

Two hypothetical examples of structured identification tests follow; the components of each test correspond to the six steps just described.

Administering and Scoring an Identification Test

With or without a trial run, the first step in administering the test is to make sure it works as planned, that it provides sufficient time for the examinee to complete the tasks, and that it does not present unwarranted hazards to the examinee. The test must be standardized to present each examinee with the same directions, the same conditions, and the same scoring criteria.

Score the test in progress by using the assessment form and following the guidelines for observation and grading that were established in advance. If applicable, provide constructive feedback to the examinees as to how they could have improved their performance.

Example One: Identification Test
Job: Geological Engineer's Apprentice

Task: To identify geological rock and mineral samples by name. The rocks and minerals may include any ten of the following:

lignite	uranium (U-238)	mica	calcium
feldspar	pumice	anthracite	asbestos
granite	gold	bituminous	silica
marble	limestone	iron ore	sulphur
quartz	shale	hornblende	pyrite

Feasibility: Distinction between lignite, anthracite, and bituminous (three types of coal) is not entry-level knowledge—test any *one* of the three. ("Coal" is an unacceptable response.) Possible hazards in using U-238; do not test. Gold is difficult to find and keep; use pyrite (fool's gold) instead.

Structure: Examiner places one high-quality sample of each of ten of these rocks and minerals on a table, in numbered sequence. Examinee identifies them by name in order from one to ten. Examiner checks "yes" or "no" on checklist.

Materials: Samples of all minerals collected except gold, U-238, and hornblende.

*Assessment
Form:*   Form follows sample format below.

#	Sample	Yes	No
1	Feldspar		
2	Pumice		
3	Pyrite		

Instructions and Scoring Criteria:

*Instructions
to Examinee:* "Look carefully at each of the rock samples on the table. Beginning with number one, give me the name of each sample. First, say the number of the sample, then give its name. You will have a total of two minutes to complete the test. If you do not know the name of one of the samples, make a guess or say 'I don't know.'"

*Scoring
Criteria:* Nine correct responses out of ten constitute a passing score.

Example Two: Identification Test
Job: Electric Typewriter Repair

Task: To identify the malfunction affecting a typewriter. The malfunction may be any *one* of the following:
> worn or broken tab set
> broken ribbon feed
> malfunctioning half-spacer
> cracked typing ball

Feasibility: Identification of problem is feasible. Repair is not feasible within testing limits.

Structure: Given a typewriter with a malfunction, a brief written description of the problem from a typist, and two pieces of paper, the repair worker will identify the problem by using the machine and finding the malfunction. Examiner will observe procedures, making checklist observations.

Materials: Typewriter—IBM Selectric III (correcting model).
Tools—Standard repair kit.

*Assessment
Form:* Procedural steps should be followed as listed here.
1. Read written description of problem.
2. Sit at typewriter and insert paper properly.
3. Practice typing, including the use of part identified by typist in description (e.g., tab set).
4. With indication of problem from typing, open cover (if necessary).
5. Examine internal machinery (if necessary).

6. State problem by identifying faulty part and why it malfunctions.

Observer should check "yes" beside each step if followed correctly, "no" if not.

Instructions and Scoring Criteria:

*Instructions
to Examinee:*   "I will hand you a written description of a problem with this IBM Selectric III. You will have five minutes to identify the problem. When you have identified it, name the faulty part and tell me why it has malfunctioned."

*Scoring
Criteria:*   A "yes" on each of the six steps and a correct identification of the problem constitute a passing score.

Supervisor Ratings

Work-sample tests and identification tests are methods of assessing various aspects of actual performance. From one perspective, supervisor ratings provide an alternative means to gathering information on an employee's "work-samples." As mentioned earlier in this chapter, unobtrusive observation occurs while a person is engaged in working, under normal circumstances: the supervisor observes and/or works with the employee, assessing the product, process—or both—of the candidate's work. Formalized ratings generated from this kind of observation, and recorded in relation to predetermined criteria, represent "supervisor ratings."

Generally, the supervisor rates the candidate's performance on work-related skills and work-related behaviors exhibited on the job. These work-related attributes should be identified by some form of job analysis and should not include opinions or attitudes unrelated to job performance. Instruments used in the observation may be checklists, rating scales, or anecdotal records (all of which are examined in Chapter Six). The instruments provide both guidelines to govern the observation and a document for recording the results.

Uses

Supervisor ratings are most often used as on-going checks of an employee's progress, for the purpose of job promotion, salary setting, etc.; but they may also be used as a way to assess trainees in various types of "apprenticeship" or "internship" programs. For example, the Georgia Department of Education uses a form of supervisor ratings, based on direct observation, to assess student teachers and provisional teachers working in the classroom. Also, architectural interns are rated by their supervisors (interning with a firm is required for architectural licensure).

Supervisor ratings may also include quantitative information based on formal analyses of products and employee accomplishments. For example, in addition to observing a line assembly worker, a factory supervisor might rate the worker on the basis of speed, number of parts produced, and formal quality control.

Advantages/Disadvantages

In addition to the advantages and disadvantages inherent in observational assessments of all kinds, supervisor ratings have other distinguishing characteristics. The advantages of supervisor ratings are these: they provide for direct measurement of skills and behaviors; and, in general, candidates are rated only on those skills and behaviors which are important on the job. In addition to the actual rating scale used for the evaluation, supervisors may provide recommendations or personal comments which could be helpful in appraising a particular candidate. Also, candidates are evaluated by persons whom they know; thus, the assessment situation is familiar to them and may produce less anxiety. If applicable to the situation, supervisors may provide very helpful feedback to the candidate for performance improvement.

The disadvantages of supervisor ratings, however, are numerous—particularly in a licensing procedure which must comply with state and federal guidelines. First, different candidates are evaluated by different supervisors, which will inevitably lead to some degree of bias for or against candidates. Second, the criteria by which to evaluate candidates are difficult to establish: they must only be those skills and behaviors proven to be job-related, not opinions, attitudes, and irrelevant characteristics. Third, scoring procedures and interpretations of both the criteria and the scores are not always reliable or consistent because of the subjective nature of judgments about employees. Fourth, in practical terms, supervisor ratings are difficult to obtain in a standardized and efficient manner, if for no other reason than that supervisors are subject to job pressures, deadlines, and so on. And fifth, as discussed earlier, supervisor ratings collected in an unsystematic fashion have not stood up in court as a valid and reliable means of screening or selecting candidates for licensure or employment. In general, they are considered biased and subjective measures.

Developing and Administering Supervisor Ratings

The structure and format of supervisor ratings vary according to the job and the situation. Ratings used for training purposes are generally less rigid and structured than ratings used for promotion or salary setting. Any ratings that will lead to comparison across employees, across departments, or in relation to an established criterion must be standardized to generate comparable results.

Development of criteria by which to judge candidates must follow from job analysis; these vary significantly according to the field. The most important consideration is to make the criteria and the instrument itself clear and meaningful. It may be difficult to develop consistent and usable definitions of what ratings mean over periods of time and for different candidates. For example, such terms as "very responsible" or "quite poised" may be applied to candidates in different ways depending upon the interaction of supervisor and candidate.

Administering this procedure, or making the observational ratings, may also create significant problems unless the procedure directs the attention of the observer toward critical aspects of job performance or product quality, and the instrument provides clear standards for judgment. As Glaser and Klaus (1963) point out, all aspects of performance cannot be assessed at any one time; thus, techniques such as time sampling, performance records, and product sampling may have to be employed. The important point here is to assess the candidate on the basis of a representative sample of performances and/or products, to ensure that the ultimate rating is fair and representative. All candidates should be rated in the same way and should have about the same number of ratings.

Peer Ratings

Peer ratings are evaluative judgments made by colleagues or "peers" about a candidate or employee. Among the professions, this same approach is known as "peer review"—a concept of great importance to the medical profession, where colleagues or peers are considered the only judges qualified to evaluate each other. Criteria for rating peers are essentially the same as those used by supervisors to rate employees.

Uses

This type of evaluation is most beneficial when used in training programs to aid the education process, to help trainees evaluate themselves, and to provide encouragement for self-awareness and personal growth. In most cases, peers review one another's products rather than any processes involved, because the processes are either not observable (as in the medical profession, where physicians examine each others' records but cannot observe confidential doctor/patient interactions); or because peers (as in a vocational training program) are not qualified to evaluate one another's procedural techniques.

Advantages/Disadvantages

Peer ratings have basically the same advantages and disadvantages as supervisor ratings, with a few more on the negative side. Feedback and evaluative judgments from peers may be less threatening than from a supervisor, and the participants can learn a great deal about themselves and the evaluation process. Peers cannot be expected to know any better than the candidate what skills and behaviors are essential on the job, or whether a person has them. The reliability and validity of peer ratings are extremely low; and peers may not be expected to be reliable or credible evaluators because they are untrained in evaluation, and they themselves are being evaluated by the same standards. Beyond the inexperience factor, peers may also be affected by the fact that they are essentially competing with the persons whom they must rate.

Self-Assessment

Self-assessment techniques, ranging from informal to formal, utilize the examinee's own personal ratings of his or her actual performance. Informal techniques may include discussions with a supervisor or teacher; more formal techniques include self-assessment tests, structured interviews, checklists, and rating scales. Self-assessment may be used in relation to specific procedures or products, or in relation to programs as extensive as a four-year training course. To accomplish a self-assessment, examinees need to know how to assess themselves, and on what criteria to base the assessment. The more frequent, clearly defined, and openly communicated the assessment process is, the greater the value to the examinee.

Uses

The primary purpose of all self-assessments is didactic: to help the student learn. For obvious reasons, self-assessment does not play a significant role in licensing procedures; but it can be useful in other kinds of programs.

Self-assessment tests can provide structured information to students or trainees on how well they have learned in a particular area. The only characteristics that distinguish self-assessment tests from other types is their purpose and the way they are administered (i.e., usually without formal administration procedures). The American Academy of Family Physicians (AAFP), for example, produces learning modules for its members as part of a six-year recertification program. Each month the physicians receive a monograph and a taped discussion of a medical subject; the physician studies the materials, completes a written simulation and a multiple-choice test, then submits a copy of the answer sheets to AAFP. Scoring the tests is only important to the physicians, for their own use; the answer sheets submitted to the AAFP provide record-keeping information to verify a physician's completion of the modules.

Inventory checklists and *job information forms* can be used as self-assessment devices for screening job applicants, defining a job's critical features (as in job analysis), or evaluating a training program. Students or workers complete the checklist or form by checking those tasks or responsibilities that they perform on the job or are capable of performing, having finished a training course.

Performance checklists or *rating scales* can be used to help students assess their performance in a structured fashion. Given a checklist or scale and an orientation to its use, students can rate how well they performed on a given task; or how their product turned out, in comparison to those of others or to specified criteria.

The key to all of these uses, and to the development of self-assessment instruments, is training the student or examinee to use the instrument properly. Since the real value of self-assessment is in its use as a self-educating device, i.e., pointing out strengths and areas which need improvement, this purpose must be communicated clearly to the examinee in advance. In this way, candidates can derive the benefits of the assessment/learning process without the potential anxiety or stress that can affect other forms of assessment.

Advantages/Disadvantages

The advantages of self-assessment derive from its educational functions: it helps students identify their own strengths and weaknesses; it helps to train them in the uses of assessment criteria and objective judgment; and it helps to demonstrate the value of defined guidelines, quality-control criteria, and step-by-step procedures. Also, this technique is often less threatening than assessment by a teacher, supervisor, or peer.

Disadvantages of self-assessment stem mainly from inexperience: students and beginning workers cannot be expected to have experience in conducting evaluations; thus, they may not be capable of making useful self-assessments. They may also be influenced significantly by self-interest or emotional involvement, or the need to appear experienced and able to demonstrate high standards; thus, the self-assessment may be inflated and lacking in objectivity (or deflated, for those lacking self-confidence).

In an education or training context, self-assessment can be a valuable training aid for the student or trainee. It is not suitable, however, for use in assessment programs of legal consequences (e.g., licensing, diploma requirements) because of its lack of objectivity and reliability.

Summary

All of these forms of actual performance assessment—work-sample tests, identification tests, and ratings by a supervisor, a peer, or the examinee—require the performance of job tasks in an actual work setting. They occur in real situations, and they may be scored on the basis of quantitative, qualitative, or both kinds of criteria. In simulated performance tests, the subject of the next chapter, examinees perform real tasks but in simulated settings.

Selected References

Asher, J.J., and Sciarrino, J.A. Realistic work-sample tests: A review. *Personnel Psychology*, 1974, 519-533.

Brown, F.G. Performance items. In *Measurement and Evaluation*. Itasca, Ill.: F.E. Peacock Publishers, Inc., 1971.

Coffman, W.E. Essay examinations. In R.L. Thorndike (Ed.), *Educational Measurement, Second Edition*. Washington, D.C.: American Council on Education, 1971.

Ebel, R.L. *Essentials of Educational Measurement, Third Edition*. Englewood Cliffs, N.J.: Prentice-Hall, Inc., 1979.

Erickson, R.C., and Wentling, T.L. Constructing measures of performance. In *Measuring Student Growth*. Boston: Allyn and Bacon, Inc., 1976.

Fitzpatrick, R., and Morrison, E.J. Performance and product evaluation. In R.L. Thorndike (Ed.), *Educational Measurement, Second Edition*. Washington, D.C.: American Council on Education, 1971.

Glaser, R., and Klaus, D.J. Proficiency measurement: Assessing human performance. In R. Gagne (Ed.), *Psychological Principles in System Development*. New York: Holt, Rinehart, and Winston, 1963.

Gronlund, N. Constructing performance tests. In *Constructing Achievement Tests, Third Edition*. Englewood Cliffs, N.J.: Prentice-Hall, Inc., 1977.

Knapp, J., and Sharon, A. *A Compendium of Assessment Techniques*. Princeton, N.J.: Cooperative Assessment of Experiential Learning, Educational Testing Service, 1975.

Muchinsky, P.M. Utility of work-samples. *Personnel Journal,* April 1975, 218-220.

Northwest Regional Educational Laboratory. *Are There Any Alternatives to Traditional Paper-and-Pencil Achievement Tests?* Pamphlet produced by the Clearinghouse for Applied Performance Testing, 1980.

Northwest Regional Educational Laboratory. *Captrends,* May 1980, 5(4).

Sanders, J.R., and Sachse, T.P. Applied performance in the classroom. *Journal of Research and Development in Education,* 1977, *10*(3).

Schriber, P.E., Peel-Gregory, B., and Priestley, M. *Competency-Based Instruction in Vocational Education: How Do I Evaluate Performance?* Produced by National Evaluation Systems, Inc., Amherst, Massachusetts; for Florida Department of Education, Division of Vocational Education, October 1980.

Turnbull, W.T. Letter to the editor. *Atlantic,* April 1980.

Chapter Five

Simulations

Simulations are most useful when actual performance tests are impractical, for any of a number of reasons: cost, danger, the serious consequences of mistakes, or the impossibility of arranging actual performance situations. For these same reasons, simulations are more often used as training or teaching tools than as assessment instruments.

Whether for training or testing, a simulation is designed to be as realistic as possible, to provide a setting or situation and a set of required tasks that are as close as possible to the real setting and actual performance. The primary value of the simulation is its ability to predict, on the basis of simulated performance, how well a candidate will perform when placed in the real situation.

The previous chapter defined actual performance assessment as the measurement of actual tasks performed in an actual on-the-job or in-the-classroom setting. A simulation measures performance in a simulated but realistic setting. By simulating performance conditions, the examiner can control most of the variables in the testing situation (unlike in a real job), and can standardize the assessment across all candidates and administrations; but he or she can still measure on-the-job behaviors and skills. The key to a simulation then is its setting or situation, which is why simulations are sometimes called "situational tests."

Simulations cover a wide range of techniques, from the equivalent of a pinball game to war maneuvers in which nearly everything but the ammunition is real. This chapter covers a number of the most important types of simulations, as listed here:

Simulated Performance
Simulated Identification Test
Written Simulation
Management Exercises
Simulator Machines

Each type is considered separately, although combinations of different techniques are certainly possible. This selection of types, however, should provide the information needed to combine various approaches or devise new simulations better suited to a specific situation.

Simulated Performance

In its broadest definition, simulated performance includes every type of simulation covered in this chapter. In keeping with the classification system used here, however—classification by mode of assessment—this category includes those assessment techniques which require physical performance in a simulated setting. The performance itself must be as faithful to the real activity as possible.

Uses

Simulated performance techniques can be used to measure a diverse domain of interrelated skills and behaviors, but usually they focus on practical and technical procedures, behavior, and management skills (analysis, problem-solving, situational assessment, managing people, etc.). Many organizations that use simulated performance assessments call them "practical exams," to distinguish them from paper-and-pencil tests.

The American Association of Workers for the Blind, for example, uses two types of practical exams: one to assess rehabilitation skills, the other to assess orientation and mobility; that is, the ability of the worker to orient a blind person to a given situation and assist him or her to become mobile, or capable of moving about without danger or discomfort. Ironically, both of these exams are scored by observation of the worker's performance.

In a second example, the Registry for Interpreters of the Deaf uses audio-visual equipment to provide a context for simulated performance and a method of scoring. A candidate enters the testing room and faces five judges, three of whom are deaf. An aural tape plays a recorded message that the candidate interprets through sign language. All of the candidate's motions are recorded on a videotape that is used to attain a "reverse interpretation": translating the candidate's signing back to words, for comparison to the taped message.

Perhaps the most useful example of simulated performance is the basic-level practical exam used by the National Registry of Emergency Medical Technicians—a test deserving of a more complete description. The National Registry itself provides a manual and a videotape designed to assist local EMT training programs in setting up assessment situations. Standardized procedures with only minor variations yield relatively standardized nationwide scores, which are reported to the Registry.

The conceptual basis of the test is founded upon three concepts (NREMT, 1980): (1) testing content relevant to on-the-job emergency situations; (2) attaining realism of stress associated with most job situations; and (3) measuring patient management, situational assessment techniques, and technical competency in the application of procedures and use of equipment.

In the testing situation, a candidate performs at each of six to eight stations—either individually or as part of a two-person team—while a station examiner observes and scores the performance. The examiner reads brief instructions to the candidate, who then must act quickly to deal with a "patient" who has an epileptic seizure, a chest wound, two broken legs, or some other problem requiring emergency care.

Two of the most interesting aspects of the exam are its stress inducements and the realism of its settings. Each station is a room with carefully selected props, or a wrecked automobile, or an area outside the building (e.g., at the foot of a ladder where someone might have fallen). Using "programmed patients," the examiner sets up each situation to resemble the scene of an accident. The patients are dressed and made up cosmetically to look like victims in pain, with broken bones, bloody wounds, etc. Each patient is usually a local actor or an experienced EMT who can simulate the situation and assist in evaluating the candidate (except in the CPR sequences, where the candidate must "revive" a mannequin). In each situation, the candidate's performance is timed with a stopwatch, and no conversation (except programmed cues) can occur between the examiner and the candidate. These two conditions, along with the situation's realism and the true-to-life reactions of the patient, create the stress usually evident in an actual situation. With the stress factors involved, a candidate's behavior and attitude can be assessed as well as the competencies required; the goal is to ensure that the candidate is serious and conscientious, and has the integrity required of an EMT.

Scoring of the candidates is done by each station examiner who sets up and observes the simulated performance. The examiner records these observations on a checklist (see Figure 5.1), and the patient may contribute to the observational judgments. Each action is rated acceptable or unacceptable, and some actions—if not taken, or taken improperly—result in automatic failure. In Figure 5.1, the checklist includes "knife removed" from the patient's chest wound; this action, if done, would be medically inappropriate, and would result in the candidate's failure.

These three examples—workers for the blind, interpreters of the deaf, and EMTs—all demonstrate the use of simulated performance techniques in the context of practical exams, in which the candidate physically performs as he or she would in a real setting. The next technique is a specialized application of this principle, designed to assess an executive's management skills.

In-Basket test. In-basket tests were first created at AIR University in the 1950s to evaluate training, and were further developed by Fredericksen (1960) of Educational Testing Service. Since then, they have been widely used in many aspects of management training and evaluation, particularly in industry, educational administration, and government.

An "in-basket" test takes its name from the "baskets" that are found on many an executive's desk: one basket for information coming *in*, one for information going *out*. The in-basket test is a

Figure 5.1

NATIONAL REGISTRY OF EMERGENCY MEDICAL TECHNICIANS
PERFORMANCE EVALUATION FORM
BASIC EMT·A

STATION A	CHEST & ABDOMINAL WOUNDS TIME										NOTE TECHNIQUE	
	:15	:30	:45	1:00	1:15	1:30	1:45	2:00	2:15	2:30	Acceptable	Not Acceptable
AIRWAY CHECKED AND CLEARED	✓										✓	
CHEST WOUND MANUALLY SEALED			✓								✓	
EFFECTIVE ACTION TO APPLY DRESSING TO CHEST WOUND					✓							
KNIFE REMOVED												
KNIFE SECURED IN PLACE							✓					✓
OXYGEN ADMINISTERED				✓							✓	
PATIENT'S REST·LESSNESS MANAGED		✓										✓
ADEQUATE PATIENT SURVEY PERFORMED		✓									✓	

PATIENT'S EVALUATION OF THE CANDIDATE

COMMENTS:

The knife was not secure. I could feel it almost falling out as I moved from side to side. The EMT did not try to reassure me and was unnecessarily rough as he tried to restrain my movements.

NOTE EXTRANEOUS ACTIONS:

Inserted airway

(REPRINTED BY PERMISSION OF THE NATIONAL REGISTRY OF EMERGENCY MEDICAL TECHNICIANS)

---

situational test that simulates the administrative tasks of a management executive.

The examinee first receives background information on the job to be performed, the position held, and the organization for which the executive is to work. With this information about the assumed job, the examinee is instructed to act as if he or she actually works in that situation. The examinee does not respond through essays, multiple-choice questions, or discussion, but actually executes the tasks required.

After receiving and to some degree assimilating the background information provided, the examinee then receives instructions, materials for "Courses of Action," and a "Reasons for Action" form. Throughout the exercise, the examinee receives "items," such as memos, letters, telephone messages, reports, manuscripts, etc., which would commonly be found in the manager's in-basket. The instructions direct the examinee to respond to the problem posed by each "item" by taking actions appropriate to the situation—writing letters, planning meetings, asking for information, setting priorities on given tasks, making notes on a desk calendar, etc. All of the products of these actions—notes, memos, letters—constitute scorable items which the candidate submits at the end of the exercise. In addition, on the "Reasons for Action" form, the examinee records why particular actions were taken.

On the assumption that each in-basket item presents an opportunity for some kind of action or behavior, a score of "1" or "0" is given to the examinee for the response (or lack of response) to each item. Scores are assigned to written responses (courses of action) produced by the examinee throughout the exercise; the "Reasons for Action" form may be used by the scorer to interpret a particular response. Scoring categories include dimensions such as the number of words in a written message or letter, conceptual analysis of the problem, courtesy to co-workers, decisiveness, showing concern for using proper channels of communication, etc.

In-basket tests have proven to be very effective as tools for training administrators, but have scarcely been tested as assessment devices for evaluating potential candidates. Also, scoring the in-basket test is a complicated, time-consuming task that requires careful definition of 50 to 60 scoring categories and standardization of scoring results. (See Figure 5.2 for an example list of scoring categories.)

Advantages/Disadvantages

The advantages of simulated performance assessments are numerous. They can provide realistic, direct assessment of on-the-job skills and behaviors, many of which could not be measured practically in any other way. As with all simulation techniques, the primary value of simulated performance is its ability to predict how a candidate will respond when placed in a real situation. As such, it is most useful as a training tool to prepare the candidate, then as an assessment device to gauge the effectiveness of the training. Since the administrator of the simulated performance can usually control most of the variables in an assessment, this technique can be used with relative success to standardize the test across candidates and across situations.

Disadvantages of simulated performance assessments stem from the time and money required to establish a realistic setting and a set of highly job-related performance tasks. The in-basket test, for example, requires a carefully planned daily schedule, a multitude of written materials, telephone cues, an entire day of an executive's time, and at least two days of an administrator's time for set-up, observation, and scoring. Finally, the most significant disadvantage can be the scoring procedure, which is usually complex, involved, and lengthy. If properly constructed and executed, the scoring method may generate valid, reliable results; but this takes a great deal of time and expertise to accomplish.

Developing a Simulated Performance Test

The key to a successful simulated performance test is planning.

Step 1: Identify the skills or behaviors to be assessed. A definition or analysis of the job for which a candidate is to be assessed can identify the most important skills or behaviors required.

Step 2: Design the problem situations and the setting. Each skill or behavior should be performed as it would be on the job; thus, a

Figure 5.2

Example: In-Basket Test List of Scoring Categories

1. Estimates number of words
2. Uses abbreviations
3. Number of subordinates involved
4. Number of peers involved
5. Number of superiors involved
6. Number of outsiders involved
7. Conceptual analysis
8. Uses program values or physical values in analysis
9. Aware of human values, feelings of others, or employee relations
10. Shows awareness of superiors
11. Evaluation and development of staff
12. Shows awareness of poor work
13. Informality to subordinates
14. Informality to peers
15. Informality to superiors
16. Courtesy to subordinates
17. Courtesy to peers
18. Courtesy to superiors
19. Courtesy to outsiders
20. Discusses with subordinates
21. Discusses with peers
22. Discusses with superiors
23. Discusses with outsiders
24. Requires further information
25. Asks for information, opinion, advice, or permission from subordinates
26. Asks for information, opinion, advice, or permission from peers
27. Asks for information, opinion, advice, or permission from superiors
28. Gives information to superiors
29. Gives suggestions to superiors
30. Gives directions and/or suggestions to subordinates
31. Explains actions to subordinates
32. Explains actions to peers
33. Explains actions to superiors
34. Communicates by writing
35. Communicates face-to-face
36. Delays or postpones decision, or temporizes
37. Arrives at a procedure for deciding
38. Concludes decision
39. Makes tentative or definite plans only
40. Takes leading action
41. Takes terminal action
42. Schedules work for a specific day
43. Schedules work for within a specific week
44. Indicates time priorities
45. Refers to peers
46. Refers to superiors
47. Follows lead by subordinates
48. Follows lead by peers
49. Follows lead by superiors
50. Follows a pre-established structure
51. Initiates a new structure
52. Encourages or notes need for quickness or promptness
53. Sets a deadline
54. Sets up checks on others
55. Sets up checks on himself or herself
56. Concern with proper channels
57. Responds with specificity
58. Item not attempted

(Reprinted by permission of Educational Testing Service.)

realistic setting must be created and a situational test structured to replicate an actual situation. The problem situation must permit the isolation of each skill or behavior to be assessed so that examiners can observe and rate each candidate in relation to these specific criterion elements.

Step 3: Acquire the resources necessary. Depending on the situation, each simulation will require certain resources—materials, props, equipment, people—for staging the assessment. These must be acquired before the simulation can be assembled and tried out.

> *Example:* In the EMT exam, administrators must acquire oxygen tanks, bandages, splints, and other medical supplies; props for each setting, such as a ladder, a wine bottle, a wrecked auto; people to role-play the parts of patients; etc.

The realism of the setting often depends on the quality and quantity of resources obtained in advance.

Step 4: Assemble the test and try it out. Once the assessment has been designed and the resources acquired, the test and its instructions can be prepared and assembled. Once assembled, the test should be tried out by the examiner(s), who can alter it as necessary and can identify the elements of the scoring criteria required. Assembly and pilot testing of the simulation should involve consideration of every possible option an examinee may choose during the test, so that scoring and continued administration can take the examinee's actions into account.

Step 5: Develop the scoring criteria, procedure, and instrument. Scoring criteria should be based on the elements—behaviors, skills, techniques—identified for testing. Each one should be assessed and scored individually. Procedures for scoring—observation by a judge or the examiner, videotaping, comments from participants, etc.—should be worked out to fit the specific assessment situation. Instruments for scoring simulated performance are usually checklists or rating scales (see Figure 5.1) and may include quantified data (as in the in-basket test, see Figure 5.2).

Administering and Scoring a Simulated Performance Test

Examinees should not be expected to have knowledge or abilities they have not been trained for, nor should they be expected to participate in a simulation that is unfamiliar to them. Each examinee must be oriented to the test situation and given careful instructions. All examinees participating in a given simulation should receive the same instructions, the same orientation, and the same test—which may require extensive effort to duplicate a simulated situation in exactly the same way for each examinee. And, of course, all examinees should be scored in the same way. The reliability and validity of the test depend heavily on standardizing the test, its administration, and its scoring.

Simulated Identification Test

A simulated identification test differs from actual performance in that the examinee does not usually identify real materials or problems and does not actually perform a particular function in a real situation. The context of the test is a controlled situation, as opposed to a real job or work situation, in which the candidate either identifies parts or problems and does nothing more, or in which the candidate responds by manipulating a model. For example, in a simulated test for a medical student, the examinee might identify the parts of the body on a mannequin and/or describe how an operation would be done, but would not perform the operation.

Uses

Simulated identification tests are most useful in those cases in which mistakes made by the examinee could have serious consequences (e.g., surgical operations, tunnel blasting, assembly of explosives) and in those cases where the actual reproduction of a malfunction for each examinee is impractical or destructive (e.g., a machine working at the wrong speed, an engine with a serious problem).

In several allied health fields, this type of test has been used successfully. For example, medical laboratory technicians are often trained and tested for their ability to identify bacteria and other microbes on prepared slides. In fields that require knowledge of diverse materials and the ability to read blueprints (e.g., engineering, architecture, construction), various forms of simulated identification tests can be useful measures. The following is a description of two simulated identification items for architects.

Examinees are shown slides of various types of buildings.

Question 1: Examinees are asked to identify orally the style of architecture represented by the building (e.g., Victorian, Bauhaus, Gothic).

(This response is scored by one or more observers on a right/wrong basis.)

Question 2: Examinees are asked to explain orally the materials used in and the basic concepts of each building type (e.g., gray marble, used to blend with surroundings).

(This response is scored by one or more observers using an analytical checklist.)

Another type of identification test for architects might show an actual section drawing (e.g., a fascia detail) and require the examinee to identify its parts or potential sources of problems (e.g., structural defects).

Advantages/Disadvantages

The further from actual performance one goes, the less direct the measure. Thus, actual performance is most direct; a simulated performance is less direct, but more so than a paper-and-pencil identification test. Directness of measure must be weighed against cost, time required, ability to control the situation, and seriousness of the consequences of mistakes in performance. A simulated identification test usually measures an examinee's cognitive understanding of how to perform a task, but not the actual ability to do it.

Equipment and materials, which may be expensive or difficult to obtain, are often required for this type of assessment. In some cases, simulated materials (e.g., a mannequin) may be less expensive and less consequential than real materials; but then the accuracy, completeness, and functioning ability of the simulated materials (e.g., a model car engine) may be questionable.

Developing a Simulated Identification Test

The steps in developing a simulated identification test are basically the same as those for the "actual performance" identification test. The differences in these assessment approaches stem from the situation, which is simulated not real; the materials, which are usually simulated; and, most importantly, the mode of response. Instead of performing a task, the examinee might identify how the task would be performed—either by selecting from multiple-choice responses, writing a response, or speaking aloud.

Administering and Scoring a Simulated Identification Test

An important aspect of scoring an identification test is to maintain simplicity by having a single yes/no scoring option for each specific segment of the test (each material identified, each malfunction, or each performance task described). Administration of the test requires standardized methods to ensure that every examinee receives the same information and each response is scored on the basis of the same criteria.

The scoring method depends on the mode of response. A multiple-choice response mode requires only an answer key, while open-ended written responses may require a set of scoring criteria to determine how to score variable responses. A spoken response would require scoring criteria and a recording instrument, such as a checklist or a rating scale.

Written Simulation

A written simulation is a paper-and-pencil exercise designed to simulate a decision-making process in which the examinee must make inquiries, make decisions based on the results of those inquiries, and take action. After working through the written portion of the problem step-by-step, the examinee either solves the problem or faces unacceptable consequences resulting from his or her own decision.

This type of simulation has a number of significant characteristics: (1) the problem is posed as it would be in a real situation; (2) the exercise requires a series of sequential, interdependent decisions analogous to the various stages of solving a problem—presentation, interpretation, analysis, resolution; (3) the examinee receives feedback after each action taken, but the examinee's decision cannot be retracted (on the basis of that feedback); and (4) a written simulation can be constructed to allow for a number of different but acceptable solutions, thereby permitting the examinee to pursue any of several reasonable approaches.

In most cases, a written simulation begins with the presentation of a situation and information related to it. This may be written, filmed, recorded, role-played, spoken, or presented graphically (e.g., site plans, renderings, or specifications). Included in the presentation are a statement of the problem and data that would be available to the person presented with a similar problem in real life. The examinee then must decide how to go about solving the problem by asking questions, making choices, consulting with experts, ordering tests, and so on. In a step-by-step process, the examinee works through the problem and reaches an acceptable— or unacceptable—solution.

A written simulation is most often presented in booklet form, in which the examinee is given a presentation, one or more initial approaches to the problem, a set of *options* (divided into sections) for each approach, and one or more *bridges* (forced or free choice). An examinee chooses an approach, then answers questions or makes decisions by choosing any number of options within a section. After choosing an option, the examinee receives feedback by erasing an opaque overlay or causing a latent image to appear (by coloring with a chemically treated pen). The examinee may then use this feedback to proceed, finish each section, and cross the "bridge" to the next section. In a *branching* problem, sections may be arranged in any sequence: the examinee finishes each section of options, then, based on the results thus far, chooses or is directed to another branch of the problem. Each section and each branch include both correct and incorrect options ("incorrect" in the sense of wasteful, not helpful, dangerous, or harmful). The examinee may reach an unsuccessful conclusion by choosing an unreasonable approach or by choosing certain incorrect options.

Uses

This type of exercise was first developed by the military to train and to test technicians in how to go about solving a technical problem, e.g., repairing an electronic transmitter, which requires a methodical procedure. It is now used in many fields—from training young people how to survive alone in the wilderness with only limited equipment, to testing sales approaches, to testing police investigators, to training and evaluating management personnel. In particular, written simulations—also called "clinical simulations" or "patient management problems"—are used widely in the medical field to train and test physicians and other medical personnel. For example, given a patient's condition upon entering the out-patient clinic, the physician must ask questions, diagnose the problem, and prescribe treatment.

Theoretically, a written simulation can be used to measure skills in eliciting and interpreting data; determining the sequence of steps required to solve a problem; utilizing resources, including consultants, experts' advice, or reference books; altering a situation by manipulating it; monitoring the procedural steps and obviating or remedying adverse results; resolving a problem effectively; and avoiding unnecessary and wasteful actions.

Figure 5.3 shows an example of a patient management problem (PMP) consisting of three parts (A, B, C).

Advantages/Disadvantages

This type of item is best suited to problems in which a candidate's ability to make decisions depends on gathering and interpreting information, and discriminating between appropriate and inappropriate actions, in situations that would normally permit the person to re-evaluate the information available and go back several times to attempt new solutions of the problem.

Figure 5.3

WRITTEN SIMULATION: SAMPLE

GENERAL INFORMATION:

You are consulted by a 49-year-old woman who complains of general malaise and a vaguely-defined pain in her right hand. She describes early-morning stiffness "all over," and states that all of these symptoms have been present for about six months. A physician that she consulted previously advised her that the pain was probably caused by trauma and that aspirin, rest, and hot packs should relieve her problem. She visited this physician again, at which time he recommended that she continue the previous treatment.

A detailed history reveals that, while she complains of generalized morning stiffness, she states that her hands, especially the right, are the source of most of her pain. She states that her "energy" is less than it used to be, and that she has lost about 12 pounds over the last 18 months. She also tells you that she has taken vitamins as well as aspirin during this time in an effort to relieve her fatigue and discomfort.

Further questioning reveals no history of injury to her right hand. Her morning stiffness is often present until noon and then subsides gradually. There is no family history of similar problems. The patient has noted no elevation in temperature. Other facts, brought out in a systems review, reveal that she has noted no change in bowel habits, that she has had no rashes or other skin changes during the last two years, yet that she feels slightly depressed and this is accompanied by a decrease in her libido.

The patient is a college graduate, happily married, and the mother of three healthy children. Her husband, a bookkeeper, is also in good health. She expresses concern over the fact that her eldest daughter, 21 years old, has recently moved in with her boyfriend. The patient has not traveled outside the United States but visited southern California the previous year.

Physical Examination

T – 37.2°C (99.1°F)
Ht – 5'6''
Wt – 118 lb
BP – 150/85 mm Hg

Physical examination is entirely normal except for a questionable decrease in the ability to flex her right wrist.

PROBLEM A:

Which laboratory studies would you feel it important to order now?

A-1. Complete blood cell count	
A-2. Erythrocyte sedimentation rate	
A-3. Serum electrophoresis	
A-4. Serum uric acid	
A-5. Serum rheumatoid factors	
A-6. HL-A B-27 determination	
A-7. Skull radiographs	
A-8. Hand roentgenograph	
A-9. Bone scan	
A-10. Serum creatinine	
A-11. Aspirate right wrist joint	

Figure 5.3

SAMPLE
(Continued)

A-12. SMA-12

A-13. FANA

PROBLEM B:

Which of the following would you include in your initial management of this patient?

B-1. Acetylsalicylic acid 300 mg. (5 gr.) with meals

B-2. Acetylsalicylic acid 300 mg. (5 gr.) every 4 hours

B-3. Amitriptilene 25 mg t.i.d.

B-4. Gold thiomalate 10 mg, I.M.

B-5. Naproxin 250 mg morning and evening

B-6. Triamcinolone acetonide 5 mg/day

B-7. Conference with patient and family

B-8. Referral to surgeon

The patient returns in two weeks and reports no improvement in her condition. Her morning stiffness is worse. The proximal interphalangeal joints of the third finger of her right hand are now swollen in a fusiform manner, warm to the touch, and tender. She reports no tinnitus or any new symptoms other than the stiffness and hand-pain. Serum salicylate level is 15 mg per dl.

PROBLEM C:

Which of the following would you now order?

C-1. Increase in acetylsalicylic acid to 2.4 gm (40 gr)/day

C-2. Administration of gold thiomalate 25 mg, I.M.

C-3. Indomethacin 25 mg q.i.d.

C-4. Naproxin 250 mg b.i.d.

C-5. Prednisolone 25 mg q. A.M.

C-6. Referral to rheumatologist

C-7. Referral to surgeon

Written simulations are advantageous in that they provide relatively realistic settings for the assessment of problem-solving or decision-making skills. Feedback from decisions, etc., is immediately available to the examinee, as it often would be in real life. The examinee has considerable freedom in choosing which approach to take in solving the problem, because alternatives are available—any of which may be correct. Written simulations purport to measure *process* of performance and not a product.

As to disadvantages: the time and expense required to develop these complex problems, including the cost of printing on special "opaque overlay" or "latent image" paper, are considerable. (It is likely that they would also require additional graphic materials such as X-rays, site plans, or topographical maps.)

Written simulations are better suited to teaching or training than to testing, in part because the candidate can learn from trying different approaches but does not suffer the consequences of failure. Examinees are presented with a finite set of options from which choices must be made: the intelligent, innovative candidate may think of other options, or may disagree with the arbitrary ratings of +, 0, - assigned to each choice. Also, the examinee would have to be exposed beforehand to this type of testing, in order to be assessed fairly on his or her skills and not on test-taking ability. In some types of simulations, an incorrect option ends the problem (thus, the candidate "fails" the test). This may occur at any stage of the problem; but may not be considered fair to the examinee, or reasonably related to a real-life job situation.

Developing a Written Simulation

Methods for developing a written simulation vary slightly from one field to another, but the basic steps are fundamentally the same.

Step 1: Identify a problem. Whether in survival training, electronic repair, or obstetrics, the first step is to identify a problem. The problem chosen should be realistic, within the realm of ability expected of the examinee, and should lend itself to a fairly straightforward solution. For example, a general practitioner might be presented with a patient whose symptoms indicate diabetes; but a GP is unlikely to encounter a patient who has Rocky Mountain Spotted Fever (an extremely rare disease).

Step 2: Identify the solution. A problem that has only one solution or has hundreds of possible solutions will probably be impractical for a written simulation. The ideal is to identify a solution that requires three or four steps and includes a number of options in each step. In the process of identifying the solution, choose the correct answer, then choose all of the appropriate choices made to arrive at the solution. For example, in a television repair simulation, the problem might be to find a faulty tube; the solution is to replace the tube. Leading to the solution are several steps: observing the nature ("symptoms") of the television's malfunctions, testing a few tubes, replacing one, and trying the television again.

Step 3: Plan the tasks to simulate. Within a written simulation are several problems (usually three to four); each problem represents one major task in reaching a solution. With the problem and the solution both identified, the next step is to fill in the sequential tasks by planning which ones to simulate. The first task is usually to gather information; the second is to formulate a hypothesis or a diagnosis; the third is to test the hypothesis; and the fourth might be to evaluate test results, conduct follow-up studies, perform management functions, or prescribe therapy.

Step 4: Write the simulation. A flowchart approach might be useful here to help sequence the tasks, to write the introductory statement(s), to write directions for the examinee, and to devise options (correct, incorrect, neutral). The introductory statement presents the information needed by the examinee to begin solving the problem: it customarily includes how, why, when, where, who, and so on (see Figure 5.3 for an example in a PMP). In addition, depending on what the tasks in the problem are, another statement might be necessary before each of the tasks (2, 3, and 4) to provide further information, enabling the examinee to continue.

Step 5: Assign scores and results to the options. Each option available to the examinee must have a positive, negative, or neutral value. In addition, some may provide results. For example, an architect might use a written simulation to approach a site planning problem. If the architect wants to test the soil on-site, he or she might order a PERC test; the "result" would provide the results of the actual test, and the score for choosing the PERC test would be positive.

Administering and Scoring a Written Simulation

The first and most important requirement for administering a written simulation is to provide a high-quality booklet, particularly if the simulation includes graphic materials (e.g., X-rays, blueprints). An examinee who cannot read the latent images or discern the details of a picture will not have a fair chance to complete the simulation. Printing quality is essential to this type of assessment if a latent image or opaque overlay is used; basic black-and-white printing does not usually present the same problems.

Second, practice materials may be required if the examinees are unfamiliar with written simulation formats. Because of the complexity of written simulations, few examinees can solve them effectively without prior exposure to this form of assessment.

Third, depending on the program and the type of simulation used, steps may have to be taken to ensure that examinees do not take advantage of the test format. In some situations, an examinee can glance at the last page and determine how to proceed in previous steps. If the simulations administered suffer from this potential difficulty, then the administration must be conducted to ensure fairness to all examinees.

Methods of scoring a written simulation are relatively simple. Most simulations have a score assigned to each option; the score is either positive, negative, or neutral (+, -, 0; or -2, -1, 0, 1, 2). Scoring the problems involves adding the number of plus scores and subtracting the negative scores from the sum. A neutral score generally does not contribute to the overall score (because the option is so obvious that it is a giveaway or is ineffective, but not harmful); although if a neutral option is not chosen, it might be scored as a negative.

Figure 5.4 shows a written simulation developed to test police

Figure 5.4

Example: Written Simulation for Police Officers

Situation: You are a police officer in an urban area walking home after an
eight-hour shift. On the way, you pass a liquor store where a
hold-up is in progress. The suspect appears to be a male
Caucasian; he has a gun in his hand and a ski mask over his face.
As you approach the store, the liquor-store owner is emptying the
cash register drawer into a paper bag. The suspect looks
extremely nervous.

Problem A:
As a witness to the hold-up, you should do which of the following? (Select as
many as are appropriate.)
A-1   Observe everything carefully. (0)
A-2   Charge into the liquor store. (−)
A-3   Call for back-up assistance immediately. (+)
A-4   Wait for the suspect to leave the store. (+)
A-5   Write down everything you see. (−)
A-6   Draw your gun and stand behind cover. (+)
A-7   Shoot a warning shot as the suspect exits. (−)

Problem B:
After you have apprehended the suspect, what should you say? (Select as
many as are appropriate.)
B-1   "Why did you do it?" (−)
B-2   "You are under arrest." (0)
B-3   "How much cash did you get?" (−)
B-4   "Is this what you do for fun?" (−)
B-5   "You have the right to remain silent." (+)
B-6   "Do you wish to make a statement?" (+)
B-7   "Anything you say can be used against you." (+)

---

officers in their ability to deal with a sudden situation involving a robbery. It consists of two problems, A and B, each of which has seven options. Each option is designated as a + (a correct choice), a 0 (ineffective, but not harmful), or a − (incorrect because it is potentially dangerous, would jeopardize the officer's legal case, or would be otherwise inappropriate). The score for each problem would be the total number of +'s minus the number of −'s; 0's would not count either way.

Management Exercises

All of the categories of assessment methods in this chapter constitute subgroups of simulations, the more general classification. Forms of "management exercises" presented here are variations on a basic theme: place the examinee in a role-playing situation and observe what happens.

Most of the methods grouped as management exercises emphasize management of someone or something; they differ from simulated performance assessments primarily because they focus on technique, not on content or factual knowledge. From this perspective, an in-basket test is considered a simulated performance because it includes assessment of "content" items (memos, letters, telephone calls, etc.); but it could also be included as a management exercise.

Brief descriptions of several major types of management exercises appear below. Each description includes an explanation of the specific approach, its uses, advantages and disadvantages, and scoring method.

Role-Playing

As a training or assessment technique, role-playing requires the examinee to assume a particular role, usually that of a person in the profession to which the examinee aspires. Presented with a problem situation, described orally or in written form, the examinee interacts with one or more other persons. The other participants may be examiners, trained actors, or other examinees. The situation itself is designed to elicit a sample of the examinee's behavior, interpersonal and communication skills, and problem-solving skills in a realistic setting. Some role-playing exercises are designed to measure the application of prior learning, while others emphasize self-discovery; the first is primarily an assessment device, while the second emphasizes training or education.

Role-playing techniques have been used primarily to assess candidates for administrative or management-level positions in business and industry, and in other professions that depend heavily on personal interactions (e.g., sales and marketing). Many role-playing situations require the examinee to assume the role of a supervisor discussing a particular problem with a subordinate, as in the military uses of role-playing to assess the leadership and human-relations skills of potential officers. Other situations involve the management of a client situation (e.g., promoting a product to a potential client, managing a patient).

In most role-playing situations, only one of the role-players is an examinee. Observers and other players rate the examinee's performance on the basis of predetermined criteria, using a checklist, rating scale, or questionnaire. Examiners may rate the candidate's *overall* performance as a "pass" or "fail"; or they may rate each aspect of the performance as pass/fail, or on a scale of one to five, poor to excellent, inadequate to superior.

The most significant advantage of role-playing techniques stems from their ability to provide a realistic but controlled setting in which to observe a candidate exhibit social interactive skills, which are otherwise not easily measurable. The examinee can be placed in a situation which closely approximates a typical job setting and can be observed exhibiting complex behaviors.

Major disadvantages of role-playing stem from the amount of time and number of personnel required for development, adminis-tration, and scoring. In addition, subjectivity is inherent in any rating or scoring system used to assess such complex perfor-mances. For these reasons, role-playing techniques most often function as training devices rather than as assessment methods.

Simulated Interviews

Simulated interviews (also known as "simulated diagnostic interviews," "simulated proposed treatment interviews," "oral simulations," "role-playing patient management problems," and "simulated office orals"), by any other name, are specialized uses of role-playing. As the label implies, they specifically measure interview skills and their attendant behaviors.

In their most common uses, simulated interviews assess candidates whose jobs require interviewing on a regular basis (e.g., journalists, performance appraisers, telephone sales, admissions officers, social workers, employment counselors). In medical and allied health fields, simulated interviews may be used to train and assess physicians, nurses, psychiatrists, psychologists, and counselors. Police officer training programs, such as those used by the New York City Police Department and the International Association of Chiefs of Police, often require simulated interviews. A police officer candidate would interrogate a suspect or interview the victim of a crime such as rape or burglary. The examinee would be rated on his or her ability to deal with people, with the public, and to investigate a crime.

The College of Family Physicians of Canada and the American Board of Orthopaedic Surgery both use simulated interviews as part of their certification exams. Programmed patients enter a consulting-examining room, present their symptoms, and answer questions posed by the physician—whose performance is observed and videotaped through one-way mirrors. Examiners rate the candidate on several factors: ability to elicit information, to exhibit desirable attitudinal skills, to solve problems, and to allay patient anxiety. Each performance factor, or competency, receives a score of 0-12; usually at least one aspect, such as allaying patient anxiety, is essential to a passing score.

Special types of simulations, known as "stress interviews," are used to assess emotional control and other attributes essential to a particular profession (e.g., police work, labor negotiations, public relations). The Central Intelligence Agency (CIA), for example, uses stress interviews to evaluate potential agents and their reactions under pressure. Interviewees may be interrupted, criticized, verbally or physically provoked, and subjected to long periods of tension-filled silence.

All of these variations on simulated interviews require the

examinee and at least one other person to play a role and to conduct an interview in a carefully structured situation. This approach is basically the same as role-playing in terms of administration, scoring, and advantages and disadvantages.

Fact-Finding Exercises

Most often used in business and corporate settings, a fact-finding or "information-seeking" exercise usually presents a specific problem that exists within a "company" or dummy corporation. Candidates receive a minimum amount of background information about the problem and about the company itself. They must then question a "resource person" available, examine documents, etc., to assemble information, analyze the information, and propose recommended solutions.

The key to most fact-finding exercises is the candidate's ability to identify essential information within a short period of time—often no more than ten minutes. Candidates must be able to distinguish relevant from irrelevant facts, understand the problem clearly, and synthesize information directly related to a solution. Examinees may be rated on their questions and attempts to procure information, on their recommended solutions, and on their answers to questions that require them to defend or justify their solutions (as a way for the examiner to discover how the solution was derived).

Although fact-finding exercises can be useful in some situations, they have two major disadvantages. First, they are often used in a small-group setting; thus, during the question-and-answer period, each candidate has the benefit of answers to others' questions. Also, one or more candidates may dominate the entire ten-minute period with irrelevant questions, thereby leaving the less aggressive persons at a distinct disadvantage. Unless group dynamics and aggressiveness are assessment criteria, these characteristics can be shortcomings. Second, unless a number of optional sources of information exist within the exercise, the examinees have little room for ingenuity or personal problem-solving styles. Thus, a person who might solve problems quietly and discreetly in other situations must pursue a "tough" line of questioning here to obtain information quickly.

Case Study

A case study may require a written response, a role-playing response, or an active performance. In most cases, one or more people receive informational case descriptions which they must analyze, then must propose solutions or diagnoses. For example, a group of five social workers might be given the case description of a divorced mother with three children who has applied for welfare benefits, even though the neighbors report that her employed ex-husband visits the family every night and leaves the next morning. The group would examine the case, discuss possible implications (e.g., the husband may be forcing himself on the family, or the mother may be trying to collect benefits for which she is ineligible), and propose a course of action.

Presentation of the case itself may be a written document only; or, it may include a videotape, interview segments, medical records, etc. A common use of case studies is in business, where candidates receive information packets on the financial situation or the management structure of a given company. Each candidate must then analyze the information and diagnose the problem, or propose a beneficial change to solve the problem.

The key to case studies is an assumption that a person's response, behavior, or course of action in relation to an exemplary case can be generalized to all cases. Thus, the selection of actual cases for the exercises is an important consideration, as is the weight placed on a conclusion or assessment extrapolated from responses to a single case. Examinees may be scored on the basis of their final solutions and recommendations or on the basis of how they derived the solution. As with most management exercises, the emphasis should be the technique or management approach used by the examinee—not the specific content or knowledge incorporated into the solution. Generalizing from the use of techniques in a given case is more reliable than generalizing from the content of a solution to the same case, since the candidate who has mastered techniques will be more likely to prove capable of applying them in any situation.

Leaderless Group Discussion

Actually a specific use of the case-study approach, a leaderless group discussion attempts to assess various aspects of group dynamics: ability to impose structure upon a group, to solve problems, to reach compromises, to demonstrate communication skills, and to adopt various behavioral roles. The participants may be assigned roles to play during the discussion, an approach which emphasizes projective techniques; or they may not be assigned roles, in which case the participants tend to act as they normally would (aggressive, passive, manipulative, etc.).

In most cases, the group is presented with a situation, case, or problem that they must manage in some way. The situation often pits group members against each other to foster competition, negotiation, or both. For example, a management team might be given a budget figure for a hypothetical company in which each member supervises one department. Participants would then have to decide who gets what portion of the budget, based on each person's persuasive abilities, corporate goals, negotiated trade-offs, and so on.

Observers score the group members' performance in relation to the goals of the exercise and the ability to work in a group situation. As a measure of group dynamics, the leaderless group discussion can be a well-structured training and assessment device, capable of identifying skills and behaviors that do not emerge from individual performance assessments.

Management Games

This final subgroup of "management exercises" includes an almost infinite number of possible simulations. Because of the inherent nature of "game" situations, these methods are used primarily for training and educating persons in specific areas, most often through a demonstration and analysis of various concepts and principles. As such, their value as assessment devices is somewhat tenuous.

One example of a management game, called "Star Maker," involves a brief explanation of the setting and the rules, a timed period of "play," and a discussion of the results. Each participant receives a certain amount of currency and the ownership to a given resource, with an understanding of the "country" in which the game takes place. Participants then buy, sell, and trade resources among themselves. Inevitably, at the end of the game, the most aggressive members of the group have absorbed most of the resources and the power, while the passive members have lost almost everything and declared that material possessions are of insignificant value.

This type of game can be used to demonstrate the effects of personality, of traditional sex roles, of non-verbal communication, and so on. Its results point out the process by which some people gain power and others do not—which may be a desirable process in business, marketing, or politics, but undesirable in counseling or teaching.

Management games are most useful when specially designed for a particular purpose and a given situation, although commercially marketed games may be available to suit a specific need. The ability of games to provide participatory demonstrations of management principles and the effects of behavior far outweigh their value as assessment instruments to judge a candidate's potential on the basis of a gaming situation.

Simulator Machines

For vocational training programs, in particular, the use of simulator machines may be the most practical approach to training and assessing candidates for certain occupations. The term *simulator machine* may conjure images of NASA astronauts floating in simulated weightlessness or airline pilots learning to fly jumbo jets while sitting in a classroom, but not all simulators are as complex—or as expensive—as these examples. Machines used as simulators may be as simple as a keyboard or as complex as a space capsule.

Whatever its level of complexity, a simulator machine is an apparatus that closely approximates an actual piece of equipment or component part of a larger machine. It is a device used to train or assess technical skills when the use of the actual apparatus would be impossible because of expense, danger, or some other impracticality. Using a simulator provides a relatively direct measure of skills, behaviors, and knowledge in a relatively realistic setting. Because the examinee must usually manipulate the simulator in some way, the apparatus may be used to measure psychomotor performance (e.g., reaction time) in addition to the knowledge and abilities required.

In some cases, particularly in training programs, the simulator itself provides assessment indicators or scores to the examinee. For example, an aircraft gunner who pushes a wrong button may be told by the machine that he or she has "exploded." But most types of machines provide little response to the examinee, who must be observed by an assessor during the performance.

Uses

The types of simulators in use are as diverse as the occupations that require any kind of apparatus, but their uses generally fit into one of two categories: training or testing an operator of an actual machine, or training or testing someone to repair equipment.

Training operators of expensive, complex machinery is usually done with simulators to eliminate the potential consequences of mistakes that occur. Pilots are trained to operate an apparatus under various circumstances, such as maneuvering a simulated aircraft through rough weather, emergency situations, or pro-grammed malfunctions. Student drivers often begin their training with simulators, operating a steering wheel, gas pedal, and brake in response to videotaped traffic circulation. One large corporation that owns oil tankers and cargo ships trains its ships' captains in a simulated bridge, which is a room filled with the equipment normally found in a ship's control room. Computer-produced graphic images projected on the "windows" of the bridge show a busy harbor with ships and small boats moving about. The captain must maneuver the ship as if this situation were as real as it seems. Other simulators are used to train operators to produce a product, rather than to demonstrate particular skills; thus, the product can be assessed in addition to or instead of the skills performed. In all of these examples, the candidates are trained and tested with the simulator until they are competent; they then enter the real situation, on the assumption that they will apply the skills they have demonstrated in a simulated setting.

The training of technicians or repair workers with the use of simulator machines usually focuses on troubleshooting skills: the ability to diagnose and solve a problem with the equipment itself. The examiner may program the machine with a malfunction prior to the training or testing session, or may manipulate controls during the session itself. Electronic technicians, machine repair workers—repair of washers and dryers, automobiles, TV sets, etc.—and electricians are often trained with simulators.

Advantages/Disadvantages
Simulators often provide the only practical means of measuring certain performance skills in a direct manner and realistic situation, when a work-sample is impossible to obtain. An instructor or examiner often has the ability to manipulate controls on the machine during an assessment, and the machine may be capable of scoring the performance itself—an exceedingly objective and reliable method. Most important, a simulator can provide assessment information as to how a candidate will perform in a real situation.

The disadvantages of simulators are relative: for an occupation, such as airline pilot, the expense of a simulator is insignificant when compared to the cost of an airplane crash that might result without the training equipment. For most fields in education and training, however, simulator machines are prohibitively costly. Using the machines can also be very time-consuming, since most simulators can only be used by one individual at a time. Scoring performance by observation may also present problems, depending on the type of machine involved. Unless carefully structured and based upon some empirical data, scoring by observation leads to an assessment based on such generally irrelevant aspects as facial expressions and body movements—instead of on the performance of the operator.

Developing a Simulator Machine Assessment
An assessment that involves the use of a simulator machine must be developed to present a situation and a set of performance requirements that are as realistic as possible.

Step 1: Learn how to use the machine. Assuming that a machine is available, the assessor must know how to use it. This includes knowing how to operate the machine, its limitations, and the functions and situations it can simulate in a testing situation.

Step 2: Design the simulation test. Given an expensive piece of equipment and the ability to test only one candidate at a time, the simulation test must be planned carefully. Whatever malfunctions are programmed to occur or maneuvers the candidate must perform should be structured and tried out in advance. When the design is complete, the assessor should take the test several times, choosing different options each time, to gauge the effectiveness of the test.

Step 3: Develop the scoring criteria and/or instruments. With the test design already prepared to accommodate a number of functions, criteria must be developed for the evaluation of a candidate in performing those functions. Considerations should include the practicality of trying to observe performance—depending on the type of machine involved.

Step 4: Train the candidates to use the simulator. Before a candidate can be tested in the use of a machine, he or she must be trained. Once trained in its basic functions, as would normally occur in a training program, each student should get the same test. (An exception to this arises when the need for multiple forms of the test exists, as in areas where test security is essential. Alternate forms of the test should then be equivalent.)

Selected References

Simulated Performance

Carlton, S., and Brault, M. *In-Basket Scoring Manual.* Princeton, N.J.: Educational Testing Service, 1971.

Eubanks, D.H., and Diefenbach, R.C. (Eds.) *Guide for Organizing and Executing a Practical Performance Examination for Basic Level Emergency Medical Technicians.* Columbus, OH: National Registry of Emergency Medical Technicians, 1980.

Fredericksen, N. In-basket tests and factors in administration performance. *Proceedings of the International Conference on Testing Problems—1960.* Princeton, N.J.: Educational Testing Service, 1960.

Simulated Identification Tests
Boyd, J.L., and Shimberg, B. *Handbook of Performance Testing: A Practical Guide for Test Makers.* Princeton, N.J.: Educational Testing Service, 1971.
National Evaluation Systems, Inc. *California Architects Licensing Project: Assessment Techniques Report.* Unpublished document, developed for the Department of Consumer Affairs, Board of Architectural Examiners, Sacramento, California, 1980.

Written Simulations
Bobula, J.A., and Page, G.G. *Manual on Construction of Written Simulations.* Chicago: Center for Educational Development, University of Illinois College of Medicine, 1973.
McGuire, C.H., Solomon, L.M., and Bashook, P.G. *Construction and Use of Written Simulations.* New York: The Psychological Corporation, 1976.
Webster, G.D., and Cassileth, P.A. *Guide to Patient Management Problems in Medical Examinations.* New York: Elsevier North-Holland, Inc., 1978.

Management Exercises
Abt, C. *Serious Games.* New York: Viking Press, 1970.
Barton, R.B. *A Primer on Simulation and Gaming.* Englewood Cliffs, N.J.: Prentice-Hall, Inc., 1970.
Bass, B.M. Analysis of the leaderless group discussion. *Journal of Applied Psychology,* 1949, *33,* 527-533.
Hermann, C.F. Validation problems in games and simulations with special references to models of international politics. *Behavioral Science,* 1967, *12,* 216-231.
Knapp, J., and Sharon, A. *A Compendium of Assessment Techniques.* Princeton, N.J.: Cooperative Assessment of Experiential Learning, Educational Testing Service, 1975.
Lamont, C.T., and Hennen, B.K.E. The use of simulated patients in a certification examination in family medicine. *Journal of Medical Education,* October 1972, *47.*
Levine, H.G., and McGuire, C.H. The use of role-playing to evaluate affective skills in medicine. *Journal of Medical Education,* September 1970, *45.*
Levine, H.G., and Noak, J.R. *The Evaluation of Complex Educational Outcomes.* University of Illinois: Department of Educational Research, 1968 (ED 039583).

Chapter Six

Observational Assessment

Although many experts refer to them as "tests," observational assessment techniques are actually methods for scoring or rating performance. Thus, they are seldom used independently, but almost always in combination with other assessment methods. For example, work-sample tests, simulated performance, design problems, and interviews can all be scored by using observational assessment techniques.

Techniques described in this chapter include the following:

Checklists
Rating Scales
Anecdotal Records

These techniques may involve the observation of a process, a product, or both; but they all share some common characteristics: (1) they include definitions of the critical components of a product or a process; (2) they involve the use of a recording form; (3) the assessor observes the behavior or product to be rated, focusing attention on the critical components listed on the form; and (4) the observer then indicates on the form whether or not the critical components were observed. Anecdotal records differ somewhat from other forms of observational assessment because they tend to be less formal and are less likely to include documented scoring criteria; they are used primarily to record events which may later be used in an evaluation process.

Prior to the descriptions of specific techniques, this chapter includes a discussion of issues and characteristics of all observational methods and a brief presentation of common variations of specific approaches. Each of the two major categories is then further defined: checklists include both quantitative and qualitative types; rating scales include numerical, graphic, descriptive-graphic, and ranking or product assessment scales.

In the simplest of terms, checklists, sometimes known as "verification items," provide a means of determining whether or not a trait or behavior is present (yes/no); rating scales provide a means of evaluating the quality (good/bad) of a trait or behavior; and anecdotal records are used to document selective descriptions of a person's behavior or performance.

Some checklists are used to record the frequency with which given behaviors occur and the duration of the behaviors; these are sometimes known as "behavior tallies." Also, some experts consider "participation checklists," which are used to evaluate a number of persons at once, as unique types of instruments. Because all checklists operate on the same principles, they will all be considered together in this chapter.

Uses

Observational assessment may be either obtrusive or unobtrusive. Behavior that occurs normally (such as a student's classroom behavior or an employee's daily conduct) may be observed unobtrusively, i.e., without an "artificial" testing situation set up and without the candidate being aware that he or she is being assessed. On the other hand, if the observer devises a specific testing situation and the examinee must perform specific behaviors while under observation, then the nature of the observation is obtrusive. *Obtrusive* observation checklists and rating scales are geared to specific traits and behaviors elicited by an assessment situation, usually an assigned task; *unobtrusive* observation ratings generally reflect a predetermined set of standards or criteria normally applied to a natural situation (classroom or work setting).

Various forms of observational assessment are widely used in fields where important knowledge and skills cannot be assessed adequately by any other method. For example, elementary education and special education teachers use observation to assess social skills, motor skills, creativity, and interest levels in various subjects, as demonstrated by the kinds of activities children spontaneously choose and in which they participate. Vocational education teachers and trainers in many fields use observational techniques to assess trainees' behavior, attitude, and application of knowledge (as opposed to actual knowledge which can be measured by other methods). In all fields that require performance assessment—business, law, medicine, arts, etc.—observational techniques can provide the means for evaluating the performance.

Instruments used during the observation, such as checklists and rating scales, serve three major functions. The first is to structure and govern the observation: to call the observer's attention to what should be observed and evaluated. Second, the instrument serves as a recording form on which to document the observations. Third, it can be useful in explaining to the examinee exactly what is expected of him or her, i.e., the basis on which the examinee will be evaluated.

To serve these functions, the instrument usually has three structural segments: (1) directions; (2) criteria for observation and recording; and (3) scoring instructions. The directions generally describe the total process or product to be assessed, conditions under which the observation should occur, materials required, instructions to the examinee (if any), and how to fill out the observational form. Criteria for observation and recording generally constitute the checklist items or rating scales, the main body of the instrument. Scoring instructions may further define the distinction between different ratings on the form. For example, if a rating form is used to determine the frequency of given actions, and the options are "often," "sometimes," "seldom," and "never," the instructions may define these terms more precisely (e.g., "often" means five times per day). Also, scoring instructions explain how to derive points or total scores; that is, a method for calculating the examinee's points on different dimensions, and for determining whether the total score is acceptable or unacceptable.

One type of rating scale includes an additional feature called an "anchor." This type, the *anchored rating scale*, provides a description of how a particular performance or behavior *should* occur in a given situation; thus, observers have a standard by which to judge how the performance does occur. For example, Cyrs and Grussing (1978) cite the use of a Behaviorally Anchored Rating Scale (BARS) to assess pharmacy students. Observers rate examinees on each specified criterion, relative to a predetermined standard of performance. This method has a potential for validity and reliability that makes it attractive for use in certification and licensing programs, in which standard-setting issues are paramount, because it provides a criterion against which to judge performance (as opposed to judging the performance of one person in relation to that of another).

The elementary-school counterpart to this approach, noted by Blood and Budd (1972) and Cartwright and Cartwright (1974), involves the concepts of *precision teaching* and *baseline data*. Observations made at an early stage provide a standard for comparison (baseline data); the teacher then attempts to modify the students' behavior and makes a second observation later; results of the second observation are compared to the original data. Major goals of this approach are behavior modification and progress monitoring.

Issues in Observational Assessment

In training and education programs, both observers and examinees raise a number of concerns pertaining to the use of observational assessment. Most of these issues derive from the inherently subjective nature of judgmental observations, sometimes justifiably; and these issues tend to become more aggravated in direct proportion to the seriousness of the assessment's consequences. The possibility of subjective errors in a licensing test, for example, poses a great concern. This section of the chapter treats these issues, in relation to all forms of observational assessment.

Time sampling. One issue related to observational assessment is the danger of distortion or unfair judgment based on the time periods when observation occurs. For example, a man who works in a large factory, where he has numerous responsibilities throughout the day, might be observed by his supervisor for a ten-minute period on one day. In spite of any attempts to pronounce fair judgments, the supervisor sees only one small sample of the worker's performance. Without a representative sample of all aspects of the worker's job, the supervisor cannot accord him a fair judgment.

Similarly, in the classroom, a teacher may record observations about Karen or Polly when she is misbehaving. Thus, the teacher only documents one aspect—however large or small—of Karen's or Polly's behavior.

One potential solution to this type of problem is the use of time sampling. Whether on the job or in the classroom, observations can be planned to occur during allotted time slots. If the time slots constitute a representative sampling, then the observations can support generalized conclusions about the person's overall performance. In addition, time sampling can help to ensure that the busy supervisor or teacher with many persons to assess on a continual basis actually spends sufficient time working with and observing each person.

To provide objective coverage of a person's observed performance, time sampling requires the observer to plan for and select specific time slots in advance of any observation. Selection of time slots should permit observation during as large a variety of activities as possible and should be as regular as scheduling allows. Any pertinent aspects of performance observed at a time other than the scheduled time should usually not be documented, or they could be noted in anecdotal records.

Scoring reliability. Performance ratings and scoring of observational assessments depend primarily on the accuracy of the scorer's observations and judgments. It is essential that a scorer or observer be trained carefully and thoroughly, both in the specific field or subject area and in how to conduct a specific observational assessment. But even among trained observers, there are at least three common errors in ratings which should be guarded against: personal bias, the halo effect, and logical error.

Personal bias errors result from a scorer's tendency to rate all individuals at the same point on a rating scale. Generous scorers tend to rate everyone high, severe scorers rate everyone low, and others lump everyone in the middle of the scale.

The *halo effect* occurs when a scorer's general impression of a person induces the scorer to rate the person the same on all dimensions or the same over a period of time on many dimensions. For example, if the scorer has a generally high opinion of an examinee, often based on only one trait such as personality or physical appearance, he or she may tend to rate the examinee highly on an entire range of characteristics.

A *logical error* occurs when a scorer mistakenly deduces more or less correlation between two distinct dimensions than actually exists. For example, a scorer might assume that high intelligence and high academic achievement traits go together. Therefore, if the scorer observes low achievement, he or she might automatically assume low intelligence as well. The second rating would be a logical error based on preconceived notions rather than the result of actual observation.

Careful training of observers, careful planning and development of the observational assessment, and an analysis of inter-rater reliability can solve most scoring problems. Training involves the selection of persons experienced in the particular field, based on selection criteria such as race, sex, geographic region, and education level; and it involves actually training the observers, through demonstration and practice, to make accurate observations and record them properly. Careful planning and development of the assessment includes the construction of the observation instrument, to ensure that it is clear, comprehensive, and meaningful; and it includes uniform guidelines for conducting the observation itself. Analyses of inter-rater reliability may be as simple as having two or more judges observe the same performance, then comparing the results; or it may involve statistical correlations of all ratings across all raters and examinees. More specific ways to pursue these solutions are presented in relation to the different forms of observational assessment.

Observational reports. The third and last issue of this section is related to the use of observation over long periods of time for the purposes of assessment. Some characteristics and behaviors cannot be observed in brief periods of time, particularly in training programs where a learning process and exposure to new experiences may not yield the desired results for months or even years. One approach to this situation, when the desired performance is expected to require a long period of time, is to develop an observational report.

In most cases, an observational report is the result of a systematic, long-term assessment that incorporates checklists, rating scales, and anecdotal records—all of which are designed to assess aspects of performance that cannot be measured adequately by other means. In some cases, this approach includes a self-assessment component, whereby the student completes the same observational assessment forms as the observer(s), to assess his or her own performance. Results of the self-assessment can be used for comparison throughout the duration of the process. The observational report approach can help to compensate for the potential problems posed by intermittent or short-term observations, particularly if its foundation is a carefully structured long-term plan coordinated with the training or education program.

The next sections of this chapter include descriptions of checklists and rating scales; suggested procedures for developing, administering, and scoring these instruments; and a description of anecdotal records.

Checklists

There are two basic types of checklists: quantitative and qualitative. Both types list a number of dimensions to be observed, and both types require an observer to choose between two opposite choices for each dimension (yes/no, right/wrong, correct/incorrect, acceptable/unacceptable, etc.). Some differences exist, however, that distinguish each type.

Quantitative checklists assess only the presence of a dimension (behavior or attribute), not its quality. For example, a quantitative checklist might be used to determine whether or not a dental hygienist follows the necessary steps when cleaning a patient's teeth; it would not assess the hygienist's speed, delicacy of movement, or quality of conversation intended to relax the patient. Figure 6.1 shows a simple form of a quantitative checklist

Figure 6.1

Example: Quantitative Checklist

Letter for Job Application		
Dimensions	Yes	No
1. States position for which person wants to apply.	—	—
2. Mentions source of information on job opening.	—	—
3. Lists qualifications.	—	—
4. Records complete home address.	—	—
5. Provides complete telephone number.	—	—
6. Requests an interview.	—	—
7. Signs name.	—	—

---

which could be used by career education teachers to assess students' letters for job applications.

In addition to the yes/no response, a checklist may have other columns to use when yes/no responses are not available. The additional column(s) may be marked "not applicable," "no opportunity to observe," etc.

Special types of checklists have been used to record the frequency or quantity of behaviors; these are usually called frequency checklists, participation checklists (or charts), or behavior tallies—depending on their uses. While most checklists are used in the observation of an individual, one at a time, frequency checklists most often serve the observation of a group of individuals, all at once. Figure 6.2 shows a sample participation checklist, designed for rating participants in a group discussion.

Figure 6.2

Example: Participation Checklist

Observation of a Group Discussion		
Participants	# of Contributions	Total
Mary K.	‖‖‖	5
Peter S.	‖‖‖‖	4
Susan T.	‖‖‖‖ ‖	6
Nancy L.	‖‖	2
Paul G.	‖‖‖	5
Mike R.	‖‖‖‖	4
Gene V.	‖‖‖‖ ‖‖‖‖	10
Cheryl C.	‖‖‖‖	4

As it is structured here, this sample provides little useful information (except that "Gene V." talked a great deal, while "Nancy L." said little). A qualitative addition to this checklist might divide contributions into relevant/irrelevant, constructive/ destructive, kinds of questions asked or responses given by the participants, etc. This kind of addition points out the distinction and relative value of quantitative and qualitative dimensions applied to different situations.

Participation or frequency checklists can be very useful to teachers, who sometimes structure them as seating plans, and to others who must observe relatively large groups. Characteristics of these checklists are basically the same as those of standard forms, as discussed in this chapter.

Qualitative checklists assess dimensions of quality, but with the same yes/no type of response as the quantitative instrument. For example, a dimension from a quantitative checklist used to assess a resume might be: "lists work experience in chronological order with most recent experience first" (yes/no). A similar dimension from a *qualitative* checklist might be: "describes work experience in appropriate language, with sufficient detail" (yes/no). Thus, the qualitative checklist requires an element of judgment to determine whether or not the observed behavior or attribute is of the desired quality. In order to ensure uniform assessment and to minimize rater bias, qualitative terminology must be clearly defined. To use the example above: "with sufficient detail" might be defined in an explanatory note as "lists the name of the company, position held, responsibilities, major tasks, and duration of employment."

Figure 6.3 shows a sample qualitative checklist used by teachers of third-graders in Hawaii. It is one of a series of checklists developed to assess the artistic creativity of students statewide, in relation to music, drama, dance, and various visual arts. In order to define the dimensions on this checklist for each art form, a set of criteria was developed for each form. The set for Visual Arts I (Drawing and Painting) is included with the checklist (numbered criteria correspond to numbered dimensions on the checklist).

Qualitative checklists may also have multiple criteria, each one requiring a yes/no response, as in the example below.

	Legibility		Accuracy	
	Yes	No	Yes	No
Handwriting	✓		✓	
Illustrations	✓			✓

Figure 6.3

Example: Qualitative Checklist

Student's Artistic Creativity		
Directions: Over a period of five weeks, observe the student's production of creative works in various modes of expression and rate the student on the checklist below.		
The student:	Yes	No
1. expresses a personal feeling or experience through art.	1	2
2. produces a complete work.	1	2
3. produces a unified work.	1	2
4. produces a work in which the different elements are in harmonious interrelationship.	1	2
5. produces an original or inventive work.	1	2
6. emphasizes the main idea or focus of the work.	1	2
7. produces a work that has more than one dimension (e.g., tone and rhythm, or line and color).	1	2
8. uses tools and materials appropriately.	1	2
9. demonstrates technical ability.	1	2

(Reprinted by permission of the Hawaii State Department of Education.)

Criteria for Visual Arts: I
(Drawing and Painting)

1. The student draws or paints a scene or design which depicts an experience from his or her own life, or expresses a personal emotion.

2. The student completes the drawing or painting (the finished product may be "rough" or primitive, and not all the space need be filled; however, it is not acceptable if the student begins to draw a specific object, e.g., a human figure, and clearly loses interest or does not finish for some other reason).

3. The finished work clearly represents a single scene, or set of related scenes (as in a cartoon), or a unified design, rather than a set of unrelated parts.

4. The different elements of the work (e.g., color, line, proportion, balance, subject matter) complement each other in such a way as to convey a single mood or scene. (For example, a picture combines vibrant colors, bold lines, intense or emotional subject matter.)

5. The student's work is original or inventive in any of the following ways: unusual or subtle combinations of color; elaborate design or detail; unusual degree of realism; creation of an elaborate fantasy world; conveys a strong sense of mood or emotion; contains high contrasts.

6. The different elements combine to create a single strong impression (e.g., size relationships are ordered so as to set off a central object or design).

7. The student has clearly paid attention to at least two of the following elements of design: line, color, proportion, balance, form, space.

8. The student uses paints and brushes properly, does not make a mess, cleans up, etc.

9. The student demonstrates technical ability in any of the following ways: mixing colors, using color; control of pencil, brush, or crayon; realistic drawing; use of space; ability to convey proportion; use of perspective; balance.

In addition, they may have a "comments" column or space in which the observer can provide constructive criticism or a rationale for a particular judgment. This feature is most useful for providing feedback to the examinee after the assessment, and/or for prescribing remedial instruction.

Uses

The uses of checklists are as varied as the kinds of performance products and processes which might be observed. A *quantitative* checklist is most useful in determining the presence of behaviors or product components which are so important that it is sufficient or useful to know simply whether or not they are present. Quantitative checklists can provide useful measures for observing procedures with definite sets of steps (see Figure 6.4) and for evaluating a product with definite components or characteristics (see Figure 6.5). They can also be useful measures of highly complex behavior (such as social behavior on the job or in the classroom); a more sophisticated instrument may result in more subjective ratings, while the simple quantitative measure can provide the most basic information about a complex process.

Qualitative checklists are useful when the mere presence or absence of quantitative dimensions does not provide adequate assessment information about the product or process. The qualitative criteria for assessment, however, must be recognized as significant within the field (or classroom subject area) and must permit uniform interpretation by scorers. The danger of bias is greater with the use of qualitative than with quantitative checklists, but both types have been used successfully in personnel selection, product assessment, employee evaluation, training, and education.

Advantages/Disadvantages

Checklists can be useful tools for guiding and recording observation when the dimensions to be exhibited are known in advance of the observation; checklists are virtually useless in highly unpredictable situations.

The advantages of a quantitative checklist lie in its simplicity:

Figure 6.4

*Example: Quantitative Checklist
(for Procedural Steps)*

Using a Wood Saw

Direction: Place a check after each step as it is performed.

The student:
1. measures the board.   _____
2. draws a line to indicate the cut.   _____
3. positions the wood for cutting.   _____
4. positions the saw.   _____
5. nicks the wood on the line.   _____
6. applies pressure on the downward stroke.   _____
7. holds the wood to prevent splitting.   _____
8. completes the cut.   _____

Figure 6.5

*Example: Quantitative Checklist
(for Product Assessment)*

Spot-Welded Aluminum Case		
Product Characteristics	Yes	No
1. Dimensions of the case match specifications.	___	___
2. Six spot welds are visible.	___	___
3. Edges have been filed.	___	___
4. Metal has been cleaned.	___	___
5. All corners are right angles.	___	___
Total:		

since the observer simply checks yes or no next to each dimension, rater subjectivity is less of a problem than in other observational assessment techniques which require finer discrimination.

On the other hand, a quantitative checklist is a fairly crude measure insofar as it does not include important dimensions such as quality, speed, and accuracy. When it is applied to processes, it sometimes has the drawback of being a fixed standard: problems can arise when an individual's performance differs from the expectations, e.g., when the examinee uses different steps or makes errors but completes the procedure with successful results.

The advantages of a qualitative checklist derive from its ability to do what the quantitative checklist cannot: provide a measure of quality. If the dimensions of quality are clearly defined and at least two observers score the product or process independently, then the judgment of quality can be informative and reliable. Otherwise, the qualitative aspects of the checklist can be the disadvantage.

Both types of checklists can be expensive and time-consuming to develop, administer, and score, particularly because they involve observations on an individual basis. And, although they are seldom used when another method would be more effective, the use of checklists for observational assessment may be open to claims of subjectivity and bias. However, they are relatively easy to use, with some prior orientation; and they can be used as guides for providing detailed feedback to the examinee about specific aspects of a product or performance.

Rating Scales

Rating scales are similar to checklists except that instead of marking yes or no next to each dimension, the observer indicates the degree or extent to which each dimension is present by indicating a point along a continuum (from yes to no, positive to negative) to represent the dimension observed. For example, instead of simply indicating that a behavior is present, the observer can indicate the frequency with which the behavior is exhibited (e.g., often, sometimes, seldom, never). Or, instead of indicating the quality of a product with a yes or no (e.g., yes, the design has quality), the observer can indicate the relative degree of that quality (e.g., the design is extremely well-unified, coherent, clearly articulated, and harmonious).

There are four basic types of rating scales: those based on numerical, graphic, or descriptive-graphic ratings; and those used for ranking. All of these types can be used in many of the same situations that checklists are used, but all usually provide more information. Certain dimensions, such as personality traits and on-the-job behavior, can be assessed more effectively over a period of time than through a single observation. Rating scales can incorporate the important factors of time and frequency.

Many behaviors and attributes are always present to some extent, so that a yes/no indication of their presence becomes meaningless. These dimensions can only be evaluated in terms of degree. For example, with respect to a salesperson's performance, a rating of "yes, the person sells the product" does not provide very useful data. With a rating scale, the salesperson's ability to sell the product could be judged on a continuum from high to low; or the continuum could include numerical ranges of the number of products sold within a given period (0-5, 6-10, etc.).

Affective traits, such as attitudes and opinions, are generally measured by rating scales rather than checklists because most affective traits cannot be considered right or wrong; they can only be measured on a continuum, between opposite poles. The measurement of affective traits may be done by an observer, based on the candidate's behaviors; or it could be accomplished through a form of self-assessment. For example, in assessing individuals' opinions of a new government policy, a typical rating scale could list the policy and require the individuals to indicate the descriptions that most accurately describe their opinions, from a range of descriptors such as "strongly agree—agree—no opinion—disagree—strongly disagree."

Most rating scales consist of a number of behaviors or attributes, listed vertically, and a scale of ratings beside each dimension, listed horizontally. The scorer, when observing for each dimension, circles, marks the line, or otherwise indicates the rating attributed to the candidates on each dimension.

In a *numerical* rating scale, the scale of possible ratings is expressed in the form of numbers. For example:

The individual is:	Never				Always
A. punctual	1	2	3	4	5
B. reliable	1	2	3	4	5
C. self-motivating	1	2	3	4	5

Because numbers can have different meanings as ratings (e.g., is "1" high or low?), numerical scales should only be used by experienced raters in fairly predictable situations. Numerical ratings should be defined in behavioral terms (actually, numerical values can be assigned to other types of descriptors to facilitate recording and scoring).

Numerical rating scales can only be used reliably in assessing behaviors when the alternatives are constant in meaning; in other words, the numbers must have the same meaning for each dimension listed. If the numbers one through five represent frequency ratings from a low of "never" to a high of "always" for the first dimension listed, then they should have the same meaning for all of the other dimensions on the list. Each listed behavior must be assessed according to the same principle. If the meaning of the numbers were to shift between frequency and quality, observers could easily become confused.

The major advantage of a numerical rating scale is its ease of use, particularly in compiling total scores (simply adding the numbers). Its major disadvantage, assuming that each number is defined in behavioral terms, is that it cannot be used to measure behaviors according to changing sets of criteria.

A *graphic* scale uses words rather than numbers as ratings. Typical ratings on a graphic scale might range from "poor" to "excellent." The observer rates the examinee by making a mark on the line somewhere between the two extremes, or on one of a number of specified points (as in the following example).

Graphic Scale

Dimension

Neatness

Legibility

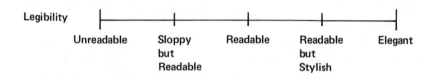

Different ratings on a graphic rating scale usually consist of one to three words placed horizontally on a continuum; they progress in logical order of quality or quantity, although they may go from best to worst or worst to best. Ratings may be the same for each dimension (e.g., poor to excellent), or they may vary from one dimension to another (as in the example above).

Graphic scales are more widely used than numerical rating scales because they are generally more self-explanatory and more flexible. One drawback of this type, however, is that a one- or two-word description often seems more precise than it really is. The distinction between "fairly neat" and "meticulous," for example, is a subjective one that will vary from observer to observer. This element of subjectivity may introduce problems in the instrument's reliability. A second drawback may arise if, for scoring purposes, the ratings must be converted to numbers (e.g., "sloppy" would be a "1" and "meticulous" a "5"). Assigning numbers to ratings that fall between the two extremes can be a spurious approach.

Descriptive-graphic rating scales attempt to reduce subjectivity by providing detailed descriptions of each point on the graphic scale. This more sophisticated approach can be useful when assessing products or processes that are highly predictable.

Detailed descriptors of desirable and undesirable attributes are only useful when there is a high likelihood of observing these particular behaviors or traits. In situations where, for example, excellence could be exhibited in a myriad of particular ways, a descriptive-graphic scale would be impractically lengthy.

Below is an example of a descriptive-graphic rating scale used to assess the overall quality of a working drawing produced by a machinist.

Descriptive-Graphic Rating Scale

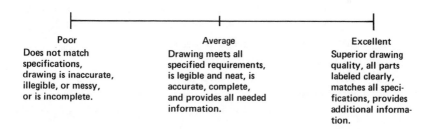

Poor	Average	Excellent
Does not match specifications, drawing is inaccurate, illegible, or messy, or is incomplete.	Drawing meets all specified requirements, is legible and neat, is accurate, complete, and provides all needed information.	Superior drawing quality, all parts labeled clearly, matches all specifications, provides additional information.

One potential drawback of this type of scale is its inability to provide precise feedback when structured in this way. A trainee whose drawing receives a rating of "poor" does not know which of the five aspects of the rating apply to the particular work (e.g., it may be clear and neat, but incomplete). In an appropriate setting, the major advantage of this scale is its precision, thus its ability to reduce subjectivity. In a setting where particular standard criteria are not usable, its precision becomes inflexible, leaving no room for differences in philosophy, creativity, or interpretation.

When constructing a rating scale of any kind, one must decide on the most appropriate number of scalar options. An odd number of options (three, five, or seven) can usually be divided into those at the high end of the scale, those at the low end, and the one in the middle. In some cases, having a neutral option is advantageous, because observers can use it to denote "average" or undistin-guished quality. However, some cases require an assignment for everyone as either high/positive/acceptable or low/negative/un-acceptable. In these cases, the "middle" option should be eliminated and an even number of options used. For example, the holistic scoring method most commonly used to assess writing samples provides only four options: "poor" and "below average" represent failing grades, "above average" and "superior" represent passing grades. Where a pass or fail grade is the desired result, every option must be above or below a specified cut line.

When deciding on the number of options to use, there are three basic criteria to consider:

(1)   Taken together, the options should cover the range of possible observations, from least to most, worst to best, etc. A scale that covers only excellent—good—fair does not meet this criterion because it provides no option to indicate poor performance.

(2)   There should not be too many options. A continuum with more than seven options to choose from becomes meaningless because the distinctions between points are extremely fine and particularly subjective. Four to five options are sufficient for most rating scales.

(3)   Options should be mutually exclusive; that is, no two options should overlap. For example, "good to excellent" and "fair to good" are overlapping judgments.

If a pass/fail line must be drawn on the rating scale, then a number of points can be assigned to each option (e.g., an "acceptable" rating is worth 2 points, "improvable" 1 point, "unacceptable" no points). Then a cut-off score can be established in one of two ways: the first is a *compensatory* or *conjunctive* model where a high score on one dimension can compensate for a low score on another dimension.

(1)   Assign numerical points to each gradation on the rating scale, then set a minimum total number of points for passing. For example, the examinee could receive a

minimum of zero and a maximum of four points for each dimension on a rating scale. If there were five dimensions on the scale, then the maximum number of points possible would be 20. A cut-off score for this scale—all five dimensions—could be set at 15.

The second is a *disjunctive* model, where a minimum score must be attained on *each* dimension.

(2) Set a minimum score for each dimension. For example, if the ratings were "often," "sometimes," or "never," it could be established that an examinee would have to attain at least a "sometimes" on every dimension. A single "never" rating would result in failure on the entire scale, even if all other dimensions were rated as "often."

A combination of the two approaches is also possible. A minimum total score could be established with the provision that an examinee could not score below a certain point on any dimension, or on one or more particularly crucial dimensions (see Figure 5.1). This approach could require a discrete cut-off score for each dimension and a total cut-off score.

With most rating scales, actual products or processes are rated against a given set of written criteria. With a *ranking scale*, a product or process is rated in comparison with similar products or processes. For example, a set of products can be compared with one another, then ranked from best to worst. If the ranking depends solely on comparisons within a group, the ranking is normative-referenced. Thus, rankings across different groups may vary considerably: a product ranked high in one group could, by comparison, be ranked low in another group.

A criterion-referenced approach to ranking, often used as a *product scale*, compares a product to a predetermined minimum standard. That is, representative samples of products are collected and arranged in order of quality (to constitute the criterion against which all products are judged); then each examinee's product is compared to this scale and graded the same as the criterion product it most closely resembles. A written description or rationale often accompanies each criterion product to explain the critical dimensions it exemplifies.

A criterion-referenced ranking scale is based on the same principle as the *anchored rating scale* mentioned earlier in this chapter. The anchored rating scale is most often used to assess a performance or process, rather than a product. The "anchor" associated with the rating scale is the criterion, usually a carefully defined description of acceptable performance, to which all observed performances would be compared and rated.

The advantage of a criterion-referenced product scale or anchored rating scale is that it can be used by different observers to assess a variety of products or performances in relation to standards that would be uniform across all observers. Thus, the result would not be a simple "good," but a "good" compared to X. Product scales have the particular advantage of providing observers with concrete examples with which to make comparisons, and from which examinees can learn how their own products may differ from those considered acceptable.

Developing Checklists and Rating Scales

The development of checklists and rating scales for observational assessment involves a number of steps, one of which is to decide which type of instrument is most appropriate to a given purpose. For this reason, and because of their basic similarities, the developmental process described below is useful for both general types.

Step 1: Identify major products or processes to be measured. As with any assessment instrument, the first step is to decide what to measure. If you begin with competencies or behavioral objectives, then an observational assessment instrument can be used to evaluate one or more than one of the specified competencies. A broad, generally stated competency may require only one checklist or rating scale; or one instrument can be used to assess multiple competencies, if they are closely related.

> *Examples:* One competency that could be assessed with one checklist might be stated as follows: The apprenticed electrician follows the appropriate procedural steps for installing a fluorescent light fixture.

Multiple competencies measurable with one rating scale might be stated as:

The apprenticed electrician: is aware of safety procedures;

has a constructive atti-tude toward safety;

follows safety proce-dures as recommended.

Step 2: Select an appropriate type of instrument. Based on what is to be measured, you can select the most appropriate type of instrument to be developed. The guidelines below summarize the uses of each type, as presented in this chapter.

Observational Assessment Instruments

Type of Instrument	Use(s)

Checklists (yes/no rating on predictable dimensions)

Quantitative	Presence of behavior; completion of steps
Qualitative	Satisfactory/unsatisfactory quality of process or product
Participation	Group participation; frequency of be-havior

Rating Scales (relative ratings)

Numerical	Time factors, frequency, quantity
Graphic	Affective traits
Descriptive-Graphic	Quality of product or process
Ranking/Product	Comparison with given standards

After selecting the basic type of instrument, begin to evaluate the most appropriate types of response options and criteria for judgment. For example, having selected the graphic rating scale for a program that requires a pass/fail grade on each dimension, decide on either four or five options for the instruments.

Step 3: Identify important factors. For each product or process to be assessed, identify the important factors to be observed in relation to each one. Depending on the competency, important factors might be steps, characteristics, aspects of quality, behaviors, or personal attributes. Depending on the program or uses for which the instruments will be developed, the method of identifying important factors will vary. For instance, a classroom teacher may simply define a competency, such as "behaves properly in the classroom," by identifying what he or she thinks are the important components of proper behavior. On-the-job assessment or licensing programs may use more systematic and less arbitrary approaches to defining important factors. These approaches may include job or task analysis surveys, interviews of job incumbents, expert judgment panels, or observation on the job.

> *Example:*   The Civil Service Commission undertook the assessment of medical technicians (Pike *et al.*, 1969). Based on observations and interests of laboratory personnel, the commission drew up a list of 13 clusters of specific tasks and responsibilities, and the abilities needed to carry them out. With the assistance of technical consultants, laboratory supervisors, and additional observations and interviews, the Commission narrowed the list to eight clusters. Each one formed the basis of a separate "anchored" rating scale, accompanied by a written description for each scale and a description of a fictitious person's performance on the dimensions given.

The most widely used way to express the important factors identified, by whatever process, is to define them as "enabling objectives." Thus, a broad competency is defined by specific skills, abilities, and attributes needed to demonstrate the competency; each specific skill or attribute becomes a dimension on the checklist or rating scale.

> *Example:* *Competency:*   The technician (or student) demonstrates proper behavior in the laboratory.
>
> *Enabling Objectives*:   The technician (or student):
> — follows directions,
> — uses equipment properly,

  — observes safety precautions,
  — keeps work area clean and orderly,
  — exhibits constructive attitude,
  — cooperates with others, and
  — uses caution when dealing with dangerous substances.

Each of these "enablers" can be used as a dimension on a checklist (e.g., the technician follows directions—yes/no) or on a rating scale (e.g., the technician follows directions—always, sometimes, never).

Step 4: Construct a draft of the instrument. After the type of instrument has been selected and the important factors to be observed have been identified, a draft version of the instrument can be constructed. Because of the complexity of such instruments and the need for completeness, the draft may require several further revisions. The draft should include the following components:

(1) statement of what is to be measured, in general terms;
(2) a list of dimensions;
(3) options for checking or rating on each dimension;
(4) directions to the observer and, if applicable, to the examinee (explaining the assessment setting, procedure to follow, equipment needed, how to record information, etc). This is particularly important for instruments that will be used by anyone other than those who develop them; and
(5) a place for examinee and observer identification (name, date, time, etc.).

When constructing the draft instrument, be careful in sequencing the tasks or attributes—in the order in which they must, or are most likely to, occur. Also, it is important not only to include desirable qualities and outcomes, but to include all possible errors or undesirable options that may occur. As stated earlier, checklists and rating scales depend upon the predictability of the assessment situation. (For further information on how to develop observational instruments, see the list of references at the end of this chapter, particularly the following: Blood and Budd, 1972;

Cartwright and Cartwright, 1974; Gronlund, 1977; Simon and Boyer, 1967; TenBrink, 1974.)

Step 5: Pretest the instrument. To ensure the accuracy and completeness of the instrument, it is advisable to conduct a "pretest." During this trial, note any particular problems that arise, anything the observer wanted to note but had no space in which to note it, and any essential dimensions that were observed but not included on the instrument. Pretesting with a sample of examinees who vary significantly in ability level will help to ensure that all possible options have been included. Pretesting with two or more qualified judges rating each performance, then comparing the results, will help determine the reliability of the instrument.

Step 6: Determine cut-off score and performance criteria. Depending upon the instrument developed and its intended use and interpretation, it may be desirable to set a predetermined cut-off score for all examinees. The cut-off score may consist of numerical scores (as described earlier), it may consist of verbal ratings, or both. The complexity and defensibility required of the cut-off score procedure depends largely on the consequences and legal implications of the program (see Chapter One).

Administering and Scoring Checklists and Rating Scales

Procedures for administering and scoring observational assessment instruments naturally depend on the instruments' uses. However, in all cases, the administration procedures should be:

(1) clearly defined, thus easily understood by anyone who will administer the assessment;
(2) pretested before the actual administration, to ensure their validity and reliability; and
(3) explained to the examinee in advance, along with the instrument, if applicable, so the examinee knows what to expect and will not be at a disadvantage.

Observers using checklists and rating scales should be selected carefully, should be familiar with and experienced in the field, and should be trained in advance to make and record observations with the instruments themselves.

One of the advantages of using checklists and rating scales is the ease of scoring possible. In most cases, ratings on all dimensions can be converted to numerical values and added together to derive total scores. This simple process is not feasible, however, if the options vary across dimensions (e.g., "1" means "poor" on dimension one, but "excellent" on dimension two). Numerical rating scales already have numerical values; in all other cases, dimensions can be assigned point values. For example, on a quantitative checklist, a "yes" may be a "1," a "no" may be a "2." With a ranking scale, the ranking assigned to a product or performance corresponds to a number assigned to the criterion product(s) or performance(s). Thus, if an examinee's product most closely resembles criterion product "3" (of 1-7), it would be rated a "3."

Anecdotal Records

Anecdotal records are factual, written descriptions of significant events in a person's life or work. They may be written by a teacher about his or her pupils, or by a supervisor about his or her employer.

The purpose of anecdotal records is to set down, as objectively as possible, events that might otherwise be forgotten or remembered incorrectly. By referring to accumulated anecdotal records, a teacher or supervisor may become aware of significant patterns of behavior that would be important for making diagnoses and recommendations.

There is no method for actually scoring anecdotal records. The notion of scoring implies judgment, and anecdotal records themselves should not be judged or evaluated; they are used only to describe particular incidents.

Uses

Anecdotal records have often been limited to recording events related to social adjustment (Gronlund, 1977). Although anecdotal records are appropriate to assessing this area, they can also be applied to other areas. They are best used to describe behavior that occurs naturally; or to describe idiosyncratic behavior that cannot be adequately conveyed by a few words on a checklist or

Figure 6.6

Example One: Anecdotal Record—Elementary School

Student _____Maria Valdez_____ Date __May 3, 1981__
Observer _____M.P._____ Grade ____3A____

Situation: The students had a free period from 9:00 to 9:30 when they could do as they pleased, within the classroom.

Incident: Maria went immediately to the bookshelf and selected several books to read. She then went to a chair in the corner by herself and read the books quietly—for the entire hour. Her facial expressions ranged from obvious delight to annoyance as she read.

Comment: Maria seems to have an exceptional ability to immerse herself in what she reads, and she reacts emotionally to what occurs in the story. Her attention span is quite remarkable.

---

rating form (e.g., a particularly surprising or illuminating action can only be recorded in an anecdotal record). Anecdotal records are especially useful in gathering information on individuals in need of extra attention.

Figure 6.6 shows an example of an anecdotal record written by an elementary school teacher. The record itself may be used as one piece of a comprehensive set of information on which to base decisions about grading, the need for additional instruction, or attitude problems.

Figure 6.7 shows an example of an anecdotal record written by a supervisor about an employee. At the time of performance evaluation, the supervisor may use anecdotal records to recall specific examples of behavior that substantiate a personal judgment about the employee; and the supervisor may use this type of record to recall not-so-recent events, since many performance evaluations are based on a six- or 12-month period.

Figure 6.7

Example Two: Anecdotal Record—Employee

| Employee | Earl Jackson | Date | March 15, 1981 |
| Supervisor | M.P. | Dept. | Editorial |

Situation: Meeting of all department heads to discuss interdepartmental coordination, attended by company president.

Incident: Each department head gave an opinion of why we had such a snafu on the social studies project. Earl interrupted several times, until it was his turn to express an opinion. He then offered no.explanation for his department's lack of progress, but proceeded to criticize the company's top-level managers in an angry, belligerent tone. He did not respond to my efforts to curb the attack.

Comment: Earl's behavior was out of place, unprofessional, and unacceptable for a person in his position. His lack of control and unconstructive approach to the problem seriously aggravated the situation and lost him the respect of his peers.

Advantages/Disadvantages

The most important advantage of anecdotal records is that they describe actual behavior. Any significant aspect of that behavior can be noted, not just those aspects that fit a predetermined rating scale or checklist.

Anecdotal records are virtually the only way to gather information from atypical but significant events. In other words, all other observational tests are designed to be used either in simulated situations, or in naturally occurring but predictable situations. The anecdotal record is the only tool for assessing the unexpected and unusual. As such, it is well-suited to use in instructional programs, particularly with young children that teachers evaluate constantly through observation. It is also useful in assessments, such as performance evaluations, which require less formal structure than, for example, a licensing test.

Selected References

Blood, D.F., and Budd, W.D. Observational tests. In *Educational Measurement and Evaluation*. New York: Harper Row Publishing, Inc., 1972.

Cartwright, C.A., and Cartwright, G.P. *Developing Observational Skills.* New York: McGraw-Hill, Inc., 1974.

Cyrs, T.E., and Grussing, P.G. *Rationale for Development of Multidimensional Assessment Procedures of Pharmacy Student Competence Through the Assessment Center Approach.* Las Cruces, N.M.: New Mexico State University, 1978.

Developing Performance Rating Methods. Tallahassee, Fla.: Department of Education, Division of Vocational Education, 1980.

Gronlund, N.E. *Constructing Achievement Tests, Third Edition.* Englewood Cliffs, N.J.: Prentice-Hall, Inc., 1977.

National Evaluation Systems, Inc. *California Architects Licensing Project: Assessment Techniques Report.* Unpublished document, developed for the Department of Consumer Affairs, Board of Architectural Examiners, Sacramento, California, 1980.

Pike, L.W. *et al. Predictions of Job Performance for Negro and White Medical Technicians: Development of the Instrumentation.* Washington, D.C.: Civil Service Commission, 1969 (ED 035013).

Schriber, P.E., Peel-Gregory, B., and Priestley, M. *Competency-Based Instruction in Vocational Education: How Do I Evaluate Performance?* Tallahassee, Fla.: Department of Education, Division of Vocational Education, 1981. Developed by National Evaluation Systems, Inc.

Simon, A., and Boyer, E.G. (Eds.) *Mirrors for Behavior: An Anthology of Observation Instruments.* Philadelphia: Research for Better Schools, 1967.

TenBrink, T.D. Constructing checklists and rating scales. In *Evaluation: A Practical Guide for Teachers.* New York: McGraw-Hill, Inc., 1974.

Chapter Seven

Oral Assessment

Anyone who has participated in some form of oral assessment, such as a job interview, either on the "question" or "answer" side of the table, has some appreciation of the difficulties of oral assessment. Oral communication is an art that requires a great deal of practice; when used as an assessment medium, it is also a science—which requires even more practice.

Oral assessment techniques are those which require some form of oral response. Technically, any non-physical performance test can be administered orally and considered an oral assessment. However, of primary interest in this chapter are techniques designed specifically as forms of oral-response assessment.

Three major techniques reviewed here are:

Oral Examination
Interview
Prepared Presentation

These assessment methods, and variations on these basic themes, are most useful in situations where examinees should have the opportunity to defend themselves or explain their reasoning; in situations where oral communication skills are essential; and in situations where written communication is impractical (e.g., testing of foreign languages, including English) or could be subject to bias. For most of these uses of oral assessment, the candidate's performance (oral response) is recorded and scored by means of a checklist or rating scale. Oral assessment is widely used to assess young children also, both in the context of psychological testing and in testing the content knowledge of children whose written communication skills have not yet developed adequately. These uses may be "scored" by anecdotal records, by checklists, or by rating scales; or they may serve only an informal purpose (unscored).

All oral-response techniques must be administered on an individual or small-group basis and must be scored during the administration. Time and cost may be relatively high for these techniques, and scoring is difficult to accomplish in a valid and reliable manner; but oral-response tests can be used to measure skills and behaviors, such as speaking skills, which cannot be measured adequately by other techniques. Oral-response tests are perhaps best suited to use in fields that require oral communication skills, such as foreign language teaching or public speaking; but they have been widely used in other fields for screening or selecting applicants for any number of positions.

Oral Examination

Oral examination methods generally take one of two forms: the *oral test* or *oral quiz*, designed to measure a generalized domain of knowledge; or the *oral defense*, designed to measure a specialized domain of knowledge, often related specifically to a product or line of inquiry developed by the examinee. The most common type of oral defense is the academic use of the "dissertation defense" or "oral comprehensive exam" in which a graduate student defends a document or a research study and demonstrates mastery of a specialized area.

As with all forms of oral assessment, an oral exam may be formal or informal, structured or unstructured. The degree of formal structure required most often depends on the purpose of the procedure and the need for legal or technical defensibility. A licensing program that includes an oral testing component, for example, will most likely impose stringent formality upon the procedure; an elementary-school teacher may assess students with daily oral quizzes that require little formality.

In an oral quiz, the questions are designed primarily to assess the store of information required for the examinee to perform effectively in a given area of competence. Questions would be prepared in advance and posed in an open-ended format; examinees may be required to give a brief answer (one to five words) or a ten- to 15-minute explanation, depending on the scope of the assessment.

In an oral defense, questions are usually based upon a product (e.g., dissertation, thesis, design project) which the examinee has developed and must defend before the examiners. In this situation, questions may be specific to the product and to the knowledge required to develop the product. For example, a research scientist may be required to explain the rationale for choosing a particular research design. Questions may also be comprehensive in nature, requiring interpretive or problem-solving responses (e.g., "If the study were conducted 20 years from now, how would the results be affected?"). This type of question might be used to test the examinee's ability to apply what he or she has learned to a different situation.

Oral examinations may be prepared formally or informally for either orals or oral quizzes. In an orals situation in which the product being defended may be unique to the individual, questions must be specific to the individual and the product (thus, the product must be submitted in advance). They may also, however, be predicated upon a common body of information related to the generation of the product that all candidates must possess. Examiners generally prepare their questions in advance and may be required to ask them in a formal fashion (e.g., one examiner at a time), perhaps in order, or in an informal fashion (to allow for spontaneous questions).

Questions for oral quizzes are most often prepared in advance of the examination, and the same questions are asked of every candidate. In this situation, two examiners—one conducting the examination and one assisting—is a sufficient number to complete the examination. The number of questions in the examination will depend upon the scope of information to be assessed and the time allowed for testing.

Uses

The California Board of Architectural Examiners includes an

oral exam (of the "quiz" variety) in its architect licensing program. In addition to passing nationally administered paper-and-pencil tests, candidates must pass the oral exam to qualify for licensure. The oral exam, administered by the Board of Examiners, is formal and carefully structured to elicit content knowledge from the examinee on subjects ranging from legal requirements to the mechanics of architectural practice. It consists of brief questions (and answers) intended to measure aspects of competence specific to California (thus, not measured on the nationwide test).

The California oral exam measures content knowledge, but other licensing boards use oral exams for different purposes. For example, the Wisconsin Examining Board of Architects, Designers, Land Surveyors, and Engineers uses an "oral exam" to assess candidates for licensure as engineers. Following a battery of written tests, each candidate submits to an oral exam/interview designed to assess character and ethical principles of practice.

Oral quizzes are most often used to assess specific mastery of a limited field of information. Oral exams of this type have been used for many years by certification agencies, such as the American Academy of Orthopaedic Surgeons (Levine and Noak, 1968). Practicing orthopaedists examine the candidates in a particular subject matter by asking questions that require mostly recall and recognition of information, some demonstration of interpretive skill, and some problem-solving. Each candidate takes five loosely structured, half-hour quizzes in various areas, questioned by the practicing orthopaedist and rated by the questioner and an examiner who participate in the session.

The Certification Examination of the College of Family Physicians of Canada (Lamont and Hennen, 1972) includes a one-hour oral examination designed to test in-depth content knowledge. Like the Orthopaedic Surgeons' oral quizzes, this exam is considered the heart of the certification process, the component that really measures the candidate's ability to demonstrate competency in the field.

Another use of oral examinations is the "oral trade test" (Knapp and Sharon, 1975), used in an interview situation. The "interview" may consist of a panel of examiners interviewing an individual or an interview of a group of individuals, similar in format to a seminar. Questions in an oral trade test are factual, related to specialized trade knowledge. Most often, the test is relatively easy for anyone who has worked in the trade; thus, it functions to eliminate those who have not attained a minimum level of trade knowledge and experience.

In education, oral examinations are used in many areas, but primarily to assess young children and to measure oral communication skills in areas which require proficiency in these skills. Informal tests of young children might be question/answer quizzes, spelling bees, or recitations (of poems, multiplication tables, etc.). Figure 7.1 shows an example of a more formal oral examination developed by National Evaluation Systems for use in Hawaii's Statewide Assessment of Foundation Program Objectives for third-graders. For a statewide program, the results of which will be used in educational evaluation and decision-making, the approach must be formally structured but easily administered and scored; it must also produce reliable results for students throughout the state. Thus, in the example, instructions, scoring criteria, and "do's and don't's" are all carefully specified.

Oral assessment in foreign language proficiency usually focuses on the ability of the student to speak the language (listening and comprehension, which may be measured at the same time, are discussed in Chapter Eight). This approach may involve brief answers, conversation, or extended discourse, either in a language laboratory or in a classroom. In most cases, specific item types are used to measure specific skills such as pronunciation, intonation, and command of vocabulary. Examples of several common formats for oral assessment in foreign language proficiency are shown in Figure 7.2 (instructions in English, content questions-and-responses in French). These can be very useful in foreign language education classrooms, used informally to encourage attention and to introduce students to new forms of testing, or used formally in oral assessment of language skills.

Another use of oral examinations in languages will undoubtedly become more popular in the near future, primarily to assess the

Figure 7.1

Example: Oral Examination (Third Grade)

Directions: The teacher will read aloud the following instructions:

"Read the story. Make sure you understand it, because when you're finished I want you to tell me about it."

New Year's Day in Japan is a very happy holiday. Many people welcome the rising sun by clapping their hands and bowing to it. The children usually wear new clothes. They go walking with their families in the public parks, call on friends and relatives, and exchange gifts. Each home is decorated with pine and bamboo (*kado matsu*). These decorations represent strength and love of country.

After the child has had time to read the story twice, take the story away. Then say:

"Tell me in your own words what the story is about. Try to start at the beginning and go to the end, and tell me everything that happened."

If the student is hesitant, you may repeat the instructions. Do not, however, prompt the student with questions such as, "How do people welcome the sun?" or "What do the children wear on New Year's Day?"

Scoring Criteria:

Mark "1" if the student:
— conveys the fact that the story is about New Year's Day in Japan,
— relates at least three of the six typical activities (greeting the sun, wearing new clothes, walking in the park, visiting friends, exchanging gifts, decorating the home), and
— does not make more than one mistake in relating the story.

Mark "2" if the student:
— neglects to state where and when the events take place,
— relates fewer than three events, and
— makes two or more factual mistakes when relating the story.

(Reprinted by permission of the Hawaii State Department of Education.)

Figure 7.2

Example: Foreign Language—Oral Assessment

Mimicry: Repeat this sentence after me. Bonjour Jeanne, comment ca va?

Oral cue: Listen to this sentence and say it back to me in plural form.

          Cue: Je rentre à midi.
  Response: Nous rentrons à midi.

Listen to my question (or direction) and respond in French.

          Cue: Demander à Pierre l'âge qu'il a.
  Response: Quel âge avez-vous (as-tu)?

Pronunciation: Pronounce each word written below (read the letter first).

     (a) soi
     (b) soir
     (c) soie

(Adapted from *Modern Language Testing: A Handbook.* Reprinted by permission of Harcourt, Brace, and World, Inc.)

---

content knowledge of students who speak English as a second language (ESL). Although considerable debate rages over this issue, many educators feel that teaching and assessing ESL students in their own language until they can speak English is not only recommended but should be required. This kind of test would basically be the same as written or oral tests of knowledge used with English-speaking students, only it would be translated into another language. For example, the New Jersey Minimum Basic Skills Program, which involves a statewide paper-and-pencil assessment of over 400,000 students annually, provides a translation of its test for Hispanics who do not speak English adequately.

In licensing and certification, many agencies have recently developed foreign-language versions of their tests, on the assumption that a candidate cannot necessarily be denied licensure because he or she does not speak English. A Vietnamese physician who emigrates to the United States, for example, could be licensed on the basis of competency demonstrated in the person's native language.

Finally, oral exams have been used to assess speaking ability in English—the ability to communicate orally. The Massachusetts Department of Education, in its Basic Skills Improvement Project, provides a speaking test component. This test poses questions to the examinee which are designed to elicit a demonstration of competency in various modes of speaking (e.g., social, business, persuasive, debate).

Uses of the *oral defense* approach generally assess comprehensive and in-depth knowledge of subject matter, interpretive and problem-solving skills, and oral communication skills. As its name implies, the oral defense emphasizes the candidate's ability to defend a product or process he or she has developed. In academic settings, oral defenses are used extensively. An analogue in the corporate setting is the contract proposal defense in which a prospective client asks technical questions of qualified bidders, who must defend their proposed plans. In both settings, questions of information, purpose, and explanation assess the candidate's knowledge of the field, application of this knowledge to solving a problem or developing a product, and ability to solve problems on the spot.

Advantages/Disadvantages

Oral examinations can be used to assess a number of complex skills which are more difficult to assess with strictly paper-and-pencil tests; these include oral communication skills, the ability to "think fast on one's feet," and the ability to bring to bear other relevant information to the problem or product at hand. Most importantly, oral examinations provide opportunity for the examinee to defend or explain his or her response. Furthermore, the opportunity exists for continued questioning on any given topic. If an examinee misinterprets a question, for example, he or she is not automatically scored as wrong: another question or rephrasing of the question may enable the examinee to demonstrate competence in the area being assessed. Finally, because defense of proposals or designs is a common activity in the corporate setting, the face validity of this type of examination can be relatively high.

One important disadvantage to oral examinations lies in the fact that the assessment is done on an individual basis. Testing individually is time-consuming for the individual and the examiner(s) in terms of both preparation and administration, and is therefore costly. Other disadvantages relate to the subjective nature of the scoring of the examinee's responses. If rating forms (e.g., checklists, rating scales) are used, then these may suffer from the same criticisms and dangers (e.g., inconsistency among raters, disagreement as to standards of assessment) as when they are used for other types of assessment. Regardless of whether or not rating forms are used, a candidate may so impress an examiner (negatively or positively) on one trait that the examiner will rate the candidate overly high or low on general competency as well as on all subsequent traits. The examinee may have interpersonal skills which could overcome any deficiencies in competence, unnoticed by the examiners.

Oral examinations may be advantageous to those who do not excel in reading comprehension; and, for those who speak English as a second language, a carefully prepared test (in understandable English, or in a foreign language) may compensate for language deficiencies. Oral examinations are best suited to situations in which oral communication skills are considered to be an important part of the competency being assessed, and when there is reason to believe that written examinations will not adequately tap the skills the assessment is intended to measure.

Developing Oral Examinations

Steps involved in developing oral examinations are similar to those required for developing paper-and-pencil tests in an open-ended format. The procedures described below pertain more to formally structured tests than to informal, unstructured tests. An informal oral exam is often based on a loose outline of areas to cover, then questions are made up as the examination progresses, often in response to the examinee's stated answers. A more formal approach requires the steps described below.

Step 1: Identify the domain of knowledge to be tested. As with all assessment methods, the first step is to define what is to be measured. In oral exams, use of objectives can provide a clear basis for domain definition, particularly in expressing those skills that cannot be measured adequately by other methods.

> *Examples:* Objective 1. Describe in detail the important aspects of a given illustration.
>
> Objective 2. Explain the mechanical functions of an air conditioner.
>
> Objective 3. Justify the choice of a specific design plan.

Step 2: Develop questions. As simple as this may sound, developing questions is the most difficult aspect of oral examinations. In a short-answer format particularly, each question must be constructed to permit only one (or two) correct response(s); at the same time, it must not lead the examinee to the correct response by the way it is stated.

> *Example:* A question on dental hygiene might be: "Discuss personal health practices which promote dental hygiene." (This question is too general; it could elicit a three-hour response.)
>
> If restated as "Discuss eating habits which promote dental hygiene," then the examinee can make a directed but brief response. The examiner can then ask about dental care, check-ups, brushing and flossing, etc.
>
> If the question said, "Discuss the value of eating apples as a way to strengthen and help clean your teeth," the examinee will be at a loss to respond with any information not already given in the question.

Step 3: Write scoring criteria. For each question, write the correct response(s) expected; then write down all of the possible responses which *could* reasonably be given to each question, indicating whether each one is correct or incorrect. (If the list of reasonable responses is too long, then the question needs revision.) When indicating the correct answer, include variations that would also be considered legitimate correct responses.

> *Example:* Who wrote the novel *1984*?
>
> > Correct answer: George Orwell (pseudonym) *or* Eric Blair (real name).

Variations can occur in any situation where there are two or more terms or names for the same thing (e.g., a tuba is also a sousaphone), or in a situation where one term has been replaced by another (e.g., in some states, a "library" is called a "media center"). Regional variations in terms, jargon, and dialect may also have to be included, if the oral exam is likely to be used with people of different backgrounds. Despite the possibility of variations, however, it is still necessary to decide which answer(s) would be correct: in some cases, variations may be considered incorrect, especially if they are outdated terms in a field that requires up-to-date knowledge.

Step 4: Develop instructions. Assuming that more than one person may administer the test, instructions should be clear and concise. They should include instructions to be read to the examinee, the questions themselves, whether or not "prodding" questions can be added (see Figure 7.1) to aid the examinee, how to record responses, and what to say to the examinee following the responses.

Step 5: Determine means of recording responses. Depending on the program, answers may be recorded on tape, on paper exactly as stated, on paper in the form of a checklist, or in all of these forms. In a simple question/answer format, the correct response(s) could be listed on the exam itself; the examiner could simply check yes or no beside each question for the examinee's response, and record any answer that is questionable.

Step 6: Pretest the instrument. A written instrument to be used as the basis for an oral quiz should be pretested to ensure that the exam functions properly. This pretest should include the experimental use of instructions, scoring criteria, and scoring instruments. With open-ended questions, an exam developer can seldom think of all the possible answers that examinees can produce; thus, a fairly large sample of pretest candidates can provide a range of responses, for comparison to those listed in the scoring criteria as correct or incorrect. Results of the pretest should be used to refine the examination. Procedures for operating recording equipment can also be pretested and corrected at this stage.

Administering and Scoring Oral Examinations

Administration procedures will depend upon the program and the specific type of oral examination used. An oral quiz can be administered fairly easily by one person reading questions from a prepared list; an oral defense requires coordination of the examiners and prior determination of who will ask questions, in what order, and so on. Taping the examinee's responses during the session is highly recommended for any situation in which proof of the test's fairness may be required; in situations where extended answers cannot be scored during the exam itself and would have to be played back for scoring after the exam; and in situations where keeping a record of the exam, for one reason or another, is essential.

There are a number of ways in which question/answer assessments can be scored, but these generally fall into two discrete categories: using written rating forms or not using them. The written rating forms that are available and useful for scoring oral examinations include checklists and various types of rating scales. Checklists are particularly useful for oral quizzes in which mastery of specific information is being assessed: relevant information can be listed and checked off as the examinee demonstrates knowledge of it. Rating scales are useful when it is important to assess to what degree an examinee demonstrates competence in one or another skill.

When written rating scales are not used, such as in an oral

defense, scoring can become more subjective. In this case, it is especially important for the examiners to agree ahead of time on their standards of competence. They will also need to consider strategies for arbitrating rating disagreements should these occur.

Another issue to consider in scoring the test is whether or not to award partial credit for partially correct or partially complete answers. The decision on this issue should be made in advance, planned into the exam procedure, and explained to the examinee along with all other instructions prior to testing.

Interview

Interviews, both structured and unstructured, are used for a wide variety of purposes in numerous types of programs. Since the primary goal of this book is to explore performance assessment methods useful in education and training, two basic types of interviews will be considered here: (1) interviews for educational and training assessment, and (2) screening interviews.

Piaget and other researchers (e.g., Ginsburg, 1975) have demonstrated the value of using informal interviews with young children as a means of psychological evaluation. Ginsburg notes that talking with children about mathematical problems, for example, will often yield great rewards: children may show signs of brilliance previously unnoticed, and they may solve problems in ways they have not been taught. Such results can be valuable as indicators of a child's intelligence and ability, but they can also provide valuable information about teaching methods; used together, these kinds of results can be extremely helpful as a basis for developing individualized instructional programs.

In terms of assessment, an interview is a situation in which the examiner(s), through dialogue, evaluate(s) the candidate in relation to predetermined standards and characteristics. The interviewer asks questions in order to gain an understanding of the candidate. Questions may be factual, affective, or a combination of both, designed to elicit responses as to the candidate's qualifications with respect to requirements for a training program, a job, a degree, a license, or a certificate. These requirements may include knowledge, skills, experience, and/or the candidate's attitude toward the profession, program, school environment, etc.

Interviews are commonly used for screening and selection purposes. *Selection interviews* are often required for candidates to obtain acceptance into courses of study or to get jobs. In these cases, examinees are evaluated with respect to their probability of success in the program or their match to the job. *Screening interviews* are used to determine which candidates may be eligible to receive licenses or certificates. In these, the assessment of attitude, character, and potential in making contributions to the field may be of high importance. In principle, screening interviews are used to "screen" out those applicants who should not be licensed, admitted to a program, etc., for one reason or another. Selection interviews are generally used to "select" the best qualified person(s) for available position(s). Selection interviews, designed to identify the *most* qualified applicants, are comparable in purpose and structure to normative-referenced tests. Since this book concerns criterion-referenced tests primarily, only screening interviews, designed to identify applicants who have not attained minimum standards, will be considered here.

A systematic job or program analysis provides the framework for the development of a structured set of interview questions to be asked of each candidate. Where such an analysis is not undertaken, the examiners must have an implicit and agreed-upon understanding of what questions are most important to include and how the examinee's responses are to be evaluated. With or without a structured set of questions, the examiner has the flexibility to branch questions in order to gain an accurate picture of an applicant's competencies in a particular area; and also to eliminate questions if, during the interview, it becomes apparent that they are not appropriate.

The specific types of questions that are included in an interview depend upon the job or program analysis. Attributes that have been judged to be important across a wide range of occupations and professions include content expertise directly related to the situation at hand, training, work experience, oral communication skills, ability to deal with professional problems, ability to work and get along with people, concern for public safety, attitude toward the professional's responsibility to clients and the community, confidence and professional demeanor, and career interests and advancement ambitions. Presenting a hypothetical situation to the examinee and asking for a reaction may also be an effective means by which to assess how the examinee might actually respond on-the-spot to a situation.

The format of interview questions tends to influence the accuracy of the information obtained from examinees. Questions should be constructed in such a way as to elicit responses that are potentially verifiable or factual, specific, and which sample actual behavior. The further the questions stray from factual information, the more likely the possibility that subjectivity may affect the interviewer's judgment.

Uses

Various forms of interviews are used in nearly all modes of education and training, with various degrees of formality and structure. In early childhood and elementary-school education, interviews are generally informal and relatively unstructured, providing a way for teachers, counselors, instructional specialists, and others to interact with children on a personal, one-to-one basis. However, in some cases, interviews can serve formal purposes.

Figures 7.3 and 7.4 show two example sections of a formally structured instrument used to interview fourth-graders. This instrument (similar to those developed for grade 8, grade 11, and for teachers) was developed and administered for a Department of Defense Dependents Schools (DoDDS) program, designed to evaluate the effectiveness of social studies curriculum in overseas schools. Interviewers talked with students and teachers to explore their attitudes toward the school, toward the host country, toward social studies, etc. Figure 7.3 shows the kinds of questions used to collect this information. The second part of the student interviews was designed to assess each student's ability to investigate and solve problems in a social studies context (Figure 7.4).

In vocational education and training programs, interviews may be used as screening devices (e.g., to screen out unqualified applicants), as student assessment techniques, and as program

Figure 7.3

Example One: Response Sheet for Grade-Four Interview

Now I am going to ask you some questions about social studies.

----

16. Can you name the things you have studied in social studies this year which you liked the MOST?
    1.
    2.
    3.

17. Could you tell me why you liked _____ (repeat 16, Answer 1)?

18. Can you think of any things you have studied in social studies this year which you really did not like?
    1.
    2.
    3.

19. Could you tell me why you disliked _____ (repeat 18, Answer 1)?

20. In general, how do you feel about social studies this year?
    POS   NEG   NEU   MIX

21. If you were the teacher, would you teach social studies differently than your teachers do?
    Y   N   DK

    If YES: How would you teach it differently?

(Reprinted by permission of Department of Defense Dependents Schools.)

Figure 7.4

Example Two: Response Sheet for Grade-Four Interview

Problem Situation I

Now I have some questions about a problem. First, listen carefully to what I read to you. Then I will ask you the questions.

Let's pretend that you have found an object. It is a piece of twisted black iron, about a foot long. It is from Africa. You want to bring it to school and show it to your class. So you have to find out everything you can about the object, then you can tell your classmates about it . . . . Is this clear so far? (Repeat as much of the introduction as necessary.) Now here is the first question.

29. What do you need to know about the object before you can tell the class about it?
    (Prompt with: Anything else?)

30. Suppose I told you that the object is a *Tonga*. It was used many years ago by the Mandingo tribe in Africa. Now, what would you do to find out more about this object?
    (If student says, "Go to library, or teacher," prompt with: And do what?)
    (If student says, "Look it up in the dictionary or encyclopedia," prompt with: What would you look up? And . . .)
    Could you look up anything else?

31. After you _____ (repeat answer to question #30), you find out the Mandingo people used Tongas to buy food and other things. Can you think of something else that is used in the same way as a Tonga?

    31A. Can you think of something we use in our lives that is like the Tonga?

32. Now, when you bring this Tonga to school, what can you tell your classmates about it? (Summarize information; draw conclusions. Prompt with: Anything else?)

33. Is there anything else your classmates might like to know about the Tonga?

(Reprinted by permission of Department of Defense Dependents Schools.)

---

evaluation instruments. Questions might be designed to gather information on student attitudes, career plans, level of maturity, and many other areas.

Various professions also use interviews as methods of assessment, but most of these uses are discussed as other types of assessment techniques. For example, specialized interviews used to assess the interviewing skills of physicians, counselors, psychiatrists, social workers, police officers, and employment personnel are actually modified uses of role-playing techniques (see Chapter Five) and oral examinations.

Screening interviews, as mentioned earlier, are most often used to eliminate unqualified candidates from a pool of applicants. As such, they do not constitute complete methods of assessment; that is, a screening interview might be the first of a battery of assessments for a given purpose. Only those who "passed" the interview could go on to more complex testing for specific knowledge and skills. For example, applicants to selective colleges and universities may be interviewed by admissions officers who look for undesirable characteristics; those who "pass" the interview would still be assessed on the basis of grades, aptitude, interests, financial stability, and so on.

Advantages/Disadvantages

The advantages of interview assessment stem from its individual and personalized nature. The interview is often cited as the only way to assess certain personal characteristics that are considered essential to effective performance in a job or an instructional setting. An interview can also offer the interviewee the opportunity to ask questions of the examiner(s), and the questions themselves can demonstrate both certain personal characteristics and the person's command of a particular field. The flexibility of an interview and its ability to be tuned to each individual can be advantageous in an informal situation (but would not provide standardized information for formal assessment).

As to disadvantages, there are a number of sources of error that can occur in rating examinees. These include disagreement among examiners on what standards of competence to employ, misunderstanding or misinterpretation by examiners of the evaluation forms, and the possible tendency by examiners to rate someone overly high or low on all traits because they were particularly impressed, positively or adversely, by one trait. Also, the consistency among examiners in interviews tends to be low, and the number of human characteristics which can be adequately assessed remains extremely limited. Moreover, interview validity, or the accuracy with which interview results predict the future success of the examinee in the job or program, is also generally low. A more limited scope in what the interview is expected to assess, particularly with regard to personality or character traits, could help solve these problems; and interview results might be used in conjunction with as much other information about the examinee's capabilities as is possible to obtain.

Because of the individual nature of interviews, the time and cost involved in this type of assessment are generally high. Preparation and administration time may be high for both examinees and assessors, and interviewing large numbers of examinees will take a long time on the part of the examiners. In general, interviews are much more effective as sources of information for instruction, training, and program evaluation than as assessment instruments. When used to collect these types of information, the interview can be less formal and less structured, emphasizing constructive information-gathering rather than the validity and reliability of assessment data.

Developing an Interview

Procedures for developing a structured interview are comparable to those used in developing oral examinations (see previous section). Questions should be based on a clearly defined domain of characteristics required for the job, training, or educational program. Each question should be clearly stated, easy to understand, and capable of being answered in a way that is efficient and useful to the interviewer. A major emphasis here is to phrase questions in a way that does not cue the respondent to a socially acceptable answer, but elicits an honest response. Scoring of the interview should be based on predetermined standards, and some form(s) of recording should be used. As with all forms of oral assessment, a pre-trial of the instrument and procedures is essential.

Administering and Scoring an Interview

A formally structured interview generally requires formal instruments (see Figures 7.3 and 7.4) to guide the interview and permit the interviewer to record a candidate's responses. Provided below is a brief set of guidelines for conducting an interview, using the interview instrument, and recording information.

Guidelines

Conducting an interview. An interview should be conducted in as objective a manner as possible to ensure standardization of responses, but should not be so mechanical and impersonal as to alienate or discomfit the candidate. The steps listed below may be helpful:

1. Choose a comfortable setting for the interview (with a table for writing).

2. Set the interviewee at ease before you begin.

3. Explain the purpose of the interview, its format, and procedures (make sure the interviewee understands all of this before you continue).

4. Ask the questions exactly as they are stated on the instrument (to elicit the kind of response for which the questions have been designed specifically).

5. Speak slowly and clearly.

6. Speak in a non-judgmental voice. (Do not express surprise, shock, disapproval, etc., to an interviewee's response.)

7. Provide positive feedback to encourage the interviewee. Feedback may be verbal ("yes," "okay," "all right") or non-verbal (attentive listening behavior, smiling, relaxed but upright posture, nodding, etc.).

8. Repeat any questions that may have been misunderstood.

9. Ask every question on the instrument, in the order in which they are presented. The order of questions is essential, since the questions should be sequenced such that each question leads into the next one.

10. Use "probes" to clarify responses. A probe may be direct (e.g., "Anything else?" "What do you mean?" etc.) or indirect (e.g., repeating the question), but it must be used carefully to avoid distortion of the question's precise intent. Any distortion of questions (which can often lead the interviewee into giving a desired response) can introduce potential bias.

Using the interview instrument. The interview instrument has two functions: to guide or structure the interview and to provide for recording the interviewee's responses. The actual questions, the sequence of the questions, and "branching" directions (e.g., "If NO, then go to Question 23") provide structure for the interview. Guidelines for recording responses are provided below:

1. For "closed" or forced-choice questions, a response may be recorded as a checkmark on one or more of the choices. In this type, the question text includes the choices.

Example: How often do you watch television—every day, a couple of times a week, once a week, or less than once a week?

every day	couple times/week	once/ week	< once/ week

2. For open-ended questions, the response must be recorded verbatim—or as close to it as possible—to ensure that the exact meaning of the response is preserved. Editing, paraphrasing, or summarizing can impose the interviewer's perceptions or preferences upon the response. Record the interviewee's own words.

Example: Do you like to watch television? (Response) Yes, some of the shows are good. An abbreviated response,

such as "yes, good shows" alters the connotation of
the response significantly.

3. Include all probes, notes, and comments in the recorded
response. If you had to ask four similar questions to get one
answer, all four questions should be recorded to provide the
correct context for interpreting the response.

4. Keep the interviewee's attention, even as you are recording
responses. One way to do this is to read back the answer as you
are writing it down; this will keep his or her attention and may
elicit corrections or additions from the interviewee.

5. Tape-record the entire interview. Interviewing time is too
valuable to waste; thus, having two copies of the responses will
ensure that at least one will not be lost, erased, etc. The taped
interview can also help you in editing the responses after the
interviews for presentation. And it provides a permanent record of
the interview that can be used for legal purposes and in verifying
the accuracy of the written version.

Scoring structured interviews can be accomplished in a number
of ways, depending on the purpose of the program. For assessment
of the individual, especially in relation to a minimum standard,
scoring may consist of a "pass" or "fail" (acceptable/unaccept-
able, etc.) decision based on agreement among the interviewers.
Or, the decision may derive from numerical ratings.

The use of evaluation forms is a standard method of scoring
interviews. These forms can be checklists, various types of rating
scales, or various types of examinee rankings. Ranking examinees
is an especially effective procedure for job selection interviews
because in these situations, only a limited number of examinees
(as few as one) may be selected. It is, therefore, to the benefit of
the examiners to rate candidates in relation to one another.

Where standard evaluation forms are not used, as in, for
example, informal employment office interviews, examiners must
again have a mutual understanding of what standards are to be
applied to the examinees' performance. Essential, too, is a process
by which to resolve rater conflict that may occur with respect to
any of the examinees.

In scoring interviews for other purposes, such as program evaluation, other techniques may be used. One widely used method is the categorization of comments by theme, which stresses quantitative compilation of opinions expressed by the interviewees; for example, 20 of 30 interviewees (66.6 percent) may have felt positive about the new training program curriculum, while six of 30 (20 percent) felt strongly that the program should never have been changed. This type of report may also include anecdotal responses from the interviews to illustrate unique opinions or representative comments made to illuminate a point beyond the scope of the interview.

Prepared Presentation

The prepared presentation is a type of oral assessment in which an examinee or group of examinees provides an organized display of some specified information. This may be entirely oral, such as a lecture or speech, or it may involve the use of audio or visual materials (as the primary focus, or as aids to illustrate or clarify the points presented). The purpose of a prepared presentation, as an assessment technique, may be to assess a particular product or the extent to which a candidate possesses a certain body of knowledge; or to assess such skills as oral communication, selection and organization of information, persuasiveness, and professional presence.

Within certain parameters, the structure and format of the prepared presentation are the responsibility of the examinee. These parameters include time (and therefore length of administration), assignment or presentation content, length of preparation time, and cost to both the examinee and the examiner(s). Determining the time allowed for the presentation may require careful consideration of the skills to be assessed and the situations in the field in which they are likely to be demonstrated. As to the assignment or basic structure of the presentation, possibilities include: (1) giving all examinees the same assignment; (2) offering a limited choice of topics or projects to be presented within a set of guidelines; or (3) allowing unlimited choice of topic and freedom of presentation. The first is most appropriate when the skills being assessed are discrete and essential for every candidate to possess. The second is useful when a process or application of skills and knowledge is being assessed since, in this case, the topic itself is of lesser importance. And the third is most effective when such skills as creativity and judgment are being assessed, or when the candidate is presenting a specialized project to colleagues and peers. The length of preparation time permitted for oral presentations may range from a few moments to days, weeks, or months, depending upon what skills are designated as top priority for assessment.

The method of scoring prepared presentations will depend upon the type of presentation that is given. Standard rating forms can be prepared and are especially useful when a number of raters or examiners are involved. Teacher evaluations, for example, involve the use of a standard rating form with a large number of raters (i.e., colleagues, supervisors, students). With a small number of raters, rating forms may be dispensed with as long as there is discussion and agreement on the standards of competence that are to be applied.

Uses

There are a number of situations in which prepared presentations are currently being used. Candidates applying for certain types of jobs (academic, professional) are frequently required to give presentations in their specialty areas before their professional peers, e.g., in the dramatic arts (musical auditions, theatrical interpretations, dramatic readings, etc.) or fields which require public speaking. Candidates for teaching certificates may be required to demonstrate their teaching skills by delivering prepared lessons or lectures. In some of these cases, the ability to utilize and integrate various media in instruction is assessed through a prepared presentation involving overhead transparencies, slides, a filmstrip, a videotape, or other audio-visual aids.

The demonstration of a product is another use of the prepared presentation, which is frequently effective in corporate settings. A completed movie, for example, can be presented to show a candidate's directing, producing, technical, or acting abilities. A candidate may present a completed invention or working model, or may be required to present a sales pitch to prospective clients. Prepared presentations of professional papers are common at professional association conventions.

Advantages/Disadvantages

Prepared presentation assessment offers many of the same advantages as other types of oral and individual assessment. It is most appropriate for measuring certain types of oral communication skills and is most applicable when those skills will be demanded of the examinee in a work or professional setting. A larger number of examiners is also possible in this type of assessment, and this approach can increase the reliability of the ratings.

The disadvantages of prepared presentation assessment also parallel those of other types of individual and oral assessment. Because of its individual nature, it is a more expensive assessment procedure than those which can be used with a large number of examinees at one time. Depending upon the type of presentation, preparation and administration time can be lengthy; time and cost will also increase as the number of raters is increased, as will possible scheduling problems.

The disadvantages of rating forms apply here if rating forms are utilized; if they are not used, and the number of examiners is limited, then the subjectivity of the scoring may increase. With a limited number of examiners, personal characteristics of the examinees that are unrelated to the assessment may have an adverse or positive effect on the examiners, and may then be reflected in their ratings.

Selected References

Ginsburg, H. Talking with children: An alternative to testing. *Educational Technology*, April 1975, *15*(4), p. 41.

Institute for Social Research. *Interviewer's Manual.* Amherst, Mass.: University of Massachusetts, Survey Research Center, 1980.

Knapp, J., and Sharon, A. *A Compendium of Assessment Techniques.* Princeton, N.J.: Cooperative Assessment of Experiential Learning, Educational Testing Service, 1975.

Lamont, C.T., and Hennen, B.K.E. The use of simulated patients in a certification examination in family medicine. *Journal of Medical Education,* October 1972, *47.*

Levine, H.G., and Noak, J.R. *The Evaluation of Complex Educational Outcomes.* University of Illinois: Department of Educational Research, 1968 (ED 039583).

Oppenheim, A.N. *Questionnaire Design and Attitude Measurement.* New York: Basic Books, 1966.

Quinto, F., and McKenna, B. *Alternatives to Standardized Testing.* Washington, D.C.: National Education Association, 1977.

Valette, R.M. *Modern Language Testing: A Handbook.* New York: Harcourt, Brace, and World, Inc., 1967.

Chapter Eight

Paper-and-Pencil Assessment

Objective tests are the most widely used assessment instruments, particularly in large-scale testing programs. Both supply-type and selection-type tests are considered objective forms of assessment because they are scored objectively; that is, they require no subjective judgment. *Selection-type* items include multiple-choice, alternate-response, and matching items. In each type of selection item, the examinee chooses one or more of the given responses. *Supply-type* items of the short-answer variety include direct questions, completions (fill-in-the-blank), identifications, and directed exercises. As an objective test item, a supply type is designed to have only one correct response which the examinee "supplies" (rather than selects). But technically, a "supply" type can be any item (essay question, design problem, etc.) that requires the examinee to supply a response.

This chapter emphasizes forms of paper-and-pencil assessment other than selection-type items. Brief descriptions and examples of multiple-choice, alternate-response, and matching items are included here to provide a basis for comparison and to demonstrate that even within the realm of selection-type items, alternatives abound. One alternative, beyond item types, is computer-adaptive testing, which is discussed under "selection-type items."

Forms of paper-and-pencil assessment covered in detail in this chapter include the following:

Short-Answer Items
Essay Questions
Design Problems
Written Reports

179

Technically, each of these types requires "performance"; that is, the examinee must perform certain skills to supply a response, however brief or extended. However, to fit within the definition of performance assessment expounded earlier, these types can only be considered to measure "performance" when they are used to measure skills closely related to a job, a training program, or educational context. For example, an *essay test* can measure job-related performance skills when used to assess journalists, lawyers, and others who must demonstrate competence in writing. Similarly, a *design problem* can measure job-related performance skills when used to assess individuals whose occupations require design skills—architects, engineers, interior designers, and others.

Beyond this limited definition, paper-and-pencil assessment methods can be adapted to a wide range of uses for assessing a significant range of skills. Examples of various uses are included for each assessment method.

Selection-Type Items

A selection-type item generally consists of a question, an incomplete statement, or simply a direction followed by a number of response options from which the examinee must *select* one or more alternatives. For some items, stimulus material may be provided (e.g., a chart, map, reading passage), and several items may be matched to one stimulus.

Standard selection types include multiple-choice, alternate-response, and matching items. Within each of these standard categories are a number of possible variations, as shown in the examples below. (For more information on the selection-type items shown here, see any of the "Selected References" listed at the end of this chapter.)

Multiple-Choice Items

Several medical and health-related professions group basic multiple-choice items in one of four categories: A, B, K, and X. These categories are used here for convenient reference.

A-Type. An A-type item is the "straight" multiple-choice item with which most people are familiar. It may have three, four, or five response options (or "alternatives"): three options are generally used in items for young children (up to grade four) and in cases where only three options are possible. Four or five options are most common, depending on the type of test (e.g., using five options tends to increase the item's ability to discriminate among examinees, thus improving its value for a normative-referenced test). Options may be lettered (A, B, C . . .) or numbered (1, 2, 3 . . .).

Examples: Which word rhymes with *sail?*
    A. ball
  *B. tale
    C. seal

Mercury (Hg) occurs naturally in what state?
  *A. liquid
    B. solid
    C. gas

If Juan earns $4.50 per hour, how much will he earn for 40 hours?
    A. $160.00
    B. $165.00
  *C. $180.00
    D. $184.50

What country lies between France and Spain?
    A. Portugal
    B. Italy
    C. Switzerland
  *D. Andorra
    E. Luxembourg

B-Type. A B-type item, which is most similar in format to a "matching" item, consists of a series of terms or statements that must be matched with each response option (A-E). For each set of response options, the series may include two to ten terms or statements.

Example: For each type of food listed below (1-6), select the
nutrient (A, B, C, D, E) found in the highest quantity
in that type of food.

A.   vitamin C
B.   protein
C.   carbohydrate
D.   fats
E.   iron

1.   broccoli   (E)
2.   bread   (C)
3.   ice cream (D)
4.   potato   (C)
5.   grapefruit (A)
6.   tuna fish   (B)

Technically, each numbered term (1-6) is considered a unique
item, to which the examinee responds by choosing A, B, C, D, or
E. This type of item is commonly used in medical tests to assess
knowledge of diseases or disorders and associated symptoms.

K-Type. A K-type item basically consists of multiple true/false
questions, to which the examinee responds by choosing one of the
following options:

A.   if only 1, 2, and 3 are correct
B.   if only 1 and 3 are correct
C.   if only 2 and 4 are correct
D.   if only 4 is correct
E.   if all are correct

This type of item, also used widely in medical exams, tests an
examinee's knowledge of several closely related aspects of a
substance, process, disease, etc.

Example: Abraham Lincoln can be accurately described as:
1. the 16th President of the United States.
2. a democrat.
3. issuer of the Emancipation Proclamation.
4. leader of the Confederacy.
   *B (1 and 3 are correct)

X-Type. Like the K-type, an X-type item is basically a multiple true/false question. The examinee responds by marking true or false beside each option (A-E).

> *Example:* Symptoms of regular use of amphetamines include:
>
> | | | | |
> |---|---|---|---|
> | A. | increased appetite | T | F |
> | B. | hyperactivity | T | F |
> | C. | increased blood pressure | T | F |
> | D. | physical addiction | T | F |
> | E. | dilation of the pupils | T | F |

In addition to these four standard forms of multiple-choice items, two others deserve mention here. The first is the *cloze* item: broadly defined, a cloze type is a fill-in-the-blank item modified to a multiple-choice format; specifically, a cloze item matches a reading passage with words deleted from it (blanks inserted). For each blank, the examinee chooses from two to five options (depending on grade level) the word that best fits the context.

> *Example:* Doctor Fane, from his second-floor office, stared out at the _____ in the street below. "That charlatan," he thought, as he _____ the man selling bottles of cure-all tonic to the gullible crowd that had _____.
>
> | (1) | | (2) | | (3) | |
> |---|---|---|---|---|---|
> | | A. response | *A. | watched | | A. separated |
> | | B. marble | | B. alerted | | B. mumbled |
> | *C. | scene | | C. followed | | C. departed |
> | | D. parlor | | D. governed | *D. | gathered |
> | | E. distance | | E. sensed | | E. rummaged |

The second is the standard A-type used in a listening test: the examinee listens to a tape or a speaker and answers each question by choosing a response. The stem (or question) of the item may or may not be included as part of the tape, before or after the listening portion is played.

> *Example:* (Taped selection from *Lohengrin*—30 seconds, played once) Who composed this piece?
>
> A. Mozart
> B. Verdi
> *C. Wagner
> D. Liszt

Alternate-Response Items

As its name implies, an alternate-response item provides two options, usually direct opposites (true/false, valid/invalid, yes/no, etc.). The examinee chooses one response for each item.

Examples:

1. Grover Cleveland was the only president who served two non-consecutive terms in office.   <u>True</u>   False

2. If A > B and B > C, then A = C.   Valid   <u>Invalid</u>

3. Zucchini, butternut, and acorn are all types of squash.   <u>Yes</u>   No

4. Saul Bellow deserved to win the Nobel Prize for Literature.   Fact   <u>Opinion</u>

Matching Items

A matching item consists of two lists, e.g., inventors and inventions, events and dates, parts of a diagram and names of the parts. The examinee must match the terms of one list to the other. One list usually contains more terms than the other (to avoid selecting correct responses by process of elimination). The example below is a matching item adapted to multiple-choice format.

Example: Match each inventor with his invention by selecting the correct sequence of answers, reading from top to bottom. (One invention is not matched.)

Inventors	Inventions
A. Thomas Edison	1. steam engine
B. Elias Howe	2. wireless telegraph
C. Guglielmo Marconi	3. cotton gin
D. James Watt	4. reaper
E. Eli Whitney	5. phonograph
	6. sewing machine

Which sequence is correct?

A. 6	*B. 5	C. 2	D. 3
4	6	3	5
1	2	5	2
3	1	4	1
5	3	1	6

Computer-Adaptive Testing

Computer-adaptive testing is a technique in which a computer is programmed to select which test items to include in an examinee's test. This selection procedure occurs while the examinee is taking the test; thus, the test is "tailored" to the ability level of each examinee. Decisions about which particular items from a large item pool should be included on a test are based upon individual performance on each item administered. The basic decision rule may be summarized as follows: if the examinee answers a test item correctly, the computer chooses a more difficult test item to administer next; if the examinee answers an item incorrectly, the computer chooses an easier item to administer next.

Because the computer individualizes the sequencing and selection of items, each participant must be seated at a computer terminal to take the test. While a number of examinees may be tested simultaneously through the use of computer time-sharing techniques, the mode of administration is essentially individual. Computer-adaptive testing is suitable for use with selection-type objective test items (e.g., multiple-choice, true/false), because the examinee must be able to indicate each response to the computer in a simple manner.

Computer-adaptive testing was developed as a means of insuring an appropriate level of difficulty for each examinee, and it is most often used as a screening device to determine where on a continuum of hypothetical underlying ability (latent trait) an examinee belongs. The item pool typically consists of test items that range from very easy to very difficult, to permit the assessment of examinees of all levels of ability and experience with the same test instrument. It is a technique that has been used extensively in military testing applications.

To the examinee, the fact that the computer is selecting and sequencing test items is not necessarily apparent; the test would appear to be the same as any other objective test with selection-type items. Because the test appears on a computer terminal, however, there may be some limitations in providing large-scale or complex illustrations and graphics with the test items. This may be overcome, though, by giving the examinee a separate booklet containing appropriate illustrations (such as site plans or working drawings), and directing the examinee to the appropriate illustration for each question.

Advantages/disadvantages. The major advantages of the computer-adaptive testing technique have to do with the technical characteristics of test analysis. Proponents of latent trait theory claim that use of the technique increases test reliability and validity; that is, one would theoretically have more confidence in the correctness of conclusions regarding the comparative ability of examinees. It should be noted that about the same level of reliability may be obtained by administering *all* items in the item pool, instead of a "customized" selection, to each examinee. Use of the technique permits the test administrator to avoid giving an examinee items that are inappropriate—too easy or too difficult. This savings in time can be significant and may perhaps allow additional testing in some other areas. An added advantage is that the test-taking motivation of examinees may increase when they perceive the test as being tailored to their ability level.

Among the major disadvantages is the significant expense involved in testing each examinee by computer. In addition, logistical considerations preclude the testing of large numbers of examinees simultaneously. Potential political problems could emerge in a licensing or certification process if each candidate were administered a different test.

Scoring computer-adaptive tests. Because each examinee will be administered a different set of test items, special scoring procedures must be used. Some examinees may see more test items than others, and some will have been administered items more difficult or easier than average. There exists, however, an extensive body of research known as "latent trait theory," which has as its basic assumption that the ability of examinees varies along a continuum. Statistical methods have been developed for locating examinees along a common scale, despite the fact that different examinees respond to different sets of test items. The theory and statistical methods involved, while rather complicated, are based upon the simple assumption that examinees who are higher up on the ability scale will be more likely to answer each test item correctly. Because test items vary in difficulty, it is possible to locate a person on the ability scale by finding the appropriate level of item difficulty for each examinee.

Short-Answer Items

A short-answer (or "open-ended") item consists of a question, an incomplete statement, or a direction to which the examinee must supply a response. Standard types of short-answer items include the direct question, completion (or fill-in-the-blank), identification (or association), and directed exercise. Each type requires a short response, but the mode of presentation differs. The first three types are basic and straightforward; but the fourth type, directed exercise, may take any of a number of forms. Each type is described briefly, with examples provided.

Direct question. This type of item presents a complete sentence in the form of a question. In response, the examinee must supply a short answer usually composed of one or two words, a number, or a symbol.

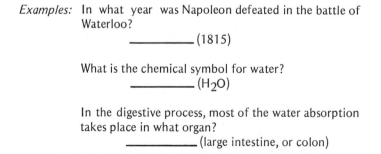

Examples: In what year was Napoleon defeated in the battle of Waterloo?
_____ (1815)

What is the chemical symbol for water?
_____ (H_2O)

In the digestive process, most of the water absorption takes place in what organ?
_____ (large intestine, or colon)

Note that each of the first two examples has only one correct response; in the third example, two responses are listed, but both mean the same. (Both "large intestine" and "colon" are acceptable names for the same organ; either one would be correct.)

As with multiple-choice items, the direct question is often preferred to other types because it presents a complete thought. Incomplete statements and fill-ins are more likely to permit more than one interpretation, thus confusing the examinee. A carefully constructed completion item, however, can be more efficient than a direct question in some cases.

Completion (fill-in-the-blank). The completion item, or "fill-in-the-blank" item, is an incomplete sentence with one or more blanks in the sentence. Most often there is only one blank, at the end of the sentence. The most important requirement in a completion item is to provide enough information in an unambiguous manner, so the examinee knows what the question is and can respond to it.

> *Examples:* The largest artery in the human body is called the
> _____. (aorta)
> The island of Great Britain includes the three countries of _____, _____, and _____. (England, Scotland, and Wales)

This second example requires three responses, which may be written in any order. Specialized forms of completion items are widely used in mathematics and foreign language tests, as shown below.

> *Examples:* If $X = 20$, then $\dfrac{X}{4} =$ _____. (5)
>
> $X^2 - 9 = 0.$ $X =$ _____. (3, -3)

> Direction: Change the tense of the verb from present to passé composé.
>
> Jeanne donne le journal à son père.
> Jeanne _____ le journal à son père. (a donné)

> Direction: Supply the correct definite article.
> José compra _____ libro. (el)

In most situations, directions for similar completion items can be given only once, and a number of clustered items would appear after the directions. As with all short-answer items, the scoring criteria must include all possible correct responses and an indication of whether or not a partial response can receive partial credit. (The "Great Britain" example above might be worth one point for three correct countries, or a total of three points—one for each correct country listed.)

Identification. An identification (or "association") item usually consists of a list of terms, names, dates, etc., to which the examinee must write a matching list of responses. Conceptually, it closely resembles a standard "matching exercise," but the examinee must supply the responses, not select them.

Example: After each country in the list below, write the name of its capital city.

Country	Capital	
1. Argentina	_____	(Buenos Aires)
2. Brazil	_____	(Brasilia)
3. Chile	_____	(Santiago)
4. Colombia	_____	(Bogota)
5. Ecuador	_____	(Quito)

Again, there is only one correct response for each blank; the directions are given only once, followed by a number of items. This type of item is a simple and efficient means of testing many "bits" of knowledge when the "bits" are closely related to one another.

Identification items are also useful in testing a sequence of events or a set of steps which must be listed in correct order. And, an identification item can be used to test the examinee's ability to identify the parts of something in a diagram (e.g., a plant, the mechanism of a hearing aid, anatomy of the human body). The examinee would be instructed to label each part.

Example: The diagram below shows the accessory organs of the digestive system. Each organ is indicated by a letter.

Beneath the diagram, write the name of the organ that corresponds to each letter.

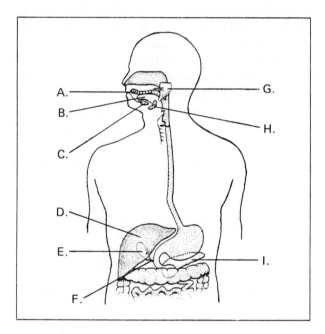

A. _____
B. _____
C. _____
D. _____
E. _____
F. _____
G. _____
H. _____
I. _____

The answer key for an identification item must include all of the correct responses, and must indicate the proper sequence if a specific sequence is required. Also, it must indicate whether the entire identification exercise should be scored as a single item, or if its components should be scored as separate items.

Directed exercise. The directed exercise usually consists of simply a statement or a direction to the examinee that describes a task, rather than a question that asks for a brief response. Depending on the test format, this type of item may or may not be followed by blanks for the response(s).

> *Examples:* List three characteristics of mammals that distinguish them from other kinds of animals.
>
> ————— (Mammals have hair.)
> ————— (Offspring of mammals are born alive.)
> ————— (Mother nurses offspring.)
>
> Name four inert gases.
> ————————— (argon)
> ————————— (neon)
> ————————— (helium)
> ————————— (xenon, etc.)

Blanks need not be numbered, unless the order of responses is important—as in this example.

> List the four strokes of a four-stroke internal combustion engine, in order of occurrence.
>
> 1. ————————— (intake)
> 2. ————————— (compression)
> 3. ————————— (combustion)
> 4. ————————— (exhaust)

Beyond these basic types, the directed exercise has enormous potential for varied uses. Anything that requires a simple drawing, for example, can be tested by a short-answer directed exercise; or it can require short writing exercises ("Write a sentence using the word *contrite*"), mathematical calculations, composition in music, etc.

> *Example:* Draw a right triangle; label the right angle and the three sides (a, b, c).

Response:

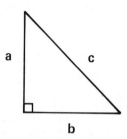

More complex problems, such as designs, can be broken down into their components, each of which can be tested separately.

Examples: 1. Complete a detail drawing of a window casing.
            2. Draw the louvers on an aluminum electronic case.
            3. Draw a simple electric circuit with a switch and one conductor, connected to a three-cell battery. (Label each part of the diagram.)

Response to (3):

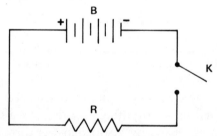

Scoring criteria for this type of directed exercise should include a correct drawing and at least one example of a drawing that is incorrect. Primarily, the purpose of the criteria is to permit objective scoring and minimize the need for judgment in scoring. Criteria should also include an indication of how to score for partial credit, if applicable.

Advantages/Disadvantages

The primary advantage of the short-answer item is that it requires the examinee to produce the correct response rather than select it from among a set of given alternatives. Thus, short-answer items minimize the incidence of guessing. Great care must be taken, however, to ensure that the items are clear and unambiguous so the examinee knows what each item means. Tests composed of short-answer items are generally considered easy to construct and are, therefore, relatively inexpensive; but this is not actually true of tests that will be used for purposes with possibly serious consequences, such as licensing tests. For a test developed and scored by the teacher and used in a classroom with a small number of students, short-answer items are probably the easiest to use.

Although useful in testing knowledge of factual information, short-answer items are not the most appropriate item types for testing more complex learning outcomes. Thus, their overall usefulness is limited to relatively simple skills.

Another disadvantage of short-answer items concerns the complications involved in scoring. The answer key must be very carefully constructed to include every possible correct response. Factors such as spelling and punctuation must also be indicated as they affect the accuracy of the response. Even with the greatest possible care in answer key construction, the scoring itself may be somewhat subjective. This may contribute to lowering the item reliability. The fact that all scoring must be done manually adds to the cost (in time and staff) of using short-answer items. But many teachers prefer this approach to other forms of paper-and-pencil assessment because it presents questions and problems as they would naturally be stated. Asking a student the question, "Who was the fourth president of the United States?" seems more natural than asking it this way: "James Madison was the fourth president of the United States, true or false?"

Developing Short-Answer Items

Since short-answer items take several forms, the first step in developing a short-answer item to assess a given skill or aspect of knowledge is to decide which form would be most appropriate (based on the information provided previously). From this point onward, the same general guidelines apply to all types (with the exceptions noted).

1. Make the item as clear and concise as possible.
2. Word the item to ensure that only one correct response is possible, and that the response is brief and definite.
3. Make sure that the item contains all of the information necessary to cue the correct response. One of the easiest mistakes for an item writer to make is to write a question with a certain perspective or certain facts in mind, but to fail to include that information in the item, thus accidentally misleading the examinee. Specifically:
   (a) Make sure that the item contains any instructions necessary to explain the task to the examinee (e.g., "Read the passage below, then answer the questions that follow.").
   (b) Make sure that the stem of the item contains a complete thought or question, rather than a fragment which the examinee must decipher in order to understand what is being asked.
   (c) Include any terminology or background information necessary to orient the examinee to the context of the item. For example: In Roman mythology, the name of the god of war is __(Mars)__. "In Roman mythology" is the lead-in that orients the examinee to the item. Without this lead-in, the item would be confusing and unanswerable.
4. Avoid "textbook language" and, even worse, taking statements from textbooks and leaving out a word or phrase for the examinee to fill in. This practice can bias an exam toward examinees who are familiar with a particular textbook or certain terminology. Also, taking sentences out of context often obscures their meaning.

Administering and Scoring Short-Answer Items

Short-answer items are usually presented in booklet form.

Generally, examinees record their responses in spaces provided within the booklet.

A detailed answer key must be prepared to aid in the scoring of short-answer items. The answer key must supply *all possible* acceptable responses for each item; therefore, the more carefully written the items, the fewer correct responses there would be, and the easier and more reliable the scoring. Test booklets are manually scored according to the answer key. Some types of responses may require detailed scoring criteria by which to assess such things as spelling, clarity, partial credit, etc., beyond the correctness of the actual response; others may simply require one-word responses or a list of numbers. Variations in single answers, particularly where more than one acceptable term exists with the same meaning, should be indicated in the scoring criteria as correct (or incorrect) responses.

Essay Question

An essay question is a question, topic, or brief statement to which an examinee must construct an extended response. Some authorities (e.g., Ahmann and Glock, 1975; Gronlund, 1977) categorize types of essay questions as "extended-response" or "restricted-response." The major difference between the two is the freedom of response possible, which stems from the limits imposed by the question itself; both types require response of greater length than short-answer items but less than, say, a written report.

An essay question can be used to measure a person's ability to make comparisons, apply principles to new situations, organize information, communicate ideas, be creative, conduct a critical study, make judgments, draw inferences, substantiate generalizations, be persuasive, use logical reasoning, integrate knowledge and applications, summarize information, and demonstrate in-depth knowledge. The key to essay questions used to measure any or all of these abilities is the fact that examinees must produce their own extended responses, in their own words.

Length of response and any other restrictions imposed upon the essay question depend upon the question's purpose. For example, essay questions used as "writing samples" generally require little content knowledge and brief responses (20-40 minutes). The question itself tends to delve into personal experience.

> *Example:* Think of a person whom you admire. Write an essay to describe the person and explain why you admire him or her.

Other essay questions may be used to measure in-depth content knowledge of a specific, limited topic. This type generally requires an extended response (45-90 minutes) and emphasizes content knowledge, not writing ability or style. The topic is chosen to represent one important aspect of an area or course of study for which the examinee is responsible.

> *Examples:* Write an essay on the major causes of the War of 1812.
> Explain the causes and effects of inflation.
> Discuss at least three principles of preventive dental care.

Finally, essay questions may be used to measure "presentation": the ability to demonstrate adequate knowledge *and* present it in an organized, unified, comprehensible way. This type emphasizes the structure and development of the essay as well as its content; thus, the topic must demand both characteristics.

> *Example:* Write an essay in defense of or in opposition to the following principle:
> "We will not have peace until we knock patriotism out of the human race" (G.B. Shaw). Use examples from literature, politics, religion, and/or psychology.

These three types of essay questions represent three points on a spectrum between brief, limited responses (of one or two paragraphs) and extended, unrestricted responses (of several pages). Each type of question fits a specific purpose and may require a different method of scoring (discussed later in this chapter).

Uses

Essay questions have been widely used in educational testing, in many subject areas, to test knowledge and such characteristics as creativity and quality of expression. Many statewide testing programs now require students to produce "writing samples" for the purpose of demonstrating the ability to communicate in written form. Some of these states utilize National Assessment of Educational Progress (NAEP) materials (e.g., Oregon, Texas, Wisconsin); other states have developed their own materials. For example, Connecticut's Ninth-Grade Proficiency Test includes math and language arts sections (multiple-choice items), a reading section (cloze test), and a writing sample (a 20-minute essay based on personal experience). The Massachusetts Basic Skills Improvement Tests also include writing samples, consisting of two questions: one essay based on personal experience, and one based on the ability to write a business letter.

Outside of education, essay questions are used in bar exams for lawyers and in many other situations. The major issue to consider in using an essay test outside the classroom, however, is its purpose. For a test to be job-related, it must measure only skills which the job requires. Thus, theoretically, an essay test should only be used to measure writing skills and/or content knowledge in fields which require such abilities on the job (e.g., journalism, speech-writing). In other areas, the use of an essay to test content knowledge would probably be less efficient and less direct than other methods more closely related to actual practice.

Advantages/Disadvantages

An essay question is best suited to a situation that requires an extended, detailed response to a narrow, specific problem or content-based question; or to a situation in which content is less important than writing ability and style. Advantages of essay questions include the following: examinees must construct their own responses, rather than select from given alternatives; essay tests require skills that cannot be tested adequately by any other means (e.g., writing ability, ability to organize information, ability to integrate knowledge and practical applications in written form);

examinees can demonstrate their abilities to be creative and original; and essay tests require the examinees to demonstrate in-depth knowledge of a particular subject, while enabling them to develop and defend their own answers. Finally, essay tests are generally considered relatively easy and inexpensive to construct.

Among the disadvantages of essay questions are two critical considerations: validity and reliability. Because of the time and effort involved in administering and taking them, essay tests can only measure a small sample of the examinee's knowledge. Thus, the test may not adequately cover the entire domain of knowledge and skills that must be tested in a given situation. Also, there are few fields in which an essay question can be shown to be valid in terms of job-relatedness: few professions require the skills needed to perform successfully on essay tests. As to reliability, scoring is the major problem. Progress in developing reliable scoring procedures has been significant in recent years, but scoring essay tests is still a costly, time-consuming, and not always reliable process. Scores may vary significantly from one "reader" or judge to the next, depending on the procedure, the experience and background of the scorers, and the criteria established for scoring.

Other concerns include the following: writing speed and writing style (vocabulary, usage, etc.) may affect an examinee's score in a way that is irrelevant to the subject being tested; and the construction of essay tests is more difficult than it seems. Essay questions must be relevant, precise, and unambiguous; they must be presented in such a way that they are neither too specific nor too general, to enable the examinee to develop a meaningful, scorable response.

Developing Essay Questions

The greatest value of an essay question is its ability to measure specific skills—such as organization, integration of ideas, and actual writing—that other methods cannot measure adequately. Each essay question should be developed in a way that will ensure its ability to measure the desired outcome.

Step 1: Determine the purpose of the essay question. As mentioned earlier, an essay question may have any of a number of purposes. First, specify in clearly stated terms the goal of each essay question to be developed.

Examples: Purpose of essay question #1: To measure the ability to express oneself clearly in expository prose, based on personal experience.

Purpose of essay question #2: To assess the ability of the eleventh-grade student to write a business letter.

Purpose of essay question #3: To measure the examinee's knowledge of _____ (a given subject, e.g., health practices, literature, construction principles).

The purpose will also help to determine the method of scoring that will be most suitable for each question.

Step 2: Select a suitable topic for each question. As with any type of test item, when designed to measure content, the topic of an essay question must be chosen carefully. To the extent possible, the topic should be: (1) significant, i.e., an important aspect of the domain from which the topic is chosen; (2) relevant to the purpose of the examinee's study or preparation; and (3) representative of the domain.

Examples: Choosing a topic for "purpose #2" (above) requires selection of a topic for a business letter. Such topics as stocks, dividends, and corporate policy might be relevant and significant for business persons, but would probably not be relevant to students in grade 11 (as the "purpose" specifies). More significant and more relevant topics might be consumer complaints, job applications, or requests (invitations to speakers, ordering a product, etc.).

In a content domain, such as "foreign policy," the topic(s) might be chosen to reflect the important aspects of a course curriculum or job description. A test on U.S. foreign policy since the Revolutionary War might require three essay questions; each one could cover a representative period of U.S. History (e.g., Monroe Doctrine, Marshall Plan, anti-communism).

The most useful method of selecting topics is often to list first all the possible general topics, then select those that seem most significant, most relevant, and most representative. This approach helps to avoid choosing trivial or obscure topics, or topics with potential bias (e.g., a topic for a "personal experience" essay that requires discussion of "sibling relationships" may be biased against those who have no siblings).

Step 3: Write a question based on the selected topic. Given a topic and a purpose, a question can be drafted; but this step requires a number of "sub-steps."

First, include all relevant information in the statement of the question. For example, a question calling for a business letter may be stated as follows:

> *Example:* You have received a record album that you ordered by mail from the E-Z Music Company, but you have discovered that it has a deep scratch across its surface. Write a letter to request that the company replace the album. Use the address below and address your letter to Ms. Colson:
>
> E-Z Music Company
> 210 Main Street
> Putney, VT 05346
>
> Be sure that your letter is direct, but courteous; and be sure that it includes the date, a salutation, and a closing.

Second, if applicable, include in the question a statement of how the response will be evaluated. This statement will clarify the purpose of the question for the examinee and will ensure that all examinees have the same understanding of what is expected from them.

> *Example:* Write an essay defending why you agree or disagree with the following statement: "No man is an island" (John Donne). Your essay will be evaluated on the basis of ideas presented, organization, and the logic of your argument.

Third, include a statement to explain length and/or time limits.

> *Example:* Write a one-page essay (no more than 250 words) to define the concept of resource allocation and how it affects job opportunities in a (given) geographical region of the United States. You will have 30 minutes to complete your essay.

Fourth, make sure that the question clearly defines the examinee's task. There has never been a shortage of examples of vague, ambiguous essay topics (e.g., "Discuss the history of Russia"). In writing the question, be sure that the examinee will understand it and know what is expected in the response.

Fifth, limit the essay question within a manageable context, especially in recognition of any time or length limits imposed (in previous steps). If you plan to allow 30 minutes for a response, try to avoid questions such as: "Discuss the evolution of humankind" or "Describe major events in the history of the world." At the same time, do not be overly specific (e.g., "Discuss the definition of the word *prolegomena*"); allow some flexibility for the examinee to produce a creative response.

Finally, review the question you have written to detect any sign of *bias.* Potential bias will appear in one of three ways: (1) vocabulary, i.e., using words that some examinees will not understand; (2) selecting a topic to which some examinees cannot relate; and, (3) slanting the question to indicate the response desired.

> *Example:* Discuss the concatenation of events which precipitated the Arab oil embargo and why decent Americans should not condone such actions.

Step 4: Pretest the essay question(s). If possible, try out the questions that have been developed, either with a small sample population of examinees or through review by qualified individuals. In addition to an examination of each question on the basis of criteria listed in the previous steps, sample responses may also provide valuable information. That is, how the examinees respond to the question will often help to identify any ambiguities, potential bias, or incompleteness in the questions.

Administering and Scoring Essay Questions

Generally, essay questions are presented in booklet form: the booklet contains a small number of questions (1-4) and several blank pages for written responses. Examinees may or may not be able to use reference works (e.g., dictionaries, almanacs, text-books, building codes), depending on the nature and purpose of the test. Most often, examinees are allowed only a certain period of time (e.g., 20-45 minutes per essay) in which to write their answers; thus, time becomes a factor in what kinds of questions can be asked and how they can be scored.

Beyond the standard approaches to essay tests, two issues often arise: optional questions and revisions. First, the use of optional questions (e.g., "choose any two of the five topics and write an essay on each") is not recommended, for two reasons: (1) different examinees will choose different topics, thereby removing any standard basis for comparison across examinees—since the tests would be different; and, (2) choices may increase the possibility that an examinee could perform well on the test but not have attained mastery of the entire field or domain. An examinee could study for one half of the domain, assuming that at least two of five given choices would be selected from the half for which he or she prepared.

Second, the question of revisions—permitting or encouraging the examinee to revise his or her response—depends on the purpose of the test. For a test designed to assess writing ability only, not content knowledge, many teachers of writing point out that a single timed session for writing an essay is unrealistic (i.e., in "real life" writers produce a first draft, then go back and revise). In response to this, some writing tests are administered on consecutive days: on the first day, the examinee writes a draft essay and submits it to the administrators; on the second day, the examinee gets the draft back and has the chance to revise it. For a test of content knowledge, this approach obviously would permit the examinee to go find the answers needed; for a test of writing ability, the chance to revise could be an effective teaching and training aid. It could also permit the direct evaluation of the student's ability to revise written materials. However, it would not seem to improve the test's realism or ability to measure writing skills. In a large-scale assessment, it certainly would increase the amount of time and administrative work required to give the test and would increase the difficulty of scoring.

There are many ways to score essay tests and many different sets of criteria that can be applied. Three widely used methods of scoring are the holistic, analytical, and primary trait (see below). Most current methods follow a basic model procedure, or slight variation thereof: two or more trained "readers" score each "essay" independently on the basis of predetermined criteria. The final score on each essay is computed as an average or a total of the two or more scores awarded by the readers. A "chief reader" or "scoring judge" settles all disputes (e.g., significant variation in the two scores).

The methods described below can be applied using this model. Choosing the one most effective method depends on the purpose of the assessment and the structure of the actual essay questions. Training and establishing evaluation criteria are essential to all three methods. (For more detailed information on these and other scoring methods, see the "Selected References" listed at the end of this chapter.)

Holistic scoring. The word "holistic," derived from the Greek root *holos,* means "whole, complete." The holistic method, also known as the "general impression" or "whole impression" approach, is based on a comparison of each essay or writing sample to a predetermined set of standards. Derived from a sample set of papers, these standards constitute the basis for training the readers or scorers who will evaluate and grade each test. For each essay question, the chief reader/trainer selects up to 20 sample papers (representing a range of responses) and discusses each one with the group of readers.

Holistic scoring standards are based on general impressions of writing samples, not on specifics such as punctuation and grammar. The purpose of the training session is to ensure that all readers internalize and apply the same standards to all papers, thereby increasing inter-rater reliability and minimizing bias. Spandel and Stiggins (1980) note that holistic scoring methods have achieved high reliability and inter-rater consistency.

In the scoring process, at least two readers judge each essay and assign it a score of 1, 2, 3, or 4. (The four-point scale is favored in most programs because it forces the readers to assign a score either above or below the "middle.") The sum of the two scores represents the examinee's grade on each essay, which generally translates to a "pass" or "fail." For example, "1" may be a poor essay, "2" below average, "3" good, and "4" superior. Thus, any total score above "4" (e.g., 2 + 3) represents a passing grade. For any essay scored by two readers where the scores differ by more than a single point (e.g., 2 and 4, 1 and 3), the chief reader determines what the score should be.

Holistic scoring enables readers to score a large number of papers (30-40 per hour) relatively quickly and inexpensively—an obvious advantage for large-scale writing assessments. However, its major drawback is that holistic scoring provides little or no information to the examinee in terms of why the essay is scored high or low and what the examinee can do to improve his or her writing skills.

Analytical scoring. Training procedures for analytical scoring are similar to those for holistic scoring, but the criteria differ. As its name implies, analytical scoring derives from careful examination of facts: isolating basic aspects of writing and scoring each one individually. Diederich (1974) identifies five major characteristics of writing: ideas, mechanics, organization, wording, and "flavor" (or style). Each paper, again judged by at least two trained readers, would be scored on the basis of *each* specific predetermined criterion. The sum of all the specific scores would be the examinee's grade.

Analytical scoring is much more time-consuming than holistic scoring, but it can provide detailed information to the examinee (e.g., specific strengths and weaknesses). As it is commonly defined, analytical scoring presumes to apply the same basic criteria to all types of writing—which could be a disadvantage. It also presumes that the "sum of the parts" will reflect the quality of the "whole"—a presumption with which synergists and writing teachers often disagree. However, generally defined as "breaking down the essay and scoring its parts," analytical scoring can be adapted to different forms of writing—and to other products as well, such as solutions to design problems—and used effectively. Specific criteria can be developed to meet the requirements of each specific essay question.

Primary trait scoring. Unlike the usual approach to analytical scoring, primary trait scoring emphasizes the specific purpose of each essay question. It assumes that each different form of writing has a different purpose (or "primary trait"). Scoring an essay requires a strict definition of its purpose, then a reading to determine how well the essay fulfills the purpose. For example, the purpose of an editorial is to persuade the reader to adopt a certain viewpoint; examinees asked to write editorials would be graded on the basis of how persuasive their editorials are. All other factors—mechanics, factual content, etc.—are secondary to this primary trait.

The primary trait approach to scoring writing samples requires a significant amount of definition to isolate the most important aspect of an essay and translate it into a scale of 1-4 or 1-5. The rest of the process resembles the holistic method. Primary trait scoring can provide valuable feedback to the examinee, however; particularly if the process includes "secondary" and "tertiary" trait scoring, as is sometimes done.

Summary. These three methods—holistic, analytical, and primary trait—are the most widely used methods for scoring writing samples. The most appropriate one for a given assessment depends on the purpose of the assessment, the kind of information desired from the scoring process, and practical factors—number of examinees, time, cost, etc. Several states (e.g., Connecticut and Massachusetts) have conducted large-scale writing assessments using the holistic scoring method. Based on experiences in these states, it is safe to say that teachers from various school districts are often willing to volunteer their time for scoring in return for training and practice in how to improve their own abilities to evaluate writing skills.

For essay questions designed to test content, the holistic and primary trait methods are of little value. The most effective approach would likely be to adapt an analysis-based scoring method to each specific question. Again, however, defining the scoring criteria in advance and training the scorers are the most important requirements.

Design Problems

Design problems *per se* are unique to fields such as architecture and engineering which require skills in design. In these fields, design problems can actually be paper-and-pencil work-sample tests because actual on-the-job performance requires design skills. Essentially, the examinee receives instructions and information related to the design that he or she must create. These may include visual presentations, such as pictures, slides, or aerial photographs, of the site for the building to be designed; they may include information about the problem presented orally; and they usually include written information. Some or all of the information may be useful to the examinee whose task is to create a design from the specifications given. One or more judges experienced in the field then evaluate the design product.

Beyond these obvious applications, design problems can provide assessment information in other areas as well. Defined in general terms, a "design" problem can be any exercise that requires an examinee to draw, create, or complete a design. Boyd and Shimberg (1971), for example, cite an electrician's test: given a drawing of a room layout, the examinee must sketch in the wiring and outlets (which must satisfy electrical codes). The work of plumbers, roofing contractors, swimming pool contractors, interior designers, sheet-metal workers, and others may all require "design" of some sort. Thus, vocational schools and training programs may find modified or "customized" forms of design problems quite useful as assessment instruments. In more academic areas, design problems can apply to art, mathematics, physics, theater production, and others.

Uses

Tests used by the National Council of Architectural Registration Boards (NCARB) have required design problems such as drawing a site plan from a topographical map and requiring the examinee to develop a series of design solutions (e.g., detail drawings, evaluations, floor plans). The National Council of Engineering Examiners requires less complicated forms of design problems (see Figure 8.1); these represent portions or separate "sub-problems" which, taken all together, could constitute a total design similar to the architect approach.

Essentially, a design problem is an applied performance assessment used to measure an examinee's ability to assimilate, organize, and utilize information through the construction of an actual design which requires principles of design, drafting, and rendering skills. In most cases, the design problem also measures the ability to apply other requirements to the design, such as building and safety codes, physical and psychological needs, space needs, and circulation needs; and the ability to fit the design to the specifications in terms of function, budget, and aesthetic considerations.

In fields which require design skills, design problems can provide an effective means of evaluating professionals for those skills that are most job-related. As with other paper-and-pencil performance tests, however, design problems cannot measure all the competencies required for a given profession: as with essay questions, design problems usually measure in-depth knowledge of very specific topics or situations.

Traditional design problems, such as those used in architect testing, can be extremely complex—as the only adequate means of measuring complex skills in a multidisciplinary profession. As the previous examples illustrate, a "design problem" can differ in complexity and scope from traditional approaches, but the underlying principles remain the same. The key is to construct design problems suited specifically to given purposes, of a complexity and scope tailored to the situations.

Basically, a design problem includes a set of instructions to the examinee that direct him or her to prepare the design and outline what is expected as a final product; and it includes information, as described earlier, upon which the design must be based. In most

Figure 8.1

Example: Design Problems for Engineers

Agricultural Engineering

Situation:
A certain broiler house is 32 ft. x 300 ft. It is to have a concrete floor with electric heating mats embedded in the floor resulting in six watts/sq. ft. of floor surface. The mats are 20 inches wide and 48 ft. long, rated for 1200 watts 240 volts each.

Requirements:
In your solution pamphlet, neatly sketch and label a recommended design of a heating system including the following:
(a) the layout of the heating mats,
(b) method of furnishing electric supply to the mats, include source and branch circuit conductors,
(c) indications and specifications of disconnecting means and the branch circuit protection for the floor heat,
(d) indications and specifications of an automatic control system for the heat, and
(e) the schematic diagram for the control circuit.

Civil Engineering

Situation:
An engineer plans to use a wood beam for a 20-foot simple span to support a 300 lb. per foot uniform load (includes the estimated beam weight). The beam's depth is limited to ten inches and as a result several 2 x 10's would be required. As an alternative, the engineer is considering a composite beam consisting of two 2 x 10's with a steel plate sandwiched between. The beam will have full lateral support. The maximum permissible deflection is not to be greater than 1/240th of the span.

Requirements:
(a) design a composite beam that will satisfy the above situation. Show all calculations, and
(b) neatly sketch, dimension, and label a cross-section view of the composite beam in requirement (a) above.

(Reprinted by permission of National Council of Engineering Examiners.)

cases, examinees may bring and use references such as dictionaries, code books, and specifications manuals (because these are available on the job; and because examinees should be familiar with the information contained in them, but need not memorize it). Also, examinees usually supply their own equipment, such as a straightedge, protractor, pens, and pencils.

Time required for a design problem may vary from five minutes to as many as 12 hours, depending on the scope of the problem and the amount of information which must first be considered.

Advantages/Disadvantages

In certain fields, design problems can be highly related to actual job performance (except for the practical constraints such as time and environment which are imposed in standardized testing situations). They can be very effective measures of in-depth knowledge and skills at multiple levels, as applied to specific areas. Complex design problems can measure the near-total integration of many related skills, as no other form of assessment can; simplified versions can measure isolated design skills—on the theory that proficiency in a number of isolated skills implies proficiency in combining these same skills. As would be expected, "isolated" design problems are easier to administer and score, but are usually less realistic.

On the negative side, complex design problems—including the scoring criteria—can be difficult, time-consuming, and costly to develop, administer, score, and report to examinees. But their validity and usefulness in design-oriented fields are unquestionable if they are constructed on the basis of skills determined to be closely related to job performance.

Developing Design Problems

Since design problems may range from the simple (comparable to a "directed exercise" of the short-answer type) to the complex, the first developmental step is to determine the scope of the problem. Subsequent steps apply to design problems at all levels of complexity.

Step 1: Determine the scope of the problem. The tasks, skills, or objectives to be measured determine, to a great extent, the scope of a design problem. The ability to produce a detail drawing of a window, for example, can be tested by requiring each examinee to produce a fairly simple window detail. A design problem can be constructed to test one skill or multiple, related skills. Designing a skyscraper or a suspension bridge requires a more complex problem or set of problems, which may or may not be broken down into component tasks (e.g., a window in the skyscraper or a concrete footing for the bridge). Skills or objectives that require integration of components, as in interior design or architecture, can only be measured effectively by complex problems calling for integrated solutions.

The second factor in determining the scope of a design problem is feasibility: a program with limited funds for developing and scoring tests may have to settle for a series of simple problems rather than complex, integrated problems. This kind of limitation, however, may demand some explanation of the results: inferring that an examinee who completes a number of simple, isolated problems satisfactorily could actually perform adequately when required to synthesize these disparate elements.

Third, consider how the problem will be scored. The scope of the problem may depend on the level of detail that can be required of the examinees and still be scored responsibly. The scoring method tentatively chosen at this point will help to guide all subsequent steps.

Step 2: Choose the design project. Selecting a design project must be done with great care, with consideration of the factors below:

    (a) The chosen project must require the skill(s) to be tested. If an engineering problem is to test volumetric calculations, aesthetic factors, and cost-benefit analysis, the problem must involve a design project that requires all three of these competencies.

    (b) The project must be free of potential bias. Particularly in nationwide tests, design problems should include projects that are fair to all examinees. For example, a design (e.g., of a house or building) that depends on climatic factors in Florida could be unfair to examinees from Minnesota.

    (c) The project should be at a reasonable, job-related level of difficulty. An entry-level architect, for example, would more likely be required to design a warehouse or a simple building type than a convention center or a metropolitan hospital. Thus, an entry-level test should include projects for which entry-level candidates would be responsible.

    (d) Practical factors must be considered. A design problem that requires two weeks of research and 32 reference books would probably be impractical for a test administration. For obvious reasons, choosing a project already completed (e.g., of an actual building) would reduce costs for development of design problems; in a test-secure program, however, choosing existing projects may give unfair advantage to some examinees who might be familiar with the actual project.

Step 3: Develop problem tasks. Having determined the steps of the problem, the skills it will measure, and the project involved, development of the problem itself can begin. Each problem must measure the skills identified, separately or in "clusters." Conceptualizing and defining each problem can be facilitated by writing brief sketches, then filling in specific information.

      Example: "Sketch" of a design problem to measure the objective stated as "The plumber is able to design a forced hot-water heating system."

              Type of house: Eight-room split-level ranch with unfinished basement.

              Specifications: water system—drilled well, electric pump, baseboards, 250-gallon oil tank (underground), two-zone heating.

              Direction: Design a forced hot-water system, showing all house levels in one diagram ("transparent walls").

From this level of information, the problem can be developed in detail.

Step 4: Develop instructions and supportive materials. The goal of this step is to develop all materials necessary to provide for the examinee who must solve the problem. These materials include:

Instructions (to examinee)—Specific directions to explain exactly what is expected in the design solution.

Information packets—Materials to provide required information, i.e., a more detailed set of specifications (as "sketched" in Step 3). These packets may also include reference works, code books, local regulations, zoning conditions, soil test results, etc.

Test materials—A list of what must be provided *to* the examinee (e.g., a response booklet, design paper) and what must be provided *by* the examinee (e.g., calculator, drafting instruments, pencils).

Instructions for administration—Directions to explain what the examiner(s) must do to administer the test, provide adequate test conditions (lighting, space, security, desks), etc.

Finally, with a problem completed, estimate the minimum and maximum amounts of time required to administer and solve it.

Step 5: Develop scoring criteria and sample solution(s). With or without a completed project (on which the design problem is based), the next step is to devise scoring criteria and sample solutions. Most design problems permit more than one correct solution (which accommodates the need to incorporate creativity in design skills); thus, "correctness" of solutions must be defined carefully in a way that can be applied to any and all possible responses.

Specific scoring criteria should be developed in relation to each objective or skill measured, if each one will contribute independently to the solution's grade (analytical scoring would be based on specified characteristics; holistic scoring might not be because it would require less specific criteria). For example, for the design of a one-story warehouse that must have at least 20,000 square feet of usable floor space, one criterion might be stated as "usable floor space: 20,000-30,000 sq. ft.; 'usable' defined as a space not used as entrance or circulation area, of at least ten sq. ft. per section (to avoid narrow or oddly shaped spaces)." The upward limit on floor space (30,000 sq. ft.) could represent the maximum space possible within budgetary and support-structure limitations.

Sample solutions should provide general types of approaches to a given problem (e.g., for a building complex, designs might be based on a square, circle, or standard "pinwheel" array). If the problem derives from a completed project, then its source would be one sample solution; others would be variations that meet all specifications.

Step 6: Pretest and revise (as necessary). If possible, pretest the instrument, including the instructions, information packets, and all materials. Formal and informal data gathered from the pretest should be reviewed carefully and the instrument revised where improvements are needed. Most important, compare the pretest solutions to the sample solutions and score them according to specified criteria—again revising as needed (on open-ended tests of any kind, scoring criteria are extremely difficult to perfect in first draft).

Administering and Scoring Design Problems

As mentioned earlier, administration of design problems involves two major functions: (1) providing adequate information to examinees, and (2) providing adequate facilities. Information includes data and specifications, provided in advance and/or during the administration; and it includes instructions in written, oral, or other form (e.g., visual). Adequate facilities, particularly for the administration of long and complex design problems, include the following: tables or desks, space for examinees to spread materials out, lighting, ventilation, relatively comfortable furniture, and low noise level. These requirements are common to all test administrations, to avoid imposing negative conditions on examinees which might affect performance, but they are particularly critical for administering design problems.

There are three basic approaches to scoring a design problem, as described in the section on essay questions—holistic, analytical, and primary trait. Each of these approaches can easily be adapted to design problems (as opposed to essays). Although reliability and consistency of scoring have sometimes been low for scoring this type of product, these problems can be overcome with the use of a carefully defined scoring procedure, clearly defined scoring criteria, training for the judges before they score the designs, and statistical analysis of scoring reliability.

The selection of judges is also important: judges should be selected in such a way as to constitute a group representative of different aspects of the profession (e.g., professors, practitioners, building inspectors) and, if possible, representative according to race, sex, and geographical area. Essentially, each judge must rate each design independently, according to standard criteria. The judges most often use checklists, rating scales, and/or comment sheets to record their ratings. It is most helpful to have the judges involved in determining the scoring criteria such that each one will have a clear understanding of how the criteria are to be interpreted.

NCARB's method of scoring its "Site Planning and Design Test," for example, involves three judges. Each judge works independently: he or she reviews an examinee response and assigns it a holistic score of 0, 1, 2, 3, or 4 (0 indicates an incomplete solution; 1-2 are "failing" scores; 3-4 "passing"). If two of three judges agree on a pass (or fail) designation, the examinee passes (or fails). In borderline cases (e.g., 2+ or 3-), a fourth person, the grading coordinator, scores the design solution.

Written Reports

As assessment instruments, written reports are used either like the essay, to evaluate an examinee's in-depth knowledge of a given subject; or, like the prepared presentation, to assess (written) communication skills, and the ability to select, effectively organize, and present materials and ideas. Essentially, the examinee chooses or is assigned a subject on which a written report is prepared and submitted as the basis for evaluation. While the examinee often has a great deal of choice about the structure and format of the report, general guidelines regarding the length of the report are usually provided for the examinee.

The report topic can either be identical for all examinees, or a limited choice of alternatives may be presented. The length of preparation time for a written report may also vary considerably and must be determined on the basis of the complexity of the assigned task. Both of these factors—topic and length—depend primarily upon the use of the report in assessment. If the purpose is to assess writing and presentation skills, then the topic matters very little; if the purpose is to assess content knowledge, then naturally the topic must be relevant to the field. For a (normative-referenced) comparison of candidates' skills, the most effective approach would be to have all candidates write reports on the same topic. This approach would provide a standard basis for comparative evaluation.

Uses

Written reports are common forms of instruction and assessment in academic areas, where students must demonstrate the ability to research, organize information, and present extended treatments of various topics. In many job situations, candidates are evaluated partially on the basis of samples of written reports. The ability to communicate effectively in written form is widely recognized as a prerequisite for success in many professions. In recent years, increasing criticism that this ability can no longer be taken for granted has resulted in more emphasis on the evaluation of writing skills for job applicants. In effect, the written report may be perceived as the professional equivalent of the work-sample test of a product in those fields where report writing is considered an essential skill. Some of these fields might include government, law, engineering and architecture (e.g., environmental impact reports), and civil service occupations of many kinds.

Advantages/Disadvantages

The advantages of a written report as an assessment technique parallel the advantages of the essay question. Examinees construct their own responses; the skills tested are difficult to assess using more objective, paper-and-pencil assessment instruments; the extended response form allows the examinee to demonstrate creativity and in-depth knowledge; and development costs are low.

In addition, the written report is often a much better approximation of a work-sample than is the essay.

Disadvantages of the written report also parallel those of other forms of written assessment. The objective scoring of the written product is a major problem. In addition, the cost of production for the examinee, in terms of time and materials, and the costs of administration, scoring, and analysis for the assessors, in terms of both time and money, may be considerable. Cost factors may be a source of potential bias, too—since candidates who have the funds will be able to produce materials of better quality (in terms of appearance, etc.) than those without funds.

Depending upon the formality of the assessment, authorship may become an issue as well. Few ways exist to verify with any degree of certainty that a candidate actually wrote the report that he or she submitted.

Administering and Scoring Written Reports

Developing and administering a written report assignment consists of little but drawing up and distributing topics and guidelines for submission formats. However, once the reports begin to come in, administrative skills and storage space become essential—to keep track of reports and maintain materials on file.

There are many ways to score written materials, as pointed out in the section on essay questions. Holistic, analytical, and primary trait scoring methods may all be used. Written reports are likely to be scored more critically than essays because candidates are generally given a significant amount of time to prepare a report, and the report is likely to be both longer and more comprehensive than an essay.

To ensure fairness, the most important requirement is to publicize the criteria for scoring before the candidates begin. Then, in the scoring itself, at least two independent judges should rate each report judiciously on the basis of the same criteria.

Selected References

Ahmann, J.S., and Glock, M.D. *Measuring and Evaluating Educational*

Achievement, Second Edition. Boston: Allyn and Bacon, Inc., 1975.

Boyd, J., and Shimberg, B. *Handbook of Performance Testing: A Practical Guide for Test Developers.* Princeton, N.J.: Educational Testing Service, 1971.

Cooper, C.R., and Odell, L. *Evaluating Writing: Describing, Measuring, Judging.* Urbana, Ill.: National Council of Teachers of English, 1977.

Diederich, P.B. *Measuring Growth in English.* Urbana, Ill.: National Council of Teachers of English, 1974.

Ebel, R.L. *Essentials of Educational Measurement.* Englewood Cliffs, N.J.: Prentice-Hall, Inc., 1978.

Gronlund, N.E. *Measurement and Evaluation in Teaching, Third Edition.* Englewood Cliffs, N.J.: Prentice-Hall, Inc., 1977.

Lippey, G. (Ed.) *Computer-Assisted Test Construction.* Englewood Cliffs, N.J.: Educational Technology Publications, Inc., 1974.

McBride, J.R. Computerized adaptive testing and its potential for military testing applications. Paper presented at annual conference of the Military Testing Association, 1976.

National Council of Architectural Registration Boards. *1981 NCARB Design Test Handbook: A Study Guide for the NCARB Site Planning and Design Test.* Washington, D.C.: NCARB, 1981.

National Council of Engineering Examiners. *Principles and Practice of Engineering: Typical Questions.* Seneca, S.C.: NCEE, 1980.

New York State Education Department, Division of Educational Testing. *Degrees of Reading Power: Description of a New Kind of Reading Test and Its Related Technology.* Albany, N.Y.: State Education Department, 1977.

Spandel, V., and Stiggins, R. *Direct Measures of Writing Skills: Issues and Applications.* Clearinghouse for Applied Performance Testing. Portland, Ore.: Northwest Regional Educational Laboratory, 1980.

Thorndike, R.L. (Ed.) *Educational Measurement, Second Edition.* Washington, D.C.: American Council on Education, 1971.

Chapter Nine

Program Requirements

Many assessment programs include tests and "other requirements." This chapter concerns the other requirements, essentially the "non-tests." Separately or in conjunction with test instruments, program requirements—as forms of assessment—should be approached with caution. Several considerations indicate the need for careful use of these assessment methods, but foremost among them is the fact that program requirements are generally based on assumptions which may not yield reliable results. For example, one common application of program requirements is the comparison of potential candidates on the basis of academic grades; but for measurement purposes, this necessarily assumes that different graders apply some comparable standards in assigning the grades. Such methods as the use of resumes and portfolios assume that candidates represent themselves fairly and sincerely, citing their own actual experiences; but few employers base personnel hiring decisions solely on this kind of assumption.

Particularly in licensing and certification programs, professional and legal guidelines for employment selection and testing tend to contraindicate the use of program requirements such as those discussed here. The reasons for this are several, primarily related to the potential for bias in unstructured and somewhat arbitrary requirements. As discussed in Chapter One, EEOC guidelines and professional testing standards stipulate that employment tests and requirements for licensing and certification meet the following criteria: (a) they must be closely related to actual job requirements; (b) they must not cause adverse impact; and (c) they must not incorporate standards set in an arbitrary or capricious manner.

Program requirements can, of course, be devised to meet these stipulations, but only with great care; these approaches to assessment are more prone to arbitrary and subjective uses than are many other more formally structured assessment methods. Personal records (e.g., transcripts, references, resumes), for example, seldom provide proof of actual on-the-job competency; by nature, they provide historical summaries of past performance (experience and education) which are seldom amenable to reliable comparisons of a normative- or criterion-referenced nature. Subjectivity in self-reporting (resumes, etc.) and in evaluation by others (e.g., assessment of a portfolio) can lead to serious problems in assessing program requirements. Also, potential bias can be a problem in establishing requirements that are easier or more difficult for one or another group to satisfy.

Beyond these shortcomings, however, program requirements can provide useful, important information for evaluation purposes. When used in conjunction with other assessment methods, in situations with clearly defined needs for such information, and in situations where practical constraints make other methods of assessment infeasible, program requirements can be of potential benefit. In some cases, they may be the *only* options available—which would often seem better than having no requirements at all.

The remainder of this chapter comprises brief discussions of a number of program requirements, with examples of how they have been, are, or might be used for assessment. Basically, the methods discussed here fall into three categories:

Personal Records
Performance Records
Apprenticeship/Internship

Each grouping includes a number of variations on the categorical theme.

Personal Records

Various types of "personal records" provide information related to a candidate's own personal background: his or her education, previous experiences, others' perceptions of the person, and training. Basically, personal records portray a candidate's aptitude or potential ability to perform competently in a job situation. Although personal records may be used for *selection* purposes, i.e., choosing the most qualified of a pool of applicants, the focus here is on the use of records for *screening,* i.e., identifying those applicants who do not have the minimum qualifications required. Records used as indicators of potential ability include the academic *transcript, recommendations* or *references, personal* (opinion) *statement,* and *apprenticeship record* or *job history.* All of these are considered in the context of program requirements; that is, proof of qualifications required to enter and/or complete a program of training, certification, or licensing. Different types of records take various forms and will reflect differences across individuals, but they are nonetheless fairly standard across fields.

The transcript is a verified record of academic courses and grades received, usually supplied by a school or special program (e.g., summer training seminar). An academic transcript provided by a school or program lists the examinee's course of study, number of credits awarded per course, and grade attained in each course; it may also include the examinee's overall grade-point average and the examinee's rank in the class. Institutions which use non-standard grading procedures usually attach an explanation of the grading system to the transcript, in an attempt to facilitate comparisons with the grades of other institutions.

Recommendations or references are descriptions, either written or verbal, of the candidates as seen by each candidate's advisor, instructor, supervisor, or colleague. They are generally sent in the form of a letter to the examiner or examining institution. If a candidate has set up some sort of placement file, then these recommendations may follow a standard format provided by the placement office. References obtained through telephone contacts are also generally recorded on a standard form provided for this purpose. In any case, information provided by the reference about the examinee includes characteristic strengths, weaknesses, and traits unique to the individual.

Personal statements are essays written by the candidate about his or her perceived strengths and personal aspirations, generally in response to a "What can you add to our program?" or "Why should we choose you?" kind of question. The content of the personal statement will be unique to each candidate within the guidelines or limitations provided by the request for the statement. Most often the personal statement requires the examinee to write about his or her strengths, unique characteristics, and career interests and ambitions. Depending upon the intended use of the statement, it may require more specific information. A personal opinion statement may be used to supplement or possibly to replace a personal interview.

An apprenticeship record or job history is a record, generally supplied by the candidate but verifiable through personal contacts, of the training and job experiences of various sorts that the candidate has held in the past and up to the current time. This particular type of personal background record is usually distinct from records or appraisal of actual performance, apprenticeship activities, or internship, all of which are discussed in later sections of this chapter. Information about an examinee's apprenticeship record or job history is generally supplied by the examinee on standard forms designed for this purpose, intended simply to verify what kinds of training courses or apprentice positions the candidate has had. Employer names and addresses, dates of employment, position titles, and descriptions of responsibilities are the types of information requested on these forms.

Uses

Candidates' personal records are commonly assessed for the purpose of making decisions about college entrance, graduate school placement, awards or promotion conferral, certification, and eligibility to take certification examinations. In order to gain admittance to some medical certifying examinations, for example, candidates must submit official transcripts documenting completion of all requirements and recommendations verifying continuous and current intern employment. Documentation of certain types of laboratory experience or participation in training programs is also required for some kinds of certification.

In architecture, the conferral of a license now depends, in part, upon the evaluation of a candidate's records. Examining boards must verify a requisite number of course credits and/or completion of a degree requirement at an accredited institution; they must verify job experience (internship); and, in most cases, must verify test scores. This is part of the normal licensing procedure, to ensure that candidates have at least the minimum requirements necessary for professional licensing.

Some associations certify only on the basis of a person's background. For example, the Association for Education of the Visually Handicapped and the American Association for Musical Therapy grant certificates on the basis of work experience, education, professional background, and completion of pre-approved programs.

Any of these qualifications might be a stated requirement that a candidate must satisfy, before or after passing a test. Program requirements may also be the only qualifications for Continuing Medical Education (CME) programs or recertification, e.g., a certain number of course credits or hours in the lab. The key to assessing program requirements is to establish prespecified standards against which the performance, products, and qualifications must be compared—which makes administrative efficiency a must in this type of assessment.

In most cases, personal records provide verification or proof of having completed prerequisite program requirements. They provide little or no reliable information as to the comparative quality of candidates' performance, only that the candidates have or have not "performed." As such, personal records seldom constitute the sole basis for assessing a candidate's qualifications; more often they are used in conjunction with test instruments and other modes of assessment.

Advantages/Disadvantages

Personal records have the advantage of providing background information about candidates which can be significantly related to future performance. The types of records gathered can also complement one another both in the information they provide about the candidates and in the sources that generate the information. In situations where time and money prohibit more extensive forms of assessment, the use of personal records can provide assessment information at a relatively low cost and with little investment of time or personnel resources.

As to the disadvantages of assessing personal records: they do not provide a complete picture of the individual, nor do they always provide a completely accurate picture. Academic transcripts, for example, provide an indication of school-related skills which may or may not transfer to a work setting. A candidate may be able to do more or less than his or her academic grades indicate. Also, as mentioned earlier, the comparability of records from different people, programs, and institutions is often less than adequate. What says that a grade of "A" in a training program in California reflects the same level of competence as an "A" in a training program in New Jersey? Assessing candidates on the basis of their opinionative personal statements of strengths and career goals may be paramount to judging people on the basis of their ability to say what the assessor wants to hear, whether or not that reflects the candidate's sincere self-appraisal. As a starting point for gathering information, personal records can be beneficial; but they are not recommended as the sole source of information for any major evaluation decisions.

Performance Records

Although the distinction is admittedly arbitrary, *performance records* differ from personal records in that they provide an evaluative indication of the quality or level of performance—not just an indication of whether a candidate has, to some degree, met the stated requirements. Performance records are qualitative, personal records quantitative. As program requirements, these forms of assessment represent evaluative reports on actual performance required by a given program. Performance records include *portfolios, writing samples, resumes, personnel files*, and *progress reports*, and, in a special case, *medical records*. These forms of assessment most often provide information for employee selection, but they can be used effectively for screening purposes as well.

The first three types of performance records could be called "required submissions," since an assessment program would require each candidate or applicant to submit a portfolio, a writing sample, and/or a resume, depending on the qualifications desired. Essentially, each type requires the candidate to present himself or herself on paper, in written or graphic form. Resumes are common enough to merit little description here, as are writing samples. A portfolio is, in principle, analogous to a resume: it is a collection of visual samples of an applicant's actual work or past performance. As a screening device, a writing sample or portfolio provides a "work-sample" by which to judge an applicant's mastery and experience in skills requisite to advancement (entrance to a training, academic, certification, or licensing program). Discussion of the resume as a form of assessment is included here because, by itself, it provides a basis for screening applicants and identifying those from whom more information will be required; thus, it leads to qualitative assessment of an applicant's performance record. More often than not, the resume accompanies a "work-sample" in written, visual, or physical form (product).

A portfolio usually includes samples of actual work (e.g., drawings, sketches) or slides or photographs of actual works (e.g., paintings, sculptures, scale models, buildings). Traditionally, the portfolio has been used to assess candidates in fine arts, commercial arts, and industrial arts—architects, cartoonists, fashion designers, commercial illustrators, drafters, etc. Recently, it has taken on a more general application to any type of unified set of materials prepared for presentation. Investors prepare financial "portfolios"; writers compile samples of various kinds of writing in a "portfolio"; and teachers (e.g., Georgia Teacher Assessment Project, 1980) compile "portfolios" to present plans and materials for instructional units.

The content, format, and composition of a portfolio usually depend on its purpose. When used for obtaining employment (like a resume), portfolio contents are generally left to the discretion of the applicant. As a consequence, what applicants choose to include in the portfolio and how they present it are both important criteria for evaluating the portfolio's quality. However, when used as a criterion for admission or licensing, the contents must usually satisfy a predetermined set of requirements. These requirements may call for samples taken from various developmental stages of the work, or for samples of different types of work (e.g., a mechanical drawing, a painting, a sketch, and a sculpture).

For evaluation purposes, comprehensive criteria may be applied to portfolios submitted in almost any field. Examples of such criteria include: completeness, organization, creativity, variety, and presentation. Further criteria, which are applicable only to specific samples included in the portfolios, may also be established. For example, in architecture, criteria used to evaluate an elevation or a site plan may include: accuracy, feasibility, neatness, conformance to specifications, etc.

The evaluation of portfolio contents is generally recorded on one or more types of checklists or rating scales. Specific purposes of the evaluative process determine the type of checklist or rating scale used. When a portfolio is used as a screening tool, whether or not the contents satisfy specific criteria would likely be recorded on a qualitative checklist. A quantitative checklist might also be used to record the presence or absence of required components. When a portfolio is used as part of a selection process, a rating scale would be used to record the *degree* to which the portfolio contents meet established criteria (e.g., the overall presentation is: extremely well-organized, fairly well-organized, or unorganized). A ranking scale would be used to *compare* the portfolios of different candidates.

With resumes and writing samples, similar procedures would be used. Resumes may have to fit specified formats, or applicants may have the freedom to present their resumes as they choose. Writing samples can be culled from existing samples, at the applicant's discretion, or created to fit given requirements. In either case, for screening purposes, the samples and resumes would be evaluated to ensure that each satisfies minimum stated requirements; for selection, all would be reviewed to identify those that are superior by comparison.

The next two types of performance records—personnel files and progress reports—are essentially specialized applications of other forms of assessment (e.g., anecdotal records, quantitative checklists, product assessment). Businesses use personnel files to document important information about employees, their training, production records, awards, raises, promotions, reprimands, etc. Progress reports provide similar information but are generally limited to training and education contexts. As assessment instruments, they provide little basis for screening candidates in most situations, except when used to identify employees eligible for promotion or to certify adequate completion of a training or academic course. Even in these cases, personnel files and progress reports really only serve as summaries and reminders of a candidate's past performance, or as documentation of decisions and performance which may be required for legal reasons.

The last type in this category is a specialized form of assessment: the use of medical records. Many physicians and other professionals in medical fields advocate the use of medical records to evaluate performance of medical personnel. For example, a family physician (who must be recertified every six years) might be evaluated by a panel of his or her peers who examine the medical records of the physician's past patients. The panel might review to evaluate the correctness of a diagnosis, whether or not the prescribed therapy fit the need, and so on.

Assessment in the medical field presents some unusual problems, thus requiring "unusual" forms of assessment adapted to specific needs. However, the general principles of assessment involved in the methods used in medical fields could be adapted to other fields as well. The use of medical records is an exemplary case.

Advocates for assessing performance on the basis of medical records (e.g., Gross, 1981; Lloyd, 1981) cite two specific reasons to justify this approach: (1) a physician's performance is usually confidential, often conducted in private with only the patient; and (2) medical professionals can only be evaluated adequately by their peers. However, the confidential aspect of medical work means that on-the-job performance normally cannot be observed by others; paradoxically, it makes after-the-fact evaluation difficult too, since medical records are also confidential. The concept of peer review is common to many professional fields, including medicine; but it can present problems beyond the issue of confidentiality, mainly related to competition among practitioners in the same field and potential bias stemming from close personal associations with the professional being evaluated.

Payne (1981) notes that more objective methods of reviewing medical records can be achieved. After collecting signed waivers from doctors and their patients, teams of evaluators can examine completed medical records, attach weights to various criteria, and set a norm for each type of diagnosis. Making sure that all medical records are complete, up-to-date, and legible is the responsibility of both physicians and the hospital administrator (for physicians associated with hospitals), and is essential to conducting objective assessment.

Uses

The key to the fair and objective use of all forms of performance records, for screening and assessment, is structure—particularly the predetermination of specific job-related requirements, made known in advance to the candidate, and evaluation on the basis of predetermined criteria closely related to these requirements. These two aspects of structuring performance records used for assessment will help to ensure that the records relate closely to the job, do not cause adverse impact, and do not derive from arbitrary standards.

As stated earlier, resumes are widely used in almost every profession, but usually for employee selection. Writing samples and portfolios are most often required submissions in professions that require, respectively, writing proficiency (e.g., journalism, copy writing, technical writing) or artistic ability (e.g., advertising, commercial art, photography). Employers use personnel files to assess performance of employees; progress reports are used in business, training, and education. The use of medical records is naturally restricted to medical fields, but the basic principles of this type of assessment could be adapted to other professions (e.g., engineering, architecture, psychiatry, teaching).

Advantages/Disadvantages

The major advantage of performance records stems from the fact that they are often closely job-related: they demonstrate the ability of the candidate to apply the skills required for actual work in a particular field. Also, in some cases (especially the portfolio), it can be advantageous to allow the candidate to choose his or her own works for inclusion in performance records—works which may be developed over a long period of time.

Disadvantages of using performance records stem largely from difficulties in standardization. Requirements, evaluation criteria, and scoring must be as standardized as possible to elicit reliable results, although some degree of subjectivity in evaluation and scoring is inherent in the methods described here.

Although performance records are appropriate for assessing certain skills and experience, they are not designed to measure a wide range of factual knowledge. The skills evident from most forms of performance records present only partial aspects of professional positions. Also, because performance records permit only after-the-fact assessment, they provide no way to evaluate the process involved: how the products were made, how much help or supervision the person may have had, how much time was involved in developing the products, and what kinds of technical resources the person had available at the time.

The resume, writing sample, and portfolio enable candidates to present the best possible image of themselves. Unfortunately, portfolios may favor those with more time, money, and resources who can put together portfolios of higher quality—at least in appearance and presentation. And, again like the resume, a portfolio may be suitable for use as a screening device to identify the incompetent, but not as the sole basis for selection or licensure. On the other hand, personnel files and progress reports seldom permit any input from the candidate directly: supervisors or teachers generally prepare these records. Integrity and conscientiousness may certainly be desirable qualities, but they cannot be inferred from the degree of accuracy in performance records.

Apprenticeship/Internship

The first two categories in this chapter—personal records and performance records—are sometimes grouped together and called "product assessments," because both types involve products of a kind but do not directly involve performance or interaction with people. An apprenticeship or internship involves the direct observation of people and their performance, and it may also include product assessment. This approach is considered a program requirement because it is one of several requirements which can lead to completion of a program, be it for licensing, training, certification, or education.

In theory, an apprenticeship or internship is a formally structured, closely monitored training program that permits the candidate to learn from direct, practical, on-the-job experience. As such, this approach to training also permits the examiner/trainer to assess the candidate's abilities before certifying him or her to graduate from the course or to perform as a professional. In practice, apprenticeships and internships are seldom as structured or as well-directed as intended; more often, they embody the "sink or swim" approach to training (a candidate gets the opportunity to learn when the supervisor thrusts him or her into a job situation and exits calmly with the life preserver). Supervisors assume that those who swim have made it, while those who sink disappear of their own accord.

As a requirement in an assessment program, an apprenticeship or internship provides the assessors with an opportunity for observing and evaluating a candidate's performance on the job. Assessment information can be collected via actual performance techniques, especially through work-samples and supervisor ratings (see Chapter Four); through observational assessment (see Chapter Six); and through the personal and performance records described earlier in this chapter.

Uses

An apprenticeship or internship is an essential requirement in a number of diverse fields that ostensibly have only two common characteristics: they require a great deal of learning which can only be achieved properly in actual practice; and failure in these fields can have serious consequences, hence the need and desire to make apprenticeship or internship a requirement in the training and assessment program. In various programs, this requirement takes a number of forms: apprenticeship in trades such as carpentry, plumbing, boilermaking, and electrical work; work-studies in dozens of vocational areas, in journalism, advertising, banking, etc.; practicums in a smaller number of fields; and internships in such fields as communications, teaching, medicine, and allied health.

In many of these fields, some form of internship or practicum is required as part of an academic program; for example, university students in mass communications often spend a semester interning at a radio or television station. These relatively informal requirements undoubtedly improve the practical value of education, but they do not lead to formal certification or licensing in many cases. In areas where the consequences of incompetence may be severe, more strict requirements for internship exist. Three examples of such programs follow.

The first example is the medical internship with which many people have some familiarity. Medical students go through several years of medical school, then two or three years of residency in which they work as "interns" in medical facilities. Training and observation of interns in residency programs is usually very strict and demanding. Most of the medical professions regulate themselves, within state and federal laws, to ensure that all training programs are adequate and that everyone certified as a medical professional is competent.

Second, architects must serve periods of internship, varying from three to eight years, in which they work in architectural firms. State licensing boards generally regulate architect licensure programs, for which requirements usually include a degree in an accredited school of architecture, and/or a number of years of internship (the number varies from state to state, and in relation to years of education), and the successful completion of state and national paper-and-pencil examinations. Some states also require oral examinations for architect licensure candidates. In the internship program, sponsored by the American Institute of Architecture (AIA), interns work in firms where they learn from and are evaluated by licensed practicing architects.

Third, most states and most teacher education programs require internship of their student teachers for at least one semester; some states then grant provisional certificates or "licenses" which permit the teacher to teach for the first year, after which the certificate must be changed or renewed. The teacher certification program in Georgia affords a good example of comprehensive program requirements (similar to those discussed here). The three major requirements for full certification are adequate course work and grades (transcript), successful completion of the Georgia Teacher Certification Test in a specific teaching field (paper-and-pencil assessment of content knowledge, based on a job analysis), and performance evaluation on the job (a form of internship). The basis of assessment for teachers on the job consists of five instruments (Georgia Teacher Assessment Project, 1980):

Instrument	Method
— Teaching Plans and Materials Instrument	— A portfolio prepared by the teacher, rated by trained evaluators
— Classroom Procedures Instrument	— Actual performance in the classroom, observed by trained evaluators
— Interpersonal Skills Instrument	— Actual performance in the classroom, observed by trained evaluators
— Professional Standards Instrument	— Interviews with the teacher and his or her colleagues
— Student Perceptions Instrument	— Questionnaire administered to students who rate their teacher's performance

To summarize, these three examples—medical practice, architecture, teaching—illustrate various forms of apprenticeship or internship; and they describe, to some extent, the kinds of assessment information provided by these program requirements.

Advantages/Disadvantages

The advantages of apprenticeship/internship stem primarily from the fact that this form of training and assessment requires actual on-the-job performance. For certification and licensing programs, these requirements are essential for training and are highly job-related, and they provide a solid basis for assessing trainees in actual work situations. As mentioned above, the potentially serious consequences of incompetence among professionals in fields such as medicine, architecture, and teaching make some form of internship a critical requirement.

Disadvantages of this approach to assessment, as with most forms of program requirements, stem from the difficulties associated with standardization. Enormous efforts to standardize both the training and assessment aspects of apprenticeship/internship are required to ensure successful results.

Summary

As discussed in this chapter, program requirements include a number of disparate approaches to assessment, all of them "non-test" methods. Personal records, such as transcripts, recommendations or references, personal statements, and job histories, provide tangible proof of having obtained the qualifications required to enter or complete a given program; but they do not involve direct assessment of performance or of the person. Performance records, such as resumes, personnel files, portfolios, and medical records, provide a means of assessing the products of a candidate's performance. Finally, apprenticeship or internship provides for the training and assessment of candidates for certification or licensure in many professions, usually under the direct supervision of instructors or employers.

Except in cases where practical constraints such as money and personnel make other forms of assessment infeasible, the use of program requirements as the sole means of assessment is not recommended. Ideally, the knowledge, skills, and abilities actually required on the job should be formally identified; and a suitable assessment program should be designed to measure each aspect of the actual requirements. Chapter Ten discusses the integration of actual requirements and assessment methods for a variety of different purposes.

Selected References

American Society of Clinical Pathologists. *Proposed Policy Manual of the Boards of Registry.* Chicago, Ill.: American Society of Clinical Pathologists, 1974.

Georgia Teacher Assessment Project. *An Introduction to the Teacher Performance Assessment Instruments: Their Uses and Limitations.* Athens, Ga.: University of Georgia, 1980.

Gross, L.J. Continuing education and competency: Some critical unresolved issues. Paper presented at the Seventh Annual Conference of the Federation of Associations of Health Regulatory Boards. San Diego, Calif.: February 1981.

Lloyd, J.S. Medical specialty board recertification: Approaches, issues, and problems. Paper presented at the Seventh Annual Conference of the Federation of Associations of Health Regulatory Boards. San Diego, Calif.: February 1981.

Medley, D.M. Alternative assessment strategies. *Journal of Teacher Education, 29*(2), March-April 1978.

National Council of Architectural Registration Boards and American Institute of Architects. *Intern-Architect Development Program: Training Guidelines.* Washington, D.C.: NCARB, 1981.

Payne, B.C. Measuring competency through review of medical records. Paper presented at the Seventh Annual Conference of the Federation of Associations of Health Regulatory Boards. San Diego, Calif.: February 1981.

Chapter Ten

Assessment Centers and Program Integration

Although it may evoke visions of a factory-like building of windowless concrete, "assessment center" is a concept, not necessarily a physical structure. A relatively new concept, the assessment center involves a standardized evaluation of knowledge, skills, and behaviors based on input from multiple sources. Simply stated, it is a battery of assessment instruments administered to examinees.

The principle of assessment centers advocates the following general approach to assessment: (1) define what is to be assessed; (2) choose the most appropriate method for assessing each defined aspect of performance; (3) administer the assessments with trained, competent administrators; and (4) standardize scores across examinees and across administrations. With these procedures as its foundation, the assessment center is a fitting conclusion to this book: a presentation of a number of assessment methods, how to use them, and how to integrate disparate methods in an overall assessment program. As such, it exemplifies the integration of the elements and principles of assessment discussed in earlier chapters.

Chapter Ten assumes a basic familiarity with the assessment methods described earlier, many of which appear again here. Hundreds of actual assessment centers (physical structures) have been developed and currently operate in this country, and they all function in basically the same way. This chapter presents a description of assessment centers, actual and conceptual, then a number of possible uses for the assessment center approach. Among them are performance appraisal, methods for teacher evaluation, and methods for student assessment—all founded on the application of the assessment center principles to education and training.

Assessment Centers

Although just a few years ago assessment centers were rare and unknown to most people, there are hundreds of actual centers in operation today throughout the country. The relatively small number of extant articles on the subject all agree on at least one point: how assessment centers began.

Historical Context

By the mid-1930s, the German military establishment had developed assessment centers to select and train military intelligence officers. The British War Office developed their own centers for similar purposes; and in 1943 the U.S. Office of Strategic Services, forerunner of the CIA, established an assessment center called "Station S" in Fairfax, Virginia.

Since military intelligence officers and secret agents must possess a rather unique range of knowledge and skills, the assessment of potential agents must be capable of measuring the entire range. At Station S, candidates were subjected to a number of assessment situations: interviews, simulations, oral tests, role-playing, paper-and-pencil tests, and so on. Candidates had to demonstrate survival skills, impersonations, facility with foreign languages, ability to write propaganda, weaponry, and self-defense. In order to simulate actual job conditions, many of the simulation exercises were designed to include stress factors.

By 1956, American Telephone and Telegraph had adapted the assessment center idea to a business setting in its Management Progress Study (Bray, 1964). AT & T's Assessment Center involved the use of business games, leaderless group exercises, interviews, and in-basket tests to assess new and existing staff members.

Since their "civilian" beginnings in AT & T, assessment centers have spread to dozens of major corporations, such as IBM; Standard Oil Co. of Ohio; Bendix; Sears, Roebuck & Co.; General

Electric; Merrill-Lynch; J.C. Penney; even the New York City Police Department. Many agencies of the federal government also use assessment centers: Internal Revenue Service, Civil Service Commission, Social Security Administration, and Federal Bureau of Investigation. Rice (1978) points out that the assessment center has gained a reputation as one of the only legally defensible methods for selecting managers, as evidenced in its current use by the Equal Employment Opportunity Commission (EEOC) itself.

The American Medical Association (AMA) has developed a number of assessment centers in collaboration with its clients, such as the American Family Insurance Group. According to Parker (1980), the American Family Insurance Group assessment center has developed and now utilizes assessment methods for every job category from clerical workers to vice-presidents.

Still, with all of this activity in establishing and operating assessment centers, the concept is relatively new in most areas of training and education. The groups listed in this section represent large corporations, associations, the federal government, and municipal organizations—groups that can presumably afford to build a physical structure and use it solely as an assessment center. Such financial support is seldom available in training and education, but the concept is just as valid. The concept of assessment centers can be adapted to the needs and constraints of different situations.

Basic Principles

Testing programs like "Station S" and AT & T's Management Progress Study were not called assessment centers at their inception; the title is relatively new. In the past ten years, however, the basic principles established in these two centers have been applied in a number of settings.

Dunnette and Motowidlo (1976) state that assessment centers are characterized by the use of multiple testing techniques; they involve the use of several trained observers during the tests to evaluate candidates' performance; and, most important, they involve simulation exercises designed to replicate important job activities and situations, and to elicit behavior that is closely similar to behavior on the job. CAPT (1979) also indicates that the unique distinguishing feature of an assessment center is its inclusion of simulations which present the candidate with problems that would be encountered on the job.

The emphasis on simulations is indeed important, but the overall concept does not reduce to this emphasis. Jaffee and Sefcik (1980) state that an assessment center is a process, an application of a specific methodology to the development of information about a candidate's job-related strengths and weaknesses. This methodology includes an analysis of the skills required of a person to succeed on the job (job or task analysis), the development of instruments to assess these critical skills in a job-related context, and the training of fair and impartial judges to process the information.

The development and operation of an assessment center, then, requires the application of these principles in the following set of procedures:

(1) identify critical elements or dimensions of the job (knowledge, skills, and abilities) through a job or task analysis;

(2) develop assessment instruments with which to assess these critical elements;

(3) select and train judges to administer, observe, and grade the assessment exercises objectively and impartially;

(4) administer the assessment exercises to the candidates;

(5) grade the candidates' performances and provide feedback, orally and in written form; and

(6) standardize the grading procedures across candidates and across administrations.

To the extent that the assessment exercises measure all, or a representative sample, of the critical job elements, the assessment center can establish its validity. To the extent that the judges observe and grade everyone impartially, and on the same basis from one group to another, the reliability of the measures can be established.

Assessment centers are most effective—and most necessary—in the evaluation of persons who must have multiple and various skills, such as managers, administrators, physicians, counselors, and so on. In most uses of assessment centers, however, the dimensions on which candidates are assessed are quite similar. Byham (1980) notes that common dimensions for assessment include the following:

- oral communication skill,
- oral presentation skill,
- written communication skill,
- job motivation (of the individual),
- initiative,
- leadership,
- planning and organization,
- ability to analyze information,
- ability to make judgments, and
- management control.

In order to measure candidates' performance on all of these dimensions, the assessment center must be well-planned, based directly on critical job elements, and conducted over a period of time long enough to permit assessment of various multiple skills—in a job-related context.

Structure

A typical assessment center administration lasts two to three days; involves anywhere from six to 30 candidates who take part in the proceedings at one time; and requires an administrator and two to ten observers to organize, moderate, and evaluate candidates' performances in the assessment exercises. The primary requirement of the two- or three-day sessions is to elicit enough job-related behaviors from each candidate on which to base an evaluative judgment.

Rice (1978) describes the assessment center activities of the Human Resources Center in Dallas, Texas; it is operated by American Airlines primarily to assess management potential among company personnel. Quick *et al.* (1980) describe an assessment center developed at the University of Texas at Arlington; it is designed to assess administration personnel for the Texas state government and derives much of its structure from the

American Airlines project. These two descriptions and a model described by Slevin (1972) provide a fairly comprehensive view of what constitutes a typical assessment center. Below is a composite description of a hypothetical assessment center for middle-level managers in a large corporation.

Day One

Morning Session. Twelve candidates enter the central conference room of a one-story building, where they will spend the next three days. They introduce themselves to each other, then an administrator presents an overview of what will happen during the next three days, what to expect, and what the goals of the session are. Meanwhile, a second administrator conducts an orientation for the four assessors or observers who will grade the candidates.

Splitting into two groups, the 12 candidates participate in *background interviews,* one-on-one, with the assessors. While the first candidates interview, the others fill out *background surveys* and *attitude questionnaires.* Following the interviews, each group of six convenes and participates in a *leaderless group discussion.*

Afternoon Session. The six candidates participate in a four-hour *in-basket exercise,* designed to gauge their performance in management roles. While this occurs, the observers compile their information and behavioral observations from the morning session, then complete preliminary write-ups for each candidate.

Evening Session. The candidates work on a *management analysis exercise,* based on a *case study,* which they will have to present individually the next day. Meanwhile, the assessors score the in-basket exercises.

Day Two

Morning Session. Candidates participate in individual interviews with assessors to discuss the in-basket exercise. Both groups of six then convene, divide into three groups of four, and participate in a *conflict resolution exercise.*

Afternoon Session. Half of the candidates participate in *simulated interviews* designed to test their interviewing and personnel management skills. The other half make their *oral presentations* on the management analysis exercise. When both groups have completed their first exercise, they reverse the roles and complete the other exercise.

Day Three

Morning Session. Candidates participate in a *fact-finding exercise,* then complete the entire session with an "exit" interview, with the same assessor who interviewed them at the beginning of the process.

In the afternoon, the assessors compile all of their information (all assessors have observed every candidate in at least two sessions) and complete ratings on each candidate as to their performance on each predetermined dimension. An extended discussion on each individual candidate follows, among all of the assessors, to agree on final ratings and identify areas in need of improvement. The assessor who conducted the background interview on each candidate then writes a developmental report on that person, based on the assessment information gathered over the past two and a half days.

Use of Results

In this hypothetical assessment center, all of the candidates were company staff members being tested for management potential. In most situations of this nature, the focus in using assessment center results is development of staff through the identification of strengths and weaknesses, and through prescriptive suggestions for training and experience to help candidates improve in their weak areas. Other assessment centers may have different emphases (e.g., selection of employees, promotion, screening), but all incorporate a process for compiling reports on each candidate and providing feedback.

Results reports are usually provided to the company's top-level management, for use in employee evaluation and promotion. The same, or slightly less complete, reports may be sent to the candidates as well; and the assessors often discuss the reports with the candidates personally. For long-range assessment purposes, longitudinal studies of performance in the assessment center may also be conducted (as in AT & T's study of newly hired college graduates).

Beyond assessment, however, is the second purpose of the center: training and development. Companies that invest significant amounts of money in an assessment do so with the goal of developing better personnel. The experience of the assessment center session itself can be very enlightening and constructive for the participants, particularly for those who have their first opportunity to experience what management situations are like. Simulation exercises provide developmental experience to the candidates in situations that closely resemble actual on-the-job conditions. In addition to the specific experiences, the assessment center provides an information base on which to construct a long-term developmental training plan. This plan specifies the candidate's weaknesses and recommends ways to overcome them through education and further experience. In many cases, the assessment center exercises also provide videotape feedback for the candidates—which can be a very effective training tool.

As mentioned in Chapter Five, one of the major advantages of using simulations—as in assessment centers—is the benefit derived from placing candidates into situations that could be dangerous or impractical under actual conditions. Within the structure of an assessment center, the use of simulation exercises can provide candidates with the opportunity to find out what actual situations will be like; and their responses and behaviors when placed in these situations provide assessors with information to judge the potential of the candidates.

Dunnette and Motowidlo (1976) offer an example of this emphasis in their descriptions of assessment centers developed and operated by the New York City Police Department and the International Association of Chiefs of Police. Many of the exercises used in these centers are role-play simulations designed to find out what the candidate (patrol officer, detective, commander, desk sergeant, etc.) would do on the job. In police work (as in the military's "Station S"), this ability to predict performance is crucial: untrained or inept police officers can easily be injured, or can cause serious harm to others. Thus, the police candidates respond to such situations as the "Hotel Call," "Burglary," "Domestic Dispute," "Accident Victim," and so on—to see how they handle these situations under stress. As with other assessment centers, the results provide developmental information on strengths and weaknesses as well as assessment data on which to base decisions regarding selection and promotion of the candidates.

Advantages/Disadvantages

It is difficult to appraise the advantages and disadvantages of assessment centers before one knows which types of assessment will be used in each case. There are, however, some distinct advantages to this approach (assuming that a range of techniques are used). First, assessment centers can be designed and used to evaluate nearly all the work-related abilities and qualities of each candidate, which is particularly important in fields where one test, e.g., multiple-choice, simply does not suffice. Second, assessment centers provide for standardized performance evaluation; that is, all candidates are rated according to the same criteria and by the same judges (who are trained and experienced). This is a vital advantage in measuring skills through observation (e.g., supervisor ratings), because it eliminates most of the differences in criteria and judgments which occur when candidates are rated by different judges.

As Parker (1980) points out, the assessment center approach helps to eliminate rater subjectivity because the assessors usually have no personal relationship with the candidates (as on-the-job supervisors would). In the assessment center, assessors make immediate judgments about the candidates on the basis of specified criteria; as opposed to supervisors, who may sit down and try to assess the performance of a staff member over the past six to 12 months, based on recall—a situation that can result in generalities. Finally, the candidates all have an equal chance at the outset, because exercises are standardized; and all have an opportunity to demonstrate a broad range of skills and abilities, because the assessment center exercises are multi-faceted.

As to disadvantages, assessment centers can be very expensive to develop and maintain because they involve many types of tests, individual and group test administrations, training of observers and evaluators, and, in many cases, the selection and financial support of full-time employees associated with the evaluation process. Slevin (1972) estimates that the cost of operating an assessment center runs at about $500 per candidate, a sum comparable to the cost of top-quality management appraisals by professional consultants. For large corporations, the investment is often worthwhile. As Cohen (1980) indicates in his cost-benefit analysis, assessment centers are relatively expensive to establish and maintain; but research reports have been overwhelmingly positive, particularly in comparison with other management tools. For groups with lesser financial endowments, however, the advantages of assessment centers may be unattainable due to prohibitive costs.

Moses (1973) notes another disadvantage to assessment centers: few individuals can be assessed at one time. This not only creates a shortage of opportunities for training and assessment, but often limits the opportunities to "select" individuals, a condition which may leave the company short on trained managers and the unselected individuals feeling slighted.

Slevin (1972) points out other potential problems. First, what he calls the "Crown Prince Syndrome" may occur with those candidates who perform exceedingly well in the assessment center. As a result, they may expect assurance of long-term job security, financial compensation, or immediate promotion. Candidates should be told from the beginning that promotions, etc., depend primarily on actual job performance, not on assessment center results. Second, assessment centers by nature create anxiety. Administration procedures should be geared to lessening anxiety, and developmental feedback should focus on diverting anxiety into constructive, self-help pursuits. Third, assessment centers may discourage individualism, initiative, and incentive, at the cost of producing managers who conform to the values of the assessors. This potential result is raised as a problem in nearly every standardized assessment program, but has yet to be verified conclusively.

Finally, many of the techniques used in assessment centers are simulations, which are less direct than actual performance. While simulations may be advantageous for situations in which errors or shortcomings can lead to serious consequences (e.g., police work), they may not be as advantageous in other situations for which job experience has no substitute. The need for comprehensive evaluation techniques must be weighed against the cost, time, and directness of measurement involved. And, the overall needs of the program must be analyzed carefully at the outset, lest too many resources and too much importance be vested in an assessment center.

Applications of the Assessment Center Concept

Thus far, discussion of assessment centers has been limited to actual centers (physical structures), primarily in use by large corporations, associations, and government agencies. With these models in mind, and with an understanding of the assessment center as a concept, discussion can proceed to applications of the concept in other settings. These other settings include small business, training, and education.

Stripped to its essentials, the assessment center approach embodies the basic concept of assessment advocated in this book. Since this concept is of major importance, it bears repeating here. In essence, the concept breaks down into three principles:

(1) define what is to be tested (domain of critical knowledge, skills, and abilities required) through some form of job or task analysis;
(2) for each aspect of the domain defined in number 1, select and/or design an assessment method to measure the specific aspects as directly as possible; and
(3) train assessors in the administration and scoring of assessment exercises and instruments, to increase the standardization and objective evaluation of all candidate performances.

The extent to which these principles can be applied, formally or informally, to a given assessment program depends on the program's goals, context, and practical constraints. The next three sections provide examples of such applications in business, training, and education, and recommendations for using the assessment center concept in other settings.

Performance Appraisal

In business settings, traditional methods of performance evaluation tend to emphasize quantitative *or* qualitative criteria for judging employees; very few methods emphasize both. *Quantitative* criteria focus on "numbers"—number of pieces produced, pages written, hours spent, and so on—but as any statistician knows, numbers can be misleading, particularly in service-oriented businesses where quality is often more important than quantity. *Qualitative* criteria focus on "words"—judgments of how well someone performs, attitudes, morale, and so on—but words can also be misleading, particularly when subjectivity and personal bias shade the rater's judgments. The fact is that both types of criteria must be considered in proper proportion to the job requirements.

Methods of appraising employee performance in business settings have taken a number of forms and an even larger number of names: performance appraisal, performance evaluation, job assessment, employee evaluation, etc. Most experts generally agree that what is currently known as *performance appraisal* (Sayles and Strauss, 1977) includes the following elements: (1) specific definition of job requirements; (2) continual or periodic evaluation of employees on the basis of job requirements; and (3) feedback to the employees. Actual procedures used in different performance appraisal systems tend to vary.

Brush and Schoenfeldt (1980) suggest, as an alternative to assessment centers, the "Integrated Appraisal Approach," which closely resembles "performance appraisal" systems. The differences between this approach and the assessment center are summarized as follows: (1) the appraisal process takes place on the job, not in simulations; (2) multiple observers pool their evaluative ratings drawn from over a long period of time; and (3) all aspects of the actual job can be appraised. These differences point out the limitations of actual (physical) assessment centers, to which employees go—away from the actual job—but they also focus attention on the application of the "assessment center concept" in a business setting, which is the subject of this section.

Uses of Performance Appraisal

Whether large or small, businesses need—and generally have—some method for evaluating personnel. The degree of formality tends to vary across different businesses according to particular needs, conditions, and directorial assay of the relative importance of conducting performance evaluations. Despite variance in degree of formality, and in the size and nature of the business, the purposes and uses of performance appraisal methods are basically the same.

There are three major uses of performance appraisal: (1) to provide an objective basis for employee promotion and job status changes (e.g., dismissal); (2) to provide information on employee strengths and weaknesses as the basis for training and development; and (3) to provide information for wage and salary administration. In addition, Sayles and Strauss (1977) state that performance appraisal can be used to collect data for long-range personnel planning (knowing who will be capable of handling a new position and when), identification of personnel for job transfers (customized to their strengths and weaknesses), and evaluation of the overall program (for management development, employee productivity, etc.).

Separating the three major purposes may be somewhat misleading, since they are usually integrated in a single program, particularly in small businesses. With the desire to obtain systematic, objective information on employee performance, and the legal "encouragement" to do so in most situations, the need for performance appraisal information in all three of these areas is apparent. From a business perspective, performance appraisal should provide a rational basis for judging an employee's competence; his or her value to the company, in order to set wage or salary levels; and the employee's strengths and weaknesses, for which the employee can be trained, promoted, transferred, or dismissed. Naturally, if the employee has potential that is valuable to the company, performance appraisal information for training purposes can be extremely helpful to the company and to the employee.

In order to apply the assessment center concept to performance appraisal in a business setting, for the purposes outlined here, the development and maintenance of the system should be based on the principles outlined previously. Actual methods for implementing these principles are described below.

Defining the Assessment Domain

The development of a rational, clearly job-related performance appraisal system depends on the ability to define the assessment domain: the set of critical knowledge, skills, and abilities required for adequate performance on the job. Several methods exist for doing this, but the one most applicable method will depend on the situation.

Job analysis. As discussed earlier, a job analysis consists of an instrument and a procedure for collecting and analyzing empirical data with which to define critical job elements. This usually takes one or both of two approaches: (1) a survey/questionnaire filled out by job incumbents in written form; (2) a standardized interview of job incumbents. From the collected data, an analysis of the job is conducted and a specific definition of important job incumbents produced.

Task analysis. Although used synonymously with job analysis, a task analysis represents the next step in order of breakdown: a task analysis involves the analysis of a specific job or duty and its breakdown into smaller components. For example, if one of a printer's duties is to prepare mechanicals, then the printer has to be able to select type, do paste-up, do mechanical drawing, design and format pages, etc. A list of component skills would be devised for each job task.

Performance expectations. A less formal, experiential approach to defining job elements is the development of "performance expectations." This usually involves cooperation between the supervisor and the employee to produce behavioral statements of job responsibilities (job definition) and performance goals (expectations). The employee then strives to attain these expectations, and the supervisor evaluates the employee on the basis of the expectations.

Management-by-objectives (MBO). Whether based on a job

analysis, task analysis, or "performance expectations" approach, the MBO system represents an integrated approach to defining positions, governing work operations, and evaluating performance. The MBO assessment is generally short-term and results-oriented in nature: the supervisor and the employee work out short-term quantitative goals for production and improving efficiency. Ongoing, systematic evaluation then occurs on the basis of these objectives, which can change from week to week, often as a result of the evaluation itself.

These four approaches provide the means for defining the domain of important job elements which form the basis for performance appraisal.

Designing Assessment Methods

The next step is to select and/or design the most appropriate method for assessing each critical job element. In order to demonstrate this procedure, the following hypothetical situation is presented. The position defined is that of manager for the Data Processing (DP) Department in a small business. Critical job elements have been defined on the basis of a weekly and quarterly MBO system and a set of performance expectations, developed and monitored by the DP manager's direct supervisor.

Although this example is rather simplified, it illustrates the completion of the first two steps: defining job elements and selecting/designing assessment methods. The DP manager's performance appraisal ratings would consist of both quantitative data and qualitative comments collected from work-samples, staff, peers, and supervisors. Collecting information from staff at different levels is important, since perceptions of a manager differ significantly at various hierarchical levels within the company; this approach also lessens the effect of the supervisor's personal bias, either positive or negative, and helps to assure the employee of fair treatment.

The following chart illustrates the results of this process—identifying critical job elements and matching appropriate assessment methods to them. The diversity of assessment methods reflects the multi-faceted nature of the job's requirements.

Matching Job Elements and Assessment Methods

Critical Job Elements	Assessment Method

Management Skills

Deals effectively with clients (internal/external).	Survey questionnaire to clients
Schedules activities.	Weekly objectives
Plans effectively for staff and activities.	Weekly objectives
Coordinates with other departments.	Interviews with department managers
Monitors quality control.	Review of records
Supervises staff.	Interviews with staff
Reports to director.	Supervisor ratings

Technical Skills

Coordinates data entry.	
Designs programs and software.	Review of records
Executes data processing.	Work-samples
Documents all processing.	Quantitative data
Advises clients (internal/external).	Questionnaire/technical review
Maintains hardware.	Equipment report

Interpersonal Skills

Communicates openly.	
Cooperates with others.	Interviews
Maintains professionalism.	Observation
Represents company to clients.	

Train Assessors

The third step in the process is to train the assessors. In a business setting the assessors are usually the managers, who appraise their subordinates, and often include members of the personnel department. The most effective ways to train managers in performance appraisal techniques are likely to be workshops or seminars, followed by actual evaluation, both of and by the manager. A manager can learn a great deal from an effective evaluation of his or her own performance; learning by example, the manager can then apply the same principles and procedures in evaluating others.

Communication skills are perhaps the most important requirements for effective performance appraisal. Many organizations schedule regular "evaluation interviews" every six or 12 months. A regular schedule accomplishes two purposes, generally: it establishes a minimum requirement for face-to-face, direct conversation between employee and supervisor about the employee's performance; and it sets a precedent for the amount of time and effort to be expended on evaluations (in addition to normal workload). The second of these purposes may be desirable financially but does not encourage on-going evaluation, which should be a regular event occurring daily or weekly on an informal basis. The most effective performance appraisals assume the regularly scheduled evaluation interview as a minimum requirement; the least effective assume it a maximum, thus trying to evaluate six or 12 months' performance in a one-hour interview.

As in all forms of assessment, feedback to the employee is the essential basis of progress and improvement. Ratings and results collected in the performance appraisal process should be discussed constructively with the employee to encourage further training and self-development.

Advantages/Disadvantages

There are numerous advantages of performance appraisal, particularly in relation to assessment centers and traditional performance reviews (e.g., supervisor ratings). Unlike the assessment center, performance appraisal occurs on the job during normal working hours. It is based on clear definitions of skills and responsibilities, tailored to each person as an individual and understood in advance by employee and supervisor—so both parties know where they stand. The use of MBO and performance expectations as a basis for appraisal makes the evaluation forward-looking and developmental, hence encouraging progress and discouraging the end-of-term "report card" syndrome. Also, with specific goals to attain, the new employee often feels more secure, more in control of his or her position, and more motivated to be productive.

Disadvantages of performance appraisal tend to derive from

misuse of the concept. For example, if the criteria for evaluation become too heavily weighted on either the quantitative or the qualitative side, the results are likely to be distorted. Also, the manager with poor communication skills will have difficulties in using this system, as will the employee/"victim" of inadequate communication. Finally, the performance appraisal system, even when used properly, provides little predictive information. As a results-oriented system, it only permits appraisal on the basis of what the employee has or has not done. In a situation where one can assume that mastery of one level indicates preparedness to move up to the next level, this shortcoming would not be a significant problem.

Teacher Evaluation

The evaluation of teachers has received a great deal of attention in the recent past, purportedly due to the national furor over declines in educational achievement. Quite conceivably, the application of the assessment center concept in educational settings could play a major role in improving methods for assessing, certifying, and increasing the performance of teachers and trainers. The roles and responsibilities of teachers are diverse and the requirements for teaching complex; also, the consequences of incompetence in the teaching profession can be considerable. Thus, teaching seems an ideal prospect for an assessment center approach to evaluation. In fact, some inroads have been made in this direction, as well as suggestions for future progress.

Teacher Evaluation Instruments

McDonald (1973) documents the progress made in a project designed to improve performance-based teacher evaluation. He contends that standard methods of assessing teacher performance, e.g., classroom observation, need to be improved because they lack sufficient controls. McDonald recommends the use of simulated teaching techniques to assess performance in controlled situations. These could include "microteaching units," in which teachers are assessed on only one specific skill at a time; and "reactive simulation devices" similar to simulations and management exercises used in assessment centers and in other non-educational settings.

Medley (1978) recommends a number of alternative assessment strategies for teacher evaluation, many of which are fairly common methods that have been adapted especially for teaching. One is the "teaching test," based on a pretest/instruction/posttest model, designed to gauge the effectiveness of teaching by measuring student progress. Another is the "sign system," based on classroom observation. Observers note the absence or presence of certain signs (behaviors, actions) that indicate positive or negative effects of teaching. The "Teacher's Briefcase" is a third method, designed on the basis of the in-basket test. And fourth, "Classroom Interaction Simulations," which are based on micro-teaching, peer teaching, and role-playing.

CAPT (1979) presents a description of a number of education-related assessment center programs. Some are used for student assessment, others for administrators. Montgomery County, Maryland, for example, conducts an assessment center for school principals. The National Association of Secondary School Principals also conducts assessment centers in various locations for assistant principals and principals.

As noted in Chapter Nine, the Georgia State Education Department has developed a multi-faceted assessment program for screening, certifying, and evaluating teachers. It includes three basic components: (1) an assessment of program requirements (transcript, recommendations); (2) a criterion-referenced test of content knowledge in each teaching field; and (3) performance-based evaluation of teachers in the classroom.

In addition to Georgia, Alabama has developed a similar program. Alabama's program also includes an entrance exam of English Language Proficiency (measuring reading, writing, language arts, and listening) and a Basic Professional Skills test (measuring knowledge of teaching skills). The testing components of these programs are based on statewide job analysis studies. Oklahoma and South Carolina have begun developing similar programs, and (as of June, 1981) at least seven other states have this approach under consideration.

All of these programs, which incorporate alternative assessment methods, speak to the need for integrated, multi-faceted evaluation of teachers. No single method will suffice because the skills required of teachers are too complex and diverse. By applying the assessment center concept, a state education department can identify the important elements of teaching, train assessors to conduct evaluations, and design assessment methods to measure each important job element. This concept can provide a means of assessing teachers and trainers in any field, from trades and industries, to special education, to basic mathematics. It can also be of tremendous value in assessing students, who are expected to learn a broad range of diverse and complex skills.

Student Assessment

The assessment center approach is specifically suited to identifying strengths and weaknesses for which further training and development may be needed. It encourages and supports growth and progress, based on accurate assessment information. What could be better suited to the needs of and goals for students of all ages?

Quinto and McKenna (1977), in a handbook produced by the National Education Association, note a serious need for alternatives to what they call "standardized testing" (used as a synonym for normative-referenced, paper-and-pencil, multiple-choice tests). They suggest a number of options: interviews with students and parents, teacher-made paper-and-pencil tests, objective- or criterion-referenced tests, and even "open admissions" (giving no tests at all). One of the suggested alternatives is the use of teacher-student *contracts.* Contracts have been used before in many situations, but the important aspect here is the congruity of this idea with the assessment center concept; its counterpart in business is the performance appraisal approach, based on defined expectations and goals. Assessment methods are selected and designed to measure progress on each element or objective defined in the contract.

Cyrs and Grussing (1978) describe the use of an assessment center in a college of pharmacy, designed to provide standardized evaluation of behavior based on multiple forms of input. The multiple forms of input measure the multiple skills required of a pharmacist in the real world. Assessment methods include: paper-and-pencil objective tests, essay tests, attitudinal measures, behavioral observations (recorded on rating scales and reported systematically), simulations, project assignments, and oral examinations.

CAPT (1979) describes assessment centers in use at Alverno College (Milwaukee, Wisconsin) and at Baylor University. Both centers stress the development of students' managerial competence and preparation for jobs in the professional world outside the schoolyard fence. Both centers have used professionals from various fields to come in and train assessors or act as assessors themselves.

Nickse (1975) describes an adult education program used in New York to educate and assess adults outside of school, to help them earn their high school diplomas. This program uses a multi-faceted assessment process to measure a number of carefully defined performance criteria. Methods include: self-assessment checklists, math and writing diagnostic tests, essay tests, interest inventories, and simulated performance tasks such as interviews with health professionals and employment counselors.

All of these student assessment programs and innovative techniques emphasize the need for defined performance criteria, trained assessors, and multiple assessment methods. They have applied the assessment center approach in structured, formalized, education settings; but the concept is equally applicable to nearly all educational situations, from private tutoring to elementary education to graduate school.

Summary

The ultimate value of the assessment center concept is its ability to provide standardized, accurate assessment information, which can be used for further progress and development; but it still recognizes the uniqueness of the individual. The day may come, in the distant future, when every able person will report to the "Assessment Center" for classification (although it will undoubtedly be called something closer to the "Ministry of Development"). But this rather awesome prospect assumes majestic advances in assessment methods and a number of more political changes that science fiction writers predict, particularly the disappearance of individualization. For the present, the use of individualized but standardized methods of assessment may encourage progress; and with the right kind of progress, the Ministry of Development may remain fiction.

Selected References

Bray, D.W. The management progress study. *American Psychologist,* 1964, *19,* 419-420.

Bray, D.W., and Campbell, R.J. Selection of salesmen by means of an assessment center. *Journal of Applied Psychology,* 1968, *52*(1).

Byham, W.C. How to improve the validity of an assessment center. *Training and Development Journal,* November 1978.

Byham, W.C. Starting an assessment center the correct way. *Personnel Administrator,* February 1980.

Brush, D.H., and Schoenfeldt, L.F. Identifying managerial potential: An alternative to assessment centers. *Personnel,* 1980, *57*(3), 68-76.

Cohen, S.L. The bottom line on assessment center technology. *Personnel Administrator,* February 1980.

Cyrs, T.E., and Grussing, P.G. Rationale for development of multidimensional assessment procedures of pharmacy student competence through the assessment center approach. Unpublished paper. Las Cruces, N.M.: New Mexico State University, 1978.

Dunnette, M.D., and Motowidlo, S.J. *Police Selection and Career Assessment.* Minneapolis, Minn.: Personnel Decisions, Inc., 1976 (ED 130042).

Jaffee, C.L., and Sefcik, J.T. What is an assessment center? *Personnel Administrator,* February 1980.

McDonald, F.J. The state of the art in performance assessment of teaching competence. Paper presented to the Multi-State Consortium, American Educational Research Association. New Orleans: February 1973 (ED 148738).

Medley, D.M. Alternative assessment strategies. *Journal of Teacher Education,* March-April 1978, *22*(2).

Millman, J. (Ed.) *Handbook of Teacher Evaluation.* Beverly Hills, Calif.: Sage Publications, Inc., 1981.

Moses, J.L. The development of an assessment center for the early identification of supervisory potential. *Personnel Psychology,* 1973, *26,* 569-580.

Nickse, R.S. Development of a performance assessment system for the central New York external high school diploma program: An educational alternative for adults. Syracuse, N.Y.: Regional Learning Service, 1975.

Northwest Regional Educational Laboratory. The assessment center method: Applications in education. *CAPT Newsletter*, September 1979, *5*(1).

Parker, T.C. Assessment centers: A critical study. *Personnel Administrator*, February 1980.

Quick, J.C., Fisher, W.A., Schkade, L.L., and Ayers, G.W. Developing administrative personnel through the assessment center technique. *Personnel Administrator*, February 1980.

Quinto, F., and McKenna, B. *Alternatives to Standardized Testing.* Washington, D.C.: National Education Association, 1977.

Rice, B. Measuring executive muscle. *Psychology Today*, December 1978.

Sayles, L.R., and Strauss, G. Performance appraisal. In *Managing Human Resources.* Englewood Cliffs, N.J.: Prentice-Hall, Inc., 1977.

Slevin, D.P. The assessment center: Breakthrough in management appraisal and development. *Personnel Journal,* April 1972.

Task Force of Assessment Center Standards. Standards and ethical considerations for assessment center operations. *Personnel Administrator,* February 1980.

Thornton, G.C. The validity of assessment centers. Unpublished paper. Fort Collins: Colorado State University, May 1971 (ED 050411).

Index

Cohen, S.L., 244
College of Family Physicians of Canada, 113, 156
Computer-adaptive tests, 39, 185-187
Connecticut Ninth-Grade Proficiency Test, 40, 197
Content specifications, 62
Continuing Medical Education (CME), 223
Contracts, teacher-student, 254
Cut-off scores, 13, 55, 148
Cyrs, T.E., 126, 254

Damrin, D.E., 31
Debra P. v. Turlington, 13
Department of Defense Dependents Schools, 167-169
Design problem, 40-41, 52-53, 179-180, 206-214
Diederich, P.B., 204
Directness of measure, 23-25
Domain, defined, 7, 248-250
Domain specifications, 49-51
Dunnette, M.D., 237, 242-243

Ebel, R.L., 68
Educational Testing Service, 33, 94, 98
English as a Second Language (ESL), 157, 159, 161
Equal Employment Opportunity Commission, 11-13, 219, 237
  federal guidelines, 11-13, 22-23, 41, 47-48, 219
Essay tests, 39-40, 56, 179-180, 195-206
Evaluation
  formative vs. summative, 24
  vs. instruction, 24-25

Fact-finding exercise, 114, 241
Fidelity (*see* Realism)
Fitzpatrick, R., 22, 31, 67

Florida Department of Professional Regulation, 71
Florida functional literacy test, 12, 22
Foreign language tests, 69, 153, 157, 159-160
Fredericksen, N., 33, 94

Gardner, F.M., 31
Georgia Department of Education, 83, 253
Georgia Teacher Assessment Project, 225, 232
Georgia Teacher Certification Test, 22, 232
Ginsburg, H., 165
Glaser, R., 31, 84
Glock, M.D., 195
Gronlund, N., 27, 76, 148-149, 195
Gross, L.J., 227
Grussing, P.G., 126, 254

Halo effect, 128
Hawaii State Department of Education, 132-134; Assessment of Foundation Program Objectives, 157-158
Hennen, B.K.E., 156
Hively, W., 60

Identification test, 26-27, 69, 75-82
In-basket test, 33, 58-59, 94-98, 240-241, 253
Instruction vs. evaluation, 24-25
Integrated Appraisal Approach, 246
International Association of Chiefs of Police, 113, 242
Internship, 41, 229-233
Interview, 36-37, 156-157, 165-175, 240, 254
Inventory (checklist), 87
Item specifications, 59-65

Jaffee, C.L., 238